Scholasticism in the Colonial Colleges

EDUCATION OF THE FOUNDING FATHERS OF THE REPUBLIC

Scholasticism in the Colonial Colleges

Education of the Founding Fathers of the Republic

By James J. Walsh, MD

ↄ

Three Font Books™

Broomall, PA

Three Font Books Φ™ is an imprint of The National Catholic Bioethics Center.™

Published by
The National Catholic Bioethics Center
600 Reed Road, Suite 102, Broomall, PA 19008

Printed in the United States

Three Font Books edition © The National Catholic Bioethics Center 2025

The Three Font Books edition is an unabridged republication of *Education of the Founding Fathers of the Republic: Scholasticism in the Colonial Colleges—A Neglected Chapter in the History of American Education*, published by Fordham University Press, 1935.

Errata from the Fordham edition have been corrected. The Three Font Books edition includes a new foreword, introduction, and afterword and contains updates to narrative and chapter style designed to make the text more useful for readers.

The numbers included in the margins of the text refer to the page numbers in the Fordham edition.

Library of Congress Control Number: 2023952390

ISBN 978-0-935372-80-9 (paperback)

Cover design by Nicholas Furton © The National Catholic Bioethics Center 2025

Cover figures (from upper left, clockwise): Benjamin Franklin, Thomas Jefferson, John Adams, and Robert Livingston.

Contents

Illustrations

AUTHOR

James J. Walsh, MD, PhD, ScD, ED, etc. (1865–1942) was a physician and Catholic intellectual. He served as the dean of the school of medicine and as a professor of medical history and nervous disease at Fordham University in New York City, where he was the founding director of Fordham University Press. He was the author of dozens of books and articles and is credited with being the first lecturer on medical history in the United States.

CONTRIBUTORS

John M. Peterson, PhD, is the assistant dean of the Braniff Graduate School of Liberal Arts, the director of the classical education graduate program, and an affiliate assistant administrative professor of humanities at the University of Dallas in Irving, Texas.

Edward J. Furton, MA, PhD, is the director of Publications and an ethicist at the National Catholic Bioethics Center in Broomall, Pennsylvania.

Jason T. Eberl, PhD, is the Hubert Mäder Chair in Health Care Ethics, a professor of health care ethics and philosophy, and the director of the Albert Gnaegi Center for Health Care Ethics at Saint Louis University in St. Louis, Missouri.

Foreword

John M. Peterson

It is hard to face how far we have fallen in our educational expectations. Therefore, we tend not to face it, looking back only with scorn on the content and methods of our fathers. This propensity is illustrated by W. H. Cowley, who, as a professor of higher education at Stanford University for three decades, sought to give coherence to the new university system, with its dizzying array of disciplines, confusing mashup of social, political, and civilizational responsibilities, and ever-increasing host of administrators and offices. He took the occasion of the death of Robert Hutchins, his great adversary in the competition to provide a vision to the future of higher education in America, to attack the latter's notion that the seven liberal arts were a worthwhile study or of any lasting significance. According to Cowley, "The seven liberal arts controlled education for only eight hundred years—from the 4th to the 12th century, that is, during the Dark Ages." Furthermore, "Universities did not come into existence until the seven liberal arts were superseded" by the "Three Philosophies," namely, "Natural Philosophy, Moral

Philosophy, and Metaphysical or Mental Philosophy."[1] Cowley could also have mentioned the practice of Scholasticism, which, through the rigorous logical exercise of disputation on difficult questions, went far beyond the rote learning of the small canon of texts on the liberal arts that constituted the earlier curriculum.

However, the three philosophies did not replace the study of the *trivium* and *quadrivium* or obviate the need for them, and Scholasticism was a means of explicating, relating, and elaborating the liberal arts, not of supplanting them. And neither the liberal arts nor Scholasticism was thoroughly rejected in subsequent centuries, and it was only in the last century and a half, as James Walsh shows in his study, that the Scholastic practices were discarded in America. Now we are left only with vestiges. The commencement programs, which once invited attendees to test graduates by calling on them to defend any of a great number of theses through scholastic disputation, now invite only celebration of them through salutatory and valedictory addresses.

Both the German research university model and the reaction to it are to blame for this. The former called for specialization and expertise rather than broad human learning, while the latter, in Cowley's words, rejected "intellectualism" in favor of "the education of the whole student."[2] While the emphasis on holistic education was not pernicious in itself, in the absence of a coherent tradition, this model for education opened the door to every new discipline, intellectual and professional, utilitarian and occupational. Colleges

---

1. W. H. Cowley, "The Seven Liberal Arts Hoax," *Improving College and University Teaching* 26.1 (Winter 1978): 97, 98, doi: 10.1080/00193089.1978.9927539. For a treatment of Cowley's career, see Brenda Sue Caldwell, "W. H. Cowley: A Life in Higher Education," PhD diss. (University of Oklahoma, 1983).

2. W. H. Cowley, "Intelligence Is Not Enough," inauguration address as Hamilton College president (1938), in *Journal of Higher Education* 9.9 (December 1938): 470, 477, doi: 10.1080/00221546.1938.11779748.

and universities put aside a common academic purpose in order to embrace social formation, athletics, and ultimately political activism. Nor did the renewed emphasis on the residential functions of higher education supplant the new emphasis on research and scholarship. Rather than insisting that every graduate be able to speak both the common language of the humanities and the scholarly language of the classics, with the ability to speak intelligently and learnedly on all broadly human questions, American colleges and universities introduced to the world graduates who were narrow-minded, both morally and intellectually.

In the chapters of this volume, one can see the expansiveness of mind and the comprehension of a broad array of human questions expected of early American college graduates. Because we are ashamed of what our education has become, we dismiss this as anachronism, justifying our departure from it by the existence of new fields of study and new challenges. Surely a static Scholasticism, a frozen liberal arts curriculum, could not be appropriate for the modern world. But we can see from Walsh's study that the Scholastic method was adaptable to new conditions. Students were able to debate questions brought to the fore by the new natural sciences; they needed not think only through Aristotelian categories, although they learned them. They were not asked to defend the same theses everywhere, and especially in theology and metaphysics, we can see where the colleges differed. But we also see the influence of Enlightenment rationalism and modern political philosophy in the questions they disputed and the theses they defended. In the colonial and post-revolutionary college, for example, every student learned something of the purpose of government, of the rights and duties of man.

One can see this education everywhere in early American history, but perhaps the most famous example is the college education of James Madison, who, along with many other prominent members of the founding generation, was a student of John Witherspoon at the College of New Jersey, later called Princeton. There he disputed, using the Scholastic methods described in this volume, Enlightenment questions, the very political and moral questions which would guide his contributions to the Virginia Declaration of Rights and, of course, the Constitution and the *Federalist Papers*. Witherspoon presided over this early formation, teaching a capstone class on moral philosophy that drew from ancient and modern sources and required graduates of the college to be able to defend theses systematically. These are schoolboy exercises of sorts, but the exercises of schoolboys expected to go on to take a leading role in deliberation on public questions of the greatest importance. This, of course, Madison went on to do.

We tend to associate Scholasticism with static forms, both philosophical and political, since it depends upon authorities, and authority must be deferred to, not challenged or overthrown. Thus, it seems a paradox that Scholastic methods would play such a role in casting off old forms and establishing a new republic with a "science of politics" that has, in the words of Alexander Hamilton, Madison's partner in writing the *Federalist Papers*, "received great improvement."[3] Certainly, the Enlightenment influence in Madison's education must not be conflated with the classical education he received. However, Scholastic methods turn out to have great flexibility in terms of political, and sometimes even moral, conclusions, for they rest upon a confidence in the human mind to master, combine, and test fundamental propositions in different

---

3. Alexander Hamilton, *Federalist* n. 9, in *The Federalist*, ed. George W. Carey and James McClellan (Indianapolis: Liberty Fund, 2001), 38. *Federalist* n. 10, written by Madison on the extended republic as a way to multiply and thus mitigate the effect of a faction, is a demonstration of this improvement. In *Federalist* n. 47, Madison refers to the separation of powers as an "invaluable precept in the science of politics," which, if not invented by Montesquieu, was "most effectually" set forth by him (250).

circumstances. While not in themselves inherently concerned with matters of prudence, which assesses contingent and transitory facts and events, Scholastic methods prepare the mind for deliberation and action by disciplining it to make all-important distinctions, so one can recognize the similar as similar, the different as different. In the founding of the American republic, nothing was more necessary than this: to learn from historical and legal precedent the lessons crucial for establishing republican government here, without falling into false conclusions by making categorical errors. Statesman and citizen alike, in a republican government resting on the prudent deliberations of a free and moral people, require such an education on some level.

Contrast this with the example of Woodrow Wilson, president of Princeton more than a century after Witherspoon and, like Madison, also president of the United States. Wilson himself attended Princeton as an undergraduate under the presidency of James McCosh, who opposed the turn to electivism and away from moral formation in higher education promoted by Harvard's Charles W. Eliot. McCosh wrote, "I would rather send a young man in whom I was interested to one of the old-fashioned colleges of the country, where he would be constrained to study Latin, Greek, mathematics, rhetoric, physics, logic, ethics, and political economy."[4] McCosh also emphasized the importance of the college in teaching young men self-government, and he argued that it could do this only insofar as it represented an authoritative tradition and a moral order. When he became president of Princeton, however, Wilson turned the school in Eliot's direction, introducing academic departments and specialized studies; moreover, he attempted to upend and take control of the old network

---

4. James McCosh, "The New Departure in College Education," in *The Liberal Arts Tradition: A Documentary History*, ed. Bruce A. Kimball (Lanham, MD: University Press of America, 2010), 340–341.

of social clubs on campus. Later, as president of the United States, he attempted to effect his progressive view of governance, which distinguished between politics and administration. The former was the arena of public expression of subjective feeling. The latter, insulated from the political process, was the realm where unelected, scientifically trained professionals engaged in the true deliberation and public action.

We see suggested by way of this little historical pastiche how a fixed and rigid curriculum may go together with a republican form of government, resting on the free deliberations of a people well-trained both morally and intellectually, whereas an education which promises many options and paths is conducive to a way of life and government that obscures its arbitrary rule under an empty and illusory freedom.

We now suffer politically, morally, and spiritually for the choices we have made, and the choices we have had, in education. Fortunately, there is a burgeoning reaction at all levels, from primary to post-secondary school. Even though this reaction has not always been motivated by rejection of electivism and professionalization— many so-called classical schools, for example, were created in order to escape the secularism and anti-Christian ire found in public institutions, more than as vehicles for any particular curricular or pedagogical revolution—among this movement, there has been a common embrace of the old *trivium* and *quadrivium*. Some schools are more wedded to these terms than others, but among the new classical schools and colleges, there is a united sense that what is needed is a unified, coherent curriculum in which every subject points to the same truth, and a needful truth at that, about man and his relation to the cosmos. This is what the classical schools have found in the old seven liberal arts.

We are now only beginning to see, after a half century of recovery and practice, what these liberal arts have been and how they can take shape in our schools. They are not disciplines or methods, specialties or skills. They are different but related ways of ordering our understanding of the same phenomena, intellectual, physical, and moral. They are different ways of seeing and pursuing the truth, comprehensive in the sense of providing an account of the whole and man's relation to it, but not comprehensive in the sense of including all subjects and paths of inquiry. Thus, they are the means by which the classical schools are rethinking curricular design, defragmenting and reinvigorating those lifeless and segmented areas of instruction which have been neutered and gutted by modern social science, mainstream education theory, and the enervating forces of relativism, historicism, and secularism: so-called social studies (instead of history), language arts (instead of literature, even English), and so on. This recovery of the *orbis intellectualis* pointed to by the *trivium* and *quadrivium* means rethinking not only the algorithmic, computational, problem-solving approach to mathematics and natural science, but all areas of study and subjects of human concern. Just as, in the medieval university, the mastery of the liberal arts was a precondition for study of theology, law, or medicine, today they can be the means of humanizing and centering exotic studies like computer science, evolutionary biology, and linguistics.

The classical movement, or, more broadly, the move to restore a more traditional and human understanding of education, represents not an anachronistic movement but a transformational, optimistic, future-oriented one. Looking back with some fondness and admiration, as this volume does, at the Scholastic methods of the early American colleges is not senseless nostalgia. Nor does it represent any sort of vanguard of a movement to restore the medieval academic world. This book is being republished now because there is a desire to rebuild decrepit educational institutions and build new ones on solid foundations. Scholastic disputation is one such foundation. We see here that it belongs not to an old, distant world but to our own, that it belongs to us and is within our grasp.

INTRODUCTION TO THE REPRINT EDITION: AMERICA'S FOUNDING IN NATURAL RELIGION

Edward J. Furton

The American Founders and Framers were educated in the Scholastic tradition of the Middle Ages. College instruction began with Boethius' trivium of grammar, logic, and rhetoric, and the quadrivium of arithmetic, geometry, music, and astronomy.[1] Upperclassmen focused on ethics and metaphysics, subjects which, because of their importance, were regularly taught by the college president.[2] The students discussed the problem of universals, the relation of

---

1. James J. Walsh, *Scholasticism in the Colonial Colleges*, 9–10. All numbers refer to the original pagination of Walsh's book.
2. Walsh, *Scholasticism*, 82. "The mental and moral philosophy of these theses, the metaphysics and ethics as taught by the college presidents and tutors, were a direct heritage from the Scholastic philosophy of the medieval universities." Walsh, *Scholasticism*, 11. "Everything contributed to make the old Scholastic philosophy and especially its metaphysics and ethics the most important

prime matter to form, the distinction between essence and existence, the norms of natural law, proofs for God's existence, and
similar topics common in the medieval university.[3] New findings
in the experimental sciences were incorporated into the curriculum, but the general content of college instruction was otherwise
entirely derived from the pre-modern era. "Scholastic philosophy
and medieval methods of teaching it," James J. Walsh observes,
"survived in all the colleges of the English colonies until well
beyond the American Revolution and indeed on into the first quarter of the nineteenth century."[4]

The core of education was "what used to be, and in philosophy classes is still, called natural theology, that is, such a knowledge of God and man's relation to Him and to the universe as may
be secured by the human mind through its own light of reason
apart from revelation."[5] Teachers recognized that knowledge of
God and morality could be acquired through reflection on nature.
This philosophical approach to religious truth had its finest and
most sophisticated expression in the Middle Ages. "The principal
object of the medieval study of philosophy," Walsh writes, "was
to furnish students with a scientific basis for the Christian faith."[6]
By "scientific basis" Walsh means an understanding of nature as a
comprehensive system of causal relations rooted in apodictic first
principles. Under this description, the disciplines of theology and
ethics were accorded a place of honor no less certain in their conclusions than those of physics and mathematics.

---

element in educational life during the last two years of their college course."
Walsh, *Scholasticism*, 79.
3. Walsh, *Scholasticism*, 14.
4. Walsh, *Scholasticism*, 1–2.
5. Walsh, *Scholasticism*, 126–127.
6. Walsh, *Scholasticism*, 12.

"Three academic exercises—the lecture, the declamation, and the disputation—lay at the heart of the education offered at seventeenth-century Harvard," observes the noted historian of American education, Lawrence A. Cremin. "The immediate goal of that education was to enable students to systematize coherently and to contend expertly, abilities highly prized in an oral culture that placed ultimate value on the discovery of philosophical and theological truth."[7] The ultimate aim was to acquire the linguistic skills necessary to engage in thoughtful debate on philosophical topics within the traditional Western understanding of nature as an ordered system of laws established by God. "The arts course began with grammar out of Priscian and Donatus, logic out of Aristotle and Boethius, and rhetoric out of Aristotle, Cicero, and Boethius, and then went to arithmetic and music out of Boethius, geometry out of Euclid, astronomy out of Ptolemy, and the three philosophies—natural, moral, and mental—out of Aristotle."[8] The latter three philosophies addressed the most complex questions in philosophy and were the capstone of colonial education.

To carry out his research, Walsh traveled to the nation's first colleges and examined the broadsheets printed for graduation day. The theses recorded there "constitute an extremely important index of the education of the college graduates . . . during the twenty-five years immediately preceding the Declaration of Independence."[9] They contain "lists of Latin propositions, one hundred or more in number, in logic, grammar, rhetoric, as well as in natural, mental, moral philosophy, and mathematics."[10] Students studied the

---

7. Lawrence Cremin, *American Education: The Colonial Experience 1607–1783* (New York: Harper & Row, 1970), 215.
8. Cremin, *The Colonial Experience*, 197.
9. Walsh, *Scholasticism*, 82.
10. Walsh, *Scholasticism*, 1.

entire set without knowing which would be selected for public defense before their fellow students, family members, and visitors. All present were free to offer comment, raise questions, or even oppose the student's argumentation. This rigorous program far surpasses today's celebratory commencements, but the students were confident that they had acquired the skills to engage in open and unstructured debate about the most advanced subjects in physics, mathematics, ethics, and metaphysics.

Implications of Walsh's Research

Walsh's book indicates that America did not have a Christian foundation, but that it rests instead on a philosophical tradition to which Christians, over the course of the centuries, have made the most notable contributions. The college curricula emphasized the study of nature through experience, especially as this was developed by Aristotle and his school. In the Middle Ages, Aristotelianism was joined to the doctrinal teachings of the Christian faith, but the colonial colleges could not do the same. Sectarianism was a major threat to unity within the country as war with Great Britain approached. The program of instruction therefore isolated the doctrinal differences among Christians. What was advanced for study was available to reason and therefore available to the members of any faith. Natural religion, the pursuit of knowledge about God and morality through the inquiries of mind, enabled teachers and students to arrive at definitive agreements about important matters in religion without stirring up the dangerous denominational differences that troubled the country.

Walsh's book confirms the view of Kody Cooper and Justin Dyer that the system of natural law advanced by the Founders and Framers was inextricably joined to natural theology, that is, to the rational conviction that God exists.[11] All the graduation

---

11. Kody W. Cooper and Justin Buckley Dyer, *The Classical and Christian Origins of American Politics: Political Theology, Natural Law, and the American Found-*

broadsheets contain the standard argument for God's existence: the cosmological proof. This argument has its origin in Aristotle's *Physics* and *Metaphysics*.[12] So too does the central theme of natural law ethics, that nature exists as a teleological system. We can know of the laws of nature because the universe presents itself to the mind as an ordered system of purposeful motion under the direction of God. All Christians, regardless of creed, accepted this. So too did prominent Deists, such as Thomas Jefferson, who united the delegates at the Second Continental Congress under the phrase "the Laws of Nature and of Nature's God." This appeal to natural religion indicates that the representatives in Philadelphia were ready to set aside their sectarian differences and unite under universal principles agreeable to reason.[13]

Contemporary scholarship holds that the Founders and Framers wanted to confine all statements on religious matters to the privacy of church and home. Walsh's study suggests a different conclusion. The division between church and state was in fact meant to be between *revealed* and *rational* religion. Supernatural doctrines that transcend reason were to be excluded from public life but religious truths agreeable to reason were to remain. The central challenge to political union at the founding were the sectarian disagreements over how to properly interpret the Scriptures. These disputes had to be set aside. The principles of natural religion, familiar to the delegates through their education, were therefore placed at the center of American public life. The existence of a Creator God, the moral content of the natural law, the divine source of human rights, and other convictions of reason became the bond of union among the people of the United States.

---

ing (Cambridge: Cambridge University Press, 2022), 1–28.

12. Aristotle's *Physics*, VIII.4–6, and *Metaphysics*, XII.1–6.

13. Cooper and Dyer, *Classical and Christian Origins*, 75–98.

If this is correct, then the United States of America rests on certain truths about God and morality that can be known by the mind independently of belief in supernatural revelation. The Declaration of Independence makes no mention of Christian revelation. Instead, it sets forth "self-evident truths," that is, truths that can be known by the mind independently of the Scriptures. The conclusion follows, therefore, that religious truths agreeable to reason are not subject to church-state separation. Contrary to prevailing opinion, they belong in American public life. The truths of natural religion are the source of our unity as "one nation under God." As we shall see, this interpretation is confirmed by the congressional deliberations over the First Amendment at the First Federal Congress, which show that church-state separation was directed at the beliefs of private religious denominations and not at the common-affirmed truths of natural religion.

The Approach to Religion through Reason

How much of the medieval theory of natural religion did the Founders accept? They accepted all of it, which is but another way of saying that they affirmed whatever could be known by reason. This was not a novel approach. John Locke, in his highly influential *Second Treatise of Government*, observes that "the state of nature has a law of nature to govern it, which obliges every one: and reason, which is that law, teaches all mankind, who will but consult it, that being all equal and independent, no one ought to harm another in his life, health, liberty, or possessions" for we are "all the workmanship of one omnipotent, and infinitely wise Maker."[14] America's founding document mirrors these words. The Declaration appeals to the Laws of Nature and of Nature's God, affirms that all human beings are created equals, and enumerates various goods that the

---

14. John Locke, *Second Treatise of Government*, ed. C. B. Macpherson (Indianapolis: Hackett, 1980), 9.

people have the right to pursue prior to the establishment of government, among them, life, liberty, and happiness.

What exactly is natural religion? For a brief description, we can do no better than the *Summa theologica* of Thomas Aquinas, which begins with the question, "Whether, besides philosophy, any further doctrine is required?" Aquinas replies that because God "surpasses the grasp of [man's] reason ... it was necessary for the salvation of man that certain truths which exceed human reason should be made known to him by divine revelation."[15] He contrasts revealed truth with religious truth that can be known by reason, which includes God's existence. Among his famous five proofs, Aquinas gives the traditional cosmological argument that is also found prominently on the broadsheets of America's colonial colleges.[16] For Aquinas, therefore, there are two paths to religious knowledge: supernatural revelation, which is the path of faith, and natural religion, which is the path of reason.[17] Each complements the other and each has a place within his system.

Similarly, his *Treatise on Law* asks, "Whether Law Is Something Pertaining to Reason?"[18] The answer, of course, is yes. The eternal law, which is the source of all intelligibility in the universe, marks out the goals or endpoints of natural motion. These aims exist as the various types of goods. Natural law, next in descending order, describes nature as it secures these ends. We can fashion laws in imitation of the higher law of Nature's God because we possess reason. For a human law to be just, however, it must follow the order of law found in nature. Although Aquinas was a devout Christian, his reasoning in these sections does not rely on belief in supernatural revelation. He holds that reason can independently

---

15. *Summa theologica* (ST), trans. Fathers of the English Dominican Province (New York: Benzinger Brothers, 1948), I.1.1 corpus.
16. ST I.2.3; ST I.3–26.
17. ST I.1.8 corpus.
18. ST I–II.90–108.

know of God, the Divine Attributes, and the tripartite division of law into eternal, natural, and human. As is clear from the colonial broadsheets, the Founders and Framers took the same view. The ideas developed in scholasticism were thus the source of the principles that informed the Declaration of Independence.

Natural religion, simply put, describes what reason can know about God and morality through its own innate powers. Supernatural faith, in contrast, assents to doctrines that transcend reason. Although the two paths have different starting points, they arrive at some of the same conclusions; for example, both affirm that God exists. Aquinas says that this duplication was necessary "because the truth about God such as reason could discover, would only be known by a few, and that after a long time, and with the admixture of many errors."[19] Other truths, however, depend entirely on supernatural revelation; for example, the doctrine of the Trinity. Christians in early America, though overwhelmingly Protestant, accepted the validity of both paths to religious truth. Those who attended America's first college did not come to learn about the supernatural mysteries of their faith. They were already fully formed Christians.

They came to learn the Western metaphysical tradition handed down from the past by the great thinkers of the ancient and medieval eras.

Theses of the Colonial Colleges

Because of his careful attention to the acquisition of knowledge through experience, Aristotle is considered the first scientist in the West. He wrote on a phenomenal range of subjects, including logic, biology, physics, astronomy, metaphysics, psychology, ethics, politics, rhetoric, and poetry. Following their rediscovery in the Middle Ages, Aristotle's philosophical works were joined to

---

19. ST I.1.1 corpus.

Christianity. His philosophy remained central to the programs of colonial education; however, there was broad agreement within the colleges that his treatises needed revision. The *Physics*, for example, with its theory of four basic elements, earth, air, fire, and water, was obviously outdated. However, little in the way of integration was attempted. Instead, the broadsheets set the metaphysical principles of ancient philosophy, such as matter and form, side by side with the latest experimental findings in the sciences.

Modern empiricism, for example, that of Locke, holds that the mind constructs its representation of the world through the abstraction of ideas from experience.[20] This approach mirrors medieval epistemology, which holds that there is nothing in the mind that is not first in the senses (*nihil in intellectu nisi prius in sensu*). Despite important methodological differences, empiricism continued the classical emphasis on nature as the source of all scientific knowledge. In the great debate between Plato and Aristotle over the source of our ideas, the colleges sided decisively with the Master of the Lyceum. Thus, as expressed by Harvard in 1767: "there are no innate ideas." And again, from Harvard in that same year: "Simple ideas are the foundation of every human cognition."[21]

(Numbers show the original pages in Walsh's book.)

Harvard

"Prime matter is without form." 15
"Form is the principle of individuation." 74
"Water, when frozen in a vacuum, does not expand." 133
"The electric spark does not liquefy bodies by calefaction." 133
"Every homogenous light, according to the degree of its refrangibility, has its own color." 133

20. John Locke, *An Essay concerning Human Understanding*, ed. Alexander Campbell Fraser, vol. 1 (New York: Dover Publications, 1959), 2.1, 121–124.
21. Walsh, *Scholasticism*, 15.

Yale

"Heat is produced by the transverse agitation very rapidly of very small particles." 20
"Earthquakes are caused by subterraneous heat." 20
"There is no such thing as spontaneous generation." 20
[A rejection of Aristotle's view.]

Princeton

"The essences of mathematical entities are immutable." 168

Although the colleges saw the need to correct Aristotle, they continued to follow his logic of inquiry, especially as laid out in the *Prior* and *Posterior Analytics*. The Philosopher, as he was called in the Middle Ages, distinguished between two types of demonstrative arguments: the first which gives knowledge of a fact and the second that which gives knowledge of the reason for a fact, with the latter the superior understanding because it identifies a cause.[22] College instruction encouraged students to form demonstrative arguments in the Aristotelian manner that identified necessary causal connections within nature. Confidence in the ability of the mind to grasp reality enabled the colleges to avoid the modern "screen of consciousness problem," the notion that somehow our concepts conceal reality from view. This unfortunate development would later undermine the notion of objectivity.

Harvard

"Simple ideas are the foundation of every human cognition." 15

---

22. *Posterior Analytics*, I.13.

"When external things are presented to our senses, we perceive the things themselves, not images nor forms of them." 89

"That we ourselves exist we know by intuition, demonstration shows us the existence of God, and the senses bear testimony to the existence of everything else." 89–90

Yale

"The knowledge of particulars is prior to that of universals." 21

"Genus and species are the handiwork of the intellect." 21

"Intellectual cognition is more certain than sensory." 21

The colleges taught that the person is a union of spiritual soul (form) and physical body (matter). The soul, as had been taught in the Middle Ages, has various vital powers, including the ability to grasp ideas in their pure form, which is the key premise in the traditional argument for the immortality of the soul. What is able to think independently of matter is able to exist independently of matter. The colleges considered mind and matter to be radically distinct realities. Neither could be reduced to the other. They did not accept the modern theory that mind originates from matter. Mind, they held, is a spiritual entity. Matter considered in its own right has no agency for thought.

Princeton

"Matter cannot, but mind can think; therefore, the mind is not material." 23

"A conscious succession of thought is not necessary to constitute personal identity." 165

Yale

"The rational soul can act without being attached to the body." 20

"The rational soul can act inorganically." 134

"That matter thinks can neither be demonstrated nor even shown to be at all probable." 135

Harvard

"The soul does not come into existence from the physical contribution of the parents." 75
"The fetus in utero has ideas." 16

The broadsheets repeatedly affirm God's existence. This is typically shown by way of the cosmological argument, the most common proof in the Western philosophical canon. The proof rests on experience, and specifically, on the impossibility of an infinite regress, that is, a causal chain that has no point of origin. In Aristotelian terms, the cosmological proof is a demonstration of a necessary fact. We have knowledge that He exists, but the cause of his existence (his Divine Essence) exceeds our knowledge. Of all the themes taught within the colonial colleges, the proof for the existence of God is the most ubiquitous, though it is noteworthy that the University of Pennsylvania also acknowledged the *a priori* argument of Anselm of Canterbury. This argument has generally been rejected as ineffective, for example, by Aquinas.

Harvard

"An infinite series implies a contradiction." 17
"Cyclogenesis is impossible; therefore, the existence of God may be clearly proved by the argument from cause-and-effect." 19

Columbia

"An infinite series plainly implies contradiction." 231
"By arguing from effect to cause, the existence of God can be demonstrated without difficulty." 232
"Nothing is the cause of itself; therefore, there must exist a first cause from eternity." 232
"There is certainly an analogy between divine and human wisdom." 231

University of Pennsylvania

"The existence of God can be demonstrated both *a priori*
and *a posteriori*." 22
"The will of God is eternal and altogether immutable." 22
"God cannot be the author of sin." 22

Princeton

"The moral perfections of God are not exercised from
natural necessity." 165
"The soul cannot but be conscious to itself of its dependence." 232

Brown

"No being can create itself; therefore, God is not created."
255

Ethics was the second most important subject. A recurring theme
across the broadsheets is that the truths of ethics are no less certain than those of mathematics. This strikes the contemporary
ear as odd, but the Founders did not have a subjective view of
morality. The laws of nature's God, both physical and moral, were
written into nature. Thus, murder was contrary to the immutable
duty to preserve innocent life. This precept would never change.
Other themes in ethics emphasized the freedom of the will, which
of course is necessary to follow the laws of nature, and the ability
of the mind to distinguish between good and evil and so perceive
moral obligation. The broadsheets also recognized the connection
between the laws of nature and the greater good of the social order.

Harvard

"Ethics is equally capable of demonstration as mathematics." 17
"No one acts unjustly unless he acts willingly." 81
"The precepts which are called the laws of nature reason
unfolds to mankind." 86

Princeton

"Truths that are known of themselves exist in ethics; therefore, moral truths can be demonstrated equally with mathematical truths." 172

"Whatever is opposed to the universal good of mankind is opposed to the law of nature." 19

"All things by the necessity of consequences are necessary, but this necessity has no influence over the will of moral agents." 165

"The faculty of distinguishing good from evil is essential to a moral agent."

"The moral sense is only indeed a mode of perceiving moral obligation."

"To be affected by a sense of the Deity and of his Providence is the greatest incitement that we have to the practice of virtue." 172

Brown

"Liberty is an attribute of the will." 24

"The light of nature teaches us to distinguish between good and evil." 257

"No one ever seeks evil as evil; therefore, that anyone should will his own damnation is in opposition to the law of nature." 257

University of Pennsylvania

"The laws of vice and virtue are eternal and immutable." 230

"God's foreknowledge does not at all take away the liberty of the human will." 233

"If a man aspires to true happiness, he must make his actions conform to the laws of God." 228

"Whatever is opposed to the common good is also opposed to the law of nature." 229

"The good or evil of an action arises partly from the object, partly from the end, and partly from the remaining circumstances." 228

The synthesis of the above themes on physics, scientific inquiry, body-soul union, proof of God's existence, and the immutable standards of natural law, are the prerequisites to modern republican political theory. Nature, created by God, contains an objective moral order that is meant to be the guide to human conduct not only at personal level but also for government. Government is necessary to secure the common good, but its laws are just only if they follow the moral order that God has inscribed into nature. Also, under the heading of politics we find an emphasis on the equality of all human beings, the affirmation that the people are the true source of political power under government, and an acknowledgement of the inevitable imperfection of all human efforts to secure justice.

Harvard

"No religion is rational without liberty of conscience." 17
"Politics treats of the external but above all the internal administration of government. The right or authority of the highest civil magistrate always springs from the people. Therefore, the highest civil magistrate has not the right of exercising any authority which is not given to him by the people." 83
"No civil law is just unless it agrees with the principles of the natural law." 119
"The closest bond of civil society is the oath; therefore, the persuasion of the existence of God is necessary for the preservation of civil society." 119
"The true equality of man is not a matter of science or honor or riches but an equality of rights." 135

Columbia

"All men are by nature equal." 229
"The right of authority among [men] does not arise from any superior dignity of nature." 229
"Where right ends, there injury begins, and the right of resistance asserts itself." 234

"All the parts of supreme government may be not improperly reduced to the legislative, federative and executive." 234–235

"That civil power is alone just which makes for the common benefit." 235

"The rights of the people are as divine as those of their rulers." 236

Brown

"Unjust laws often impel men to make revolution." 259

"No form of Commonwealth can be organized by human wisdom that can be entirely without fault; therefore, a just distribution of punishment and rewards cannot be hoped for from our courts." 263

The colonial colleges gave the Founders and Framers a common theological and moral understanding. Truth, understood as the correspondence of the mind to reality, gave them a set of objective propositions that they could affirm through mutual agreement. At the core of this agreement was a system of natural motion under the direction of God. Medieval scholasticism thus provided the philosophical materials to secure political consensus among those who gathered in Philadelphia to sign the Declaration of Independence. As Walsh puts it, "so it was by medieval methods and largely through the study of medieval subjects that the men were educated who signed the Declaration of Independence—for the majority of the signers were college men—but also formed the minds of the men who gave us the Constitution of the United States and of the various States of the Union."[23]

Religious Persecution in Early America

The centuries of religious persecutions that ravaged England and Europe arrived in America in much milder form, yet serious sectar-

---

23. Walsh, *Scholasticism*, 30.

ian divisions persisted. Most of the colonies had a particular branch of Christianity established in law as the official faith of their citizens. Virginia, for example, taxed all citizens for the maintenance of an Anglican clergy, mandated attendance at Anglican services, and considered marriages performed outside the Church of England invalid, thus making bastards of children who could not be assured of their inheritance under the law.[24] This type of sectarian conflict had to be set aside at the Second Continental Congress. In place of the domineering claims within the colonies that one branch of Christianity had the authority to rule over the others, the Founders returned to the principles of natural religion that they had studied in the colleges. Church-state separation, therefore, began at the moment the United States was founded. The First Amendment merely codified what the delegates had decided a decade earlier when they signed the Declaration.

Although the colleges taught a common curriculum, they still exhibited notable doctrinal differences. Harvard and Yale were founded by Congregationalists, Brown University (College of Rhode Island) by Baptists, and Princeton (College of New Jersey) by Presbyterians. Anglicans founded Columbia University (King's College), the University of Pennsylvania (College of Philadelphia), and the College of William and Mary. Harvard, for example, denied the need of baptism for salvation, while Brown University affirmed its necessity.[25] Calvinism took a decidedly more negative view of the use of reason within religion, and this affect the curriculum. In his *Institutes of the Christian Religion*, John Calvin argued that the Fall of Adam and Eve had thoroughly corrupted human nature, making it "totally depraved." As a result, the graduation broadsheets of Calvinist institutions sometimes suggest that little

---

24. John Ragosta, *Religious Freedom: Jefferson's Legacy, America's Creed* (Charlottesville: University of Virginia, 2013), 46.

25. Walsh, *Scholasticism*, 17.

progress would have been made in moral or theological under-standing without the benefit of revelation.

Given their small size and the difficulties of travel, we can understand why the colleges did not want to restrict admission to members of their own faith. For the most part, they opened their doors to all—with the notable exclusion of Catholics. None had the onerous religious tests that were common in England.[26] Some stipulated that ministers of other denominations should have seats on their Board of Trustees.[27] This religious toleration stood in con-trast to the reality of the colonies, where disfavored minorities were routinely deprived of common privileges given to members of the established church. Connecticut had made Congregationalism its official faith and oppressed all other denominations, and especially the Anglicans. In Virginia, the preaching of doctrines contrary to those of Anglicanism were forbidden. Those who dared to do so—often energetic Baptist preachers from the Calvinist tradition—were prosecuted, fined, and imprisoned.[28]

Those at the Second Continental Congress thus found them-selves working alongside delegates whose colonies might imprison them if they were to go there and speak openly about their faith. These divisions would certainly not be resolved in Philadelphia. They had caused wars and persecutions for centuries. Anglicans,

---

26. "None of the colleges founded about the middle of the 18th century in this country ... imposed such tests. Religious tests were still in existence of the English universities and it was difficult for a non-Conformist to secure an education and almost impossible for Catholics." Walsh, *Scholasticism*, 153.

27. The Columbia charter called for representation from the other ministers of the city including the Reformed Dutch Protestant Church, the Ancient Lutheran Church, the French (Huguenot) Church, and the Presbyterian Church. Walsh, *Scholasticism*, 178. The president of Brown University and most of the board had to be Baptist, but there were also to be four members of the Congregational Church, five Episcopalians, and five Quakers. Walsh, *Scholasticism*, 249.

28. Ragosta, *Religious Freedom*, 52–55.

Congregationalists, and Presbyterians made up the majority of the delegates in the assembly, but smaller groups of Lutherans, Dutch Reformed, Deists, and Freethinkers were also there. The presence of Charles Carroll of Carrollton, the lone Catholic to sign the Declaration, was particularly remarkable given the wholesale animosity toward the Catholic Church. He too, of course, was trained in the scholastic tradition.[29] Given the role the Catholic faith has played in preserving, developing, and transmitting this traditional philosophical understanding to modernity, it was certainly fitting that Charles be there.

The curious nature of Quaker beliefs provoked particularly intense hostility, despite their reputation for gentleness and pacifism. The 1659 "An Act for the Suppressing the Quakers, Virginia" stated that the Society of Friends sought "to destroy religion, laws, and all bonds of civil society, leaving it arbitrary to every vain and vicious person whether men shall be safe."[30] The act prohibited their assemblies, prevented the circulation of their writings, and forbade ship captains from landing them on Virginia soil. Those found within the colony were imprisoned and expelled. Anyone who returned was sent away a second time and faced possible execution if caught again. In his *Notes on Virginia*, Jefferson observes that "if no execution took place here, as did in New England, it was not owing to the moderation of the [Anglican] church, or spirit of the legislature, as may be inferred from the law itself; but to historical circumstances which have not been handed down to us."[31]

---

29. Walsh, *Scholasticism*, 50–51.
30. "An Act for the Suppressing the Quakers [sic]," Virginia (1659), in *The Sacred Rights of Conscience*, ed. Daniel L. Dreisbach and Mark David Hall (Indianapolis: Liberty Fund, 2009), 113, spelling modernized.
31. Thomas Jefferson, *Notes on Virginia, Query 17*, in *The Life and Selected Writings of Thomas Jefferson*, ed. Adrienne Koch and William Peden (Random House: New York, 1944), 253.

A particularly infamous case is recorded by the General Court of Massachusetts.[32] Three Quakers were discovered within the colony, cast out, but soon returned. The two men were hanged, but the court granted leniency to the woman. "Mary Dyer upon the petition of her son, and the mercy and clemency of this Court, had liberty to depart within two days, which she hath accepted of."[33] Yet, before long, she returned and was also hanged. The case caused an uproar in Boston, with many considering the treatment unduly harsh. Mary Dyer had simply wanted to live close to her son and other relatives. The Court disagreed and justified its conduct through a public report. The law and the expulsions should have been sufficient warning to Dyer and the other Quakers of the seriousness of their fault, the Court averred, and these factors "vindicate us from the clamorous accusation of severity."[34]

Maryland was founded by Catholics. The early settlers were protected by Cecil Calvert, Lord Baltimore, the colony's first Proprietor, through the "Maryland Act for Church Liberties" (1638).[35] Ten years later, "An Act concerning Religion" (1649) extended this legal protection to Christians generally. The Act is historically important because it was the first to offer some measure of security for the free exercise of religion, yet its severity is nonetheless disturbing. Punishments were threatened for anyone who did willfully

---

32. "A Declaration of the General Court of the *Massachusets* [sic] Holden at *Boston* in *New-England*, October 18, 1659. Concerning the Execution of Two Quakers," in Dreisbach and Hall, *Sacred Rights*, 112–113.

33. "A Declaration of the General Court," in Dreisbach and Hall, *Sacred Rights*, 113. Spelling modernized.

34. "A Declaration of the General Court," in Dreisbach and Hall, *Sacred Rights*, 113.

35. "Maryland Act for Church Liberties, 1638," in *The American Republic: Primary Sources*, ed. Bruce Frohnen (Indianapolis: Liberty Fund, 2002), 64.

"wrong, disturb, trouble, or molest any person whatsoever within this province professing to believe in Jesus Christ for or in respect of his or her religion or the free exercise thereof."[36] Ten shillings were exacted for each offense. "If the party so offending as aforesaid shall refuse or be unable to recompense the party so wronged, or to satisfy such fine or forfeiture, then such offender shall be severely punished by public whipping and imprisonment."[37]

Among the terms singled out for potential abuse were "heretic, schismatic, idolator, Puritan, independent, Presbyterian popish priest, Jesuit, Jesuited papist, Lutheran, Calvinist, Anabaptist, Brownist, antinomian, Barrowist, Roundhead, separatist, or any other name or term in a reproachful manner related to matter[s] of religion."[38] The sacred names honored among Christians were shielded under the same act, with execution for certain offenses.

> That whatsoever person or persons within this province and the islands thereunto belonging shall from henceforth blaspheme God, that is curse Him, or deny our Savior Jesus Christ to be the Son of God, or shall deny the Holy Trinity, the Father, Son, and Holy Ghost, or the Godhead of any of the said Three Persons of the Trinity or the Divinity of the Godhead, or shall use or utter any reproachful speeches, words, or language concerning the said Holy Trinity, or any of the said Three Persons thereof, shall be punished with death and the confiscation or forfeiture of all of his or her lands and goods to the Lord Proprietary and his heirs.[39]

---

36. "An Act concerning Religion, Maryland (1649)," in Dreisbach and Hall, *Sacred Rights*, 106. Spelling modernized.
37. "An Act," in Dreisbach and Hall, *Sacred Rights*, 106. Spelling modernized.
38. "An Act," in Dreisbach and Hall, *Sacred Rights*, 104. Spelling modernized.
39. "An Act," in Dreisbach and Hall, *Sacred Rights*, 104. Spelling modernized.

Penalties were less severe for words spoken against the Virgin Mary, the Apostles, and the Evangelists, but they included public whippings and imprisonment.

Such harsh penalties seem shocking today, but they were common in the colonial period.[40] Differences over doctrinal matters were a constant source of tension and violence. The Unitarians, a radical offshoot of Calvinism, rejected the doctrine of the Trinity and affirmed that God is a Unity of Being. Prominent Puritan ministers, such as Thomas Hooker and Roger Williams, held similar views. A Unitarian minister passing through Maryland who openly denied that God is a Trinity was subject to execution and the forfeiture of all his property. The punishment thus extended even to descendants. The difficulty in these disputes is that whether God is a Trinity or a Unity depends on interpretations of scriptural matters that are beyond the power reason to fully understand. Such disagreements, therefore, are in principle impossible to resolve on rational grounds. Although the Maryland Act was offered by Catholics to advance religious toleration, it achieved this aim only by controlling and censoring the religious opinions of its citizens.

Unfortunately for Catholics, when the Anglicans achieved a majority in the Maryland legislature, the assembly enacted oppressive measures against their faith. "Anti-Catholicism stood at the

---

40. In 1641, the General Court of Massachusetts Bay approved a legal code that assigned death for a variety of infractions. The first of the fifteen laws is: "If any man, after legal conviction shall have or worship any other God, but the Lord God, he shall be put to death. Exod. 22, 20. Deut. 13.6 & 10. Deut. 17 2.6." "Capital Lawes," in *American Heritage: A Reader*, ed. Hillsdale College History Faculty (Hillsdale, MI: Hillsdale College Press, 2011), 33–35. Virginia had similar legislation: "That no man speak impiously or maliciously against the holy and blessed Trinity, or any of the three persons, that is to say, against God the Father, God the Son, and God the Holy Ghost, or against the known articles of the Christian faith, upon pain of death." "Laws of Virginia, 1610," in *American Heritage*, 10.

very center of Maryland's legal, religious, and political cultures."[41] Catholics were unable to attend college "because of religious intolerance and the administration of test oaths calculated to prevent their securing any higher education."[42] Despite these disadvantages, Baltimore became the first Catholic diocese in the United States and John Carroll (1735–1815) the nation's first bishop. Like other members of the Carroll family, John was educated by the Jesuits at the College of St. Omer in Artois, France. He entered the Jesuit order, but renounced his association after Pope Clement XIV suppressed the Society of Jesus in 1773. Bishop Carroll is noteworthy for his founding of Georgetown University in 1789, the first Catholic institution of higher learning in the United States.

His cousin, Charles, was the last surviving signer of the Declaration, and a good friend of John Adams, as their several letters attest. The Carroll house still stands today behind St. Mary's Church in the historic city of Annapolis. A little-visited site on Spa Creek, the building is most notable for an elevated passageway that runs between the Redemptorist rectory and the side of the house. During periods of anti-Catholic unrest, the priest would cross through the enclosed passage to celebrate Mass within the Carroll home. Despite his patriotism and strong financial support for the war, Charles's commitment to the Catholic faith prevented him "from enjoying the privilege of voting, legal protection, and citizenship."[43] He was nevertheless the principal drafter of the state's constitution and played a prominent role in Maryland politics.[44]

---

41. Bradley J. Birzer, *American Cicero: The Life of Charles Carroll* (Washington DC: Regnery Press, 2010), 42.

42. Walsh, *Scholasticism*, 50–51.

43. Birzer, *American Cicero*, 33.

44. Birzer, *American Cicero*, 124–125.

In the *Federalist Papers*, James Madison cites his arrangement of the Maryland Senate as a model for the Federal Constitution.[45]

The Carrolls looked favorably on the American experiment in self-government. They saw in the Declaration of Independence and the Constitution a steady movement toward complete freedom of religious practice. In his old age, Charles remarked that he did not sign the Declaration solely to escape British rule, but also to advance the cause of religious toleration. The example of an assembly of men drawn from different Christian denominations, joined together in a new republic, would be "a useful lesson to all governments." Freedom of worship would advance, "founded on mutual charity, the basis of our holy religion." Having experienced religious persecution first-hand, Charles noted with pleasure the growth of toleration among the various Christian denominations, also reflected in public law. "Happily, this wise and salutary measure has taken place for eradicating religious feuds and persecutions."[46]

Natural Religion and the First Amendment

Charles's nephew, Daniel (the older brother of Bishop John Carroll), was a Representative from Maryland in the First Federal Congress. Like Charles, he too had a distinguished career in politics and signed both the Articles of Confederation and the US Constitution. He had the honor of serving on the committee that finalized the House version of the First Amendment to the Bill of Rights, joined there by Madison and other distinguished figures. Given the persecution of Catholics in colonial America, Daniel had a particular interest in ensuring that freedom of religion would be secure under the new Constitution. He was also made a member of the Conference Committee that reconciled the House and Senate ver-

---

45. Alexander Hamilton, John Jay, and James Madison, *Federalist Papers: A Commentary on the Constitution of the United States* (New York: The Modern Library, 1937), n. 63.

46. Birzer, *American Cicero*, 116.

sions, giving us the religion clauses as we have them today: "Congress shall make no law respecting an establishment of religion, or prohibiting the free exercise thereof."

An examination of the federal record—kept by Madison—shows that the distinction between rational and revealed religion remained very much at the center of the discussions over how best to phrase the religion clauses. The major concern was that one denomination of Christianity, or perhaps several conspiring together, would acquire sufficient power in the US Congress to make their faith the official religion of the United States. There were repeated efforts to do just that, as Jefferson reports, especially among the Congregationalists and the Anglicans (renamed Episcopalians).[47] A review of the congressional record shows that the supernatural beliefs of particular faiths were at issue, not the truths of natural religion. This confirms the above thesis that the United States rests on religious convictions that are knowable by reason and that are therefore in principle separable from Christianity. The committee certainly had no intention of confining the founding truths to private life.

The first substantive remark comes from Rep. Peter Silvester of New York, who thought the initial language for consideration, "no religion shall be established by law, nor shall the equal rights of conscience be infringed," might be misinterpreted. The text, he said, "was liable to a construction different from what had been made by the committee [and] might be thought to have a tendency to abolish religion altogether."[48] This possibility led Roger Sherman of Connecticut to propose that the committee strike the language. "Congress hath no authority whatever delegated to

---

47. Jefferson to Dr. Benjamin Rush, September 23, 1800, in Koch and Peden, *Selected Writings of Jefferson*, 510–511.

48. "House Debate over Religion Clauses (1789)," in Dreisbach and Hall, *Sacred Rights*, 427.

them by the Constitution to make religious establishments."[49] This remark indicates that the object of congressional concern was the possibility that one denomination of Christianity would gain the supremacy and make its faith the National Church of the United States. Sherman observes that Congress does not and should not have that power under the Constitution.

This brings us to Daniel Carroll. At this point in the discussion, removing the language entirely is on the table, but Carroll resisted this. He not only favored the language but thought it a necessary addition.

> As the rights of conscience are, in their nature, of peculiar delicacy, and will little bear the gentlest touch of the governmental hand; and as many sects have concurred in opinion that they are not well secured under the present constitution, he said he was much in favor of adopting the words. He thought it would tend more towards conciliating the minds of the people to the Government than almost any other amendment he had heard proposed. He would not contend with [the] gentleman about the phraseology, his object was to secure the substance in such a manner as to satisfy the wishes of the honest part of the community.[50]

Carroll understood, as did Sherman, that the religion clauses of the First Amendment were intended to deny the federal government any authority over matters of faith within the states. There are "many sects," he says, that do not feel safe under the new Constitution and that would like better security for their practice of religion. Carroll is clearly talking about revealed religion, not natural religion.

---

49. "House Debate," in Dreisbach and Hall, *Sacred Rights*, 427.
50. "House Debate," in Dreisbach and Hall, *Sacred Rights*, 427.

Madison, who speaks next, proceeds to identify what he believes is the point at issue: "That Congress should not establish a religion, and enforce the legal observation of it by law, nor compel men to worship God in any manner contrary to their conscience."[51] In an effort to better capture this sense, Madison thought

> that if the word national was inserted before religion, it would satisfy the minds of honorable gentlemen. He believed that the people feared one sect might obtain a pre-eminence, or two combine together, and establish a religion to which they would compel others to conform. He thought if the word national was introduced, it would point the amendment directly to the object it was intended to prevent.[52]

Here again the discussion concerns matters of faith, not religious truths that are agreeable to reason. Although Madison's recommendation was not accepted by the committee, the aim was to prevent the Congress from interfering in the practice of religion within the states.

Joseph Story, the celebrated commentator on the US Constitution, confirms this interpretation in his *Commentaries* of 1779–1845:

> The real object of the amendment was, not to countenance, much less to advance Mahometanism, or Judaism, or infidelity, by prostrating Christianity; but to exclude all rivalry among Christian sects, and to prevent any national ecclesiastical establishment, which would give to an hierarchy the exclusive patronage of the national government. It thus cut off the means of religious persecution (the vice and pest of former ages,) and of the subversion of the rights of conscience in matters of religion, which had

---

51. "House Debate," in Dreisbach and Hall, *Sacred Rights*, 427.
52. "House Debate," in Dreisbach and Hall, *Sacred Rights*, 428.

been trampled upon almost from the days of the Apostles to the present age.[53]

The amendment, Story says, was to prevent a "national ecclesiastical establishment," that is, a National Church. This was to be accomplished by excluding "all rivalry among Christian sects" at the federal level and thus preserving "the rights of conscience in matters of religion."

Freedom of Religious Expression

Walsh's book appeared prior to the US Supreme Court's disastrous series of decisions on church-state relations beginning in the 1940s.[54] The Court began to claim for itself the authority to decide matters pertaining to religion within the states. As we saw just above, the religion clauses of the First Amendment were expressly designed to prevent that from happening. The Court's jurisdiction concerns congressional legislation, not state legislation. If Congress can make no law, then the Court has nothing to adjudicate. But the Court reversed the plain meaning of the text. In *Everson v. School Board* (1947), the Justices held that the establishment clause of the US Constitution means that "neither a state nor the federal government can set up a church. Neither can pass laws which aid one religion, aid all religions, or prefer one religion over another."[55] This pairing of "state government" and "federal government" has no foundation in the text.

In 1962, *Engel v. Vitale* further ruled that it was unconstitutional for New York State to require public school students to recite the following prayer at the beginning of each day: "Almighty God, we acknowledge our dependence upon Thee, and we beg

---

53. *Commentaries on the Constitution of the United States*, n. 1865, in Dreisbach and Hall, *Sacred Rights*, 436.

54. Ronald B. Flowers, *That Godless Court? Supreme Court Decisions on Church-State Relationships* (Louisville, Kentucky: 1994), 15–19.

55. Flowers, *Godless Court?*, 64–65.

Thy blessings upon us, our parents, our teachers and our country. Amen." Such prayers were commonplace and had been since the beginning of the republic. What the New York Assembly authorized was nothing more than what had been stated in the Declaration of Independence. If God exists and has created us, as the Founders declared, then we are indeed dependent on Him. This is not a revealed doctrine that depends on the interpretation of passages taken from the Bible, but a conclusion of reason. A nondenominational prayer such as that above cannot be a violation of the Constitution because it is but a deduction from the founding principles. If that is not admitted, then we arrive at the conclusion that the public profession and teaching of the Declaration of Independence is a violation of the Constitution.

Jefferson is often faulted for these opinions. The courts like to cite his "wall of separation between church and state," but he applied the word "church" to the sectarian doctrines of private religious establishments, not to natural religion. Jefferson wrote the phrase in response to an appeal from the Danbury Baptists of Connecticut who complained to him about their ill-treatment within a state that had made Congregationalism its official religion. "What religious privileges we enjoy (as a minor part of the State) we enjoy as favors granted, and not as inalienable rights: and these favors we receive at the expense of such degrading acknowledgments, as are inconsistent with the rights of freemen."[56] Jefferson knew that if he announced a national day of prayer and fasting, as he had been asked to do, the Baptists of Connecticut would suffer persecution. They would be forced to attend Congregationalist churches, listen to heretical sermons, and if they refused, face fines or imprisonment. Of course, as the principal author of the Declaration, Jefferson had no intention of suppressing the founding document.

---

56. "Letter from Danbury Baptist Association to Thomas Jefferson (Oct. 7, 1801)," in Dreisbach and Hall, *Sacred Rights*, 526.

He favored the free expression of all religious opinions. His *An Act for Establishing Religious Freedom* appeared only a few months after the Declaration. The operative clause has two parts, the first separating church and state, and the second guaranteeing freedom of religious expression.

> *Be it therefore enacted by the General Assembly,* That no man shall be compelled to frequent or support any religious worship, place or ministry whatsoever, nor shall be enforced, restrained, molested, or burthened in his body or goods, nor shall otherwise suffer on account of his religious opinions or belief; but that all men shall be free to profess, and by argument to maintain, their opinions in matters of religion, and that the same shall in nowise diminish, enlarge, or affect their civil capacities.[57]

The passage of Jefferson's bill in 1786 effectively brought the favored status of the Episcopal Church in Virginia to an end. From then on, dissenting citizens were free to openly express their religious opinions without fear of fines or imprisonment.

The bill, of course, did not resolve sectarian differences within the state, but it did encourage agreements across denominational lines. Jefferson expected that the free expression of religious opinion would lead to a renewed consensus on those truths that are agreeable to reason. He wanted schools funded by the state to teach these truths about God and morality. Cremin captures this well in his summary of the three major aims of the *An Act for Establishing Religious Freedom*.

> First, the assumption that rational men need education to arrive at religious truth quite as much as to achieve political wisdom; second, the insistence that such elemental education as they need for their quest derives more appropriately from state-sponsored schools than from state-

---

57. *An Act for Establishing Religious Freedom,* in Koch and Peden, *Selected Writings of Jefferson,* 290.

sponsored churches; and third, the belief that, given a widespread diffusion of knowledge, the cause of religious truth is best served by permitting all churches to proffer their doctrines in a private capacity.[58]

Jefferson wanted public religious instruction, not carried out by state-sponsored churches, as had been the practice, but by state-sponsored schools. These would advance natural religion. Instruction in the supernatural doctrines of America's various denominations would be confined to private life.

Some might reply that Jefferson's *An Act for Establishing Religious Freedom* was meant to eliminate all religious conviction from public life, both rational and revealed, but the text itself disproves this. Its opening line is, "Well aware that Almighty God hath created the mind free."[59] This is a theological premise in natural religion, and from it everything else in the bill follows. As in the Declaration, Jefferson makes no appeal to any doctrine of the Christian faith. He speaks instead in the language of reason. God has created the mind free and therefore any effort to compel religious assent is immoral. The Virginia Assembly voted as a majority to enact Jefferson's bill into law despite the fact that it rests on theological premises. If it had been their intention that all religious conviction should be eliminated from public life, the legislation would have suppressed itself. That did not happen. They understood that Jefferson's bill assumes the distinction between rational and revealed religion.

Teaching the Founding Truths

Today's public schools should be free to teach that God's existence can be known by reason, that God is the Creator of the universe, that God has inscribed an objective moral order into nature, that

---

58. Cremin, *The Colonial Experience*, 442.

59. *An Act for Establishing Religious Freedom*, in Koch and Peden, *Selected Writings of Jefferson*, 289.

this order of law is the standard for all human conduct, that the natural virtues are necessary to human happiness, that the human being is a composite of body and soul, that our highest power is reason, that truth is the correspondence of the mind to reality, that the soul survives death, and that God is just and will assign rewards and punishments accordingly. Every one of these propositions was accepted on rational grounds by the Founders and Framers. They drew these ideas from the Western philosophical tradition. What flows from them are the principles of modern republicanism: that all human beings are created equal, that God endows the people with their rights, and that the written laws of government must follow the laws of nature if they are to be just.

The line of separation between church and state, as Walsh's research shows, is between revealed religion, which requires faith in supernatural revelation, and natural religion, which derives from philosophical reflection on nature. When the Founders met at the Second Continental Congress, they put aside their sectarian differences and united under religious truths agreeable to reason. These could be affirmed regardless of any commitment to a private religious creed. George Washington's series of letters to the religious congregations of America exemplifies how this rational understanding of religion offered a welcoming hand to all people of faith. He assured members of every denomination settled in America that the nation would protect their right to freely practice their religion. Their supernatural doctrines, of course, would have to be confined to private life, but these beliefs would be nurtured by a common and public understanding of God and morality that was agreeable to reason.

In the mid-twentieth, century the Supreme Court began to treat the founding principles as if they were the supernatural doctrines of some private religious establishment. The Justices were apparently unaware of the two paths to religious truth as described by the Western philosophical tradition. They also badly sullied Jefferson's name. His draft of the Declaration of Independence is what enabled the delegates to overcome their sectarian divisions and unite under a common theological and moral conception. "The Laws of Nature and of Nature's God" recalled to the representatives their education in the America's first colleges, which placed natural religion at the center of the curricula. The Founders joined the nation under religious truths that can be known by reason. The result of their effort, as Jefferson said, was the Declaration of Independence, "an expression of the American mind."[60] That expression was meant to always remain at the center of American public life, but it was suppressed by a defective interpretation of the First Amendment.

---

60. Jefferson, Letter to Dr. Henry Lee (May 8, 1825) in Koch and Peden, *Selected Writings of Jefferson*, 656.

scholasticism in the colonial colleges

education of the
founding fathers
of the Republic

james j. walsh

PREFACE

Scholasticism, the philosophy of the schoolmen and of the medieval universities, the group of subjects which occupied most of the
attention of European university students for a thousand years or
more, is usually thought to have gone out of vogue at the end of
the Middle Ages or to have disappeared with the New Learning at
the Reformation. That almost universal impression is entirely mistaken. The proof of the serious fallacy that has gained acceptance in
this matter is to be found in the easily ascertainable fact that Scholasticism continued to be the philosophic teaching of European but
also American universities and colleges down until well on in the
nineteenth century.

The evidence for this is abundant and convincing in the
archives of our colonial colleges. A set of very precious official
documents attest it. On commencement day, the candidates for
the degree of BA were required in all the colleges of this country
in the seventeenth and eighteenth centuries to defend a series of
propositions, about one hundred more or less, that were printed
at the expense of the students and were distributed to such of the
audience as cared to take part in the public disputation which was
held, as Cotton Mather tells us, on commencement morning.

x These propositions summarized the studies in philosophy which represented the principal occupation of the students during the last two years of their college course and for a considerable portion of the preceding two years.

This fact, which is manifest at once and is quite indisputable when our American colonial college theses are studied, especially in connection with the college regulations as regards the holding of disputations regularly every week, is the most surprising revelation that we have had in the history of American education for several generations. It seems quite impossible to the great majority of our educators that Scholasticism should have continued to maintain its foothold in European and American colleges down to the beginning of the nineteenth century. Scholasticism has always been looked upon as a thing of the distant past, but as a matter of fact, the men who organized our government of the people, by the people, and for the people in its present form were most of them trained mentally in accordance with this medieval mode of thought and teaching.

The Founding Fathers of our republic, then, were educated according to the academic traditions which had been formulated in the earlier Middle Ages by Boethius, sometimes hailed as the father of Scholasticism, developed under St. Anselm in the eleventh century, reaching their culmination in the mind of Aquinas and the group contemporary with him in the thirteenth century, when there came the conciliation of Scholastic doctrines with Aristotle, thus welding together the whole course of philosophic thought.

xi A number of the professors of philosophy to whom I submitted the colonial college theses reechoed the expression of the distinguished historian of Harvard that it is a matter of pride and congratulation that our American colleges were in their inception linked with the age-old traditions of education which have come down to us from the Greeks of the golden age of Athens and represent the core of the college curriculum until well on in the nineteenth century.

The chapters on the history of education at each of the colonial colleges were submitted to the history departments of the present-day institutions, and suggestions made by them were invariably taken.

I have to thank his Excellency, Right Reverend James H. Ryan, rector of the Catholic University, Right Reverend John A. Ryan, professor of ethics at the same institution, Reverend John X. Pyne, SJ, professor of philosophy at Fordham University, and a number of other Jesuit teachers of Scholastic philosophy, a group of professors in the diocesan seminary of Philadelphia at Overbrook, who discussed the theses with me on several occasions, Reverend Lucian Johnston of Notre Dame of Maryland in Baltimore, and finally Reverend M. D. Chenu of the Institute of Medieval Studies at Ottawa for their kindness in examining for me the theses of the colonial colleges to determine their Scholastic quality. All these men, either at the present time or within a few years, have been engaged in teaching Scholastic philosophy and are agreed that the great majority of these theses are, as in the words of Father Chenu, "pure Scholastic formulas."

xii

I have to thank Reverend Dr. Peter Guilday, professor of American Church history at the Catholic University, Washington, for valued advice as well as the reading of the proofs, and Reverend Michael J. Mahony, SJ, professor of philosophy at Fordham University, for similar aid.

I owe special thanks to Professor Samuel E. Morison, historian of Harvard University, who asked for an article on "Scholasticism in the Colonial Colleges" for the *New England Quarterly* (July 1932). His appreciation of the significance of the commencement theses in the history of American education encouraged further study of the documents.

Author's Introduction:
Scholasticism in the
Colonial Colleges

What would seem to be undoubtedly the most important group of *1* documents for the history of education during the colonial period in this country, but also for a full generation after the Declaration of Independence, has been strangely neglected or profoundly misunderstood. These are the so-called commencement theses printed on broadsides (large sheets of paper some 20 x 24 inches) and comprising lists of Latin propositions, one hundred or more in number, in logic, grammar, rhetoric, as well as in natural, mental, moral philosophy and mathematics. The thesis sheets were printed for distribution among members of the audience who, on commencement morning, might choose to take part in the public act which was held as the culminating exercise of the examination. These broadsides were of a size and shape that made their preservation somewhat difficult, so that many of them were lost and many others tucked away in libraries, so that they were not easy to get at and attracted little attention. When studied they afford definite proof of a fact that has been but very little appreciated, indeed usually quite ignored. This is that Scholastic philosophy and medieval methods of teaching it survived in all the colleges of the English colonies until well beyond the American revolution and indeed on into the first quarter of the nineteenth century.[1]

All the colleges in the various English colonies, even those founded in the second half of the "century of enlightenment," used these theses, differing slightly in content and terminology but alike in purpose and essence. The Harvard College library has original imprints or photostats of many of the theses issued at her commencements since 1642.[2]

Four of the sets of theses that were issued by the College of New Jersey at Princeton about the middle of the eighteenth century are available for study in the Princeton University Library.[3] The John Hay Library at Providence has more than thirty of the theses

---

1. William Coolidge Lane, late librarian of Harvard, wrote an excellent account of the Harvard theses from the bibliographical point of view under the title "Early Harvard Broadsides," *Proceedings of the American Antiquarian Society* 24.2 (October 1914): 264–304. Miss Lao Genevra Simons, professor of mathematics at Hunter College, New York, has a description of commencement theses in "Introduction of Algebra into American Schools in the Eighteenth Century," *Department of the Interior, Bureau of Education, Bulletin* 18 (1924), but touches only the mathematical theses. Like many other workers in Americana, I am greatly indebted to Mr. Wilberforce Eames for suggestions and assistance in the study of the theses and their significance. I am also indebted for many courtesies to the librarians of Harvard, Yale, Princeton, Pennsylvania, William and Mary, Columbia, and Brown.

2. Checklist in Lane, "Early Harvard Broadsides." The Harvard College Library has since acquired photostats of all theses not represented in its collection by originals. Most of the known theses for the seventeenth century are printed in John Langdon Sibley, *Biographical Sketches of Harvard University, in Cambridge, Massachusetts*, vols. 1–4 (Cambridge, MA: Harvard University Press, 1873, 1881, 1885, 1933).

3. 1750, 1752, 1760, 1762.

issued at the College of Rhode Island (Brown University).[4] None *3*
has been preserved from King's College (Columbia), but receipted
bills for their printing prove their existence.[5] Three surviving theses
sheets of the College of Philadelphia (University of Pennsylvania)
are in the collection of the Historical Society of Pennsylvania.[6]

None from William and Mary (founded at Williamsburg
in 1693) is extant, but there is a well-substantiated tradition that
they were printed and distributed at Williamsburg, and the college
authorities there still hope to find copies which may have escapade
the vicissitudes of the Civil War in some of the Virginia homes.
Yale has more than fifty of her theses.[7]

At the top of each thesis sheet comes, in various-sized capitals,
a fulsome dedication to the governor of the province—in Pennsylvania to the proprietor—followed by slightly less flowery compli-
ments in proper gradation of type to lesser colonial officials, college
officers, the clergy, and patrons of learning in general. There follow
the Latinized names of those who are about to receive the bachelor's
degree, with the declaration that they are ready to defend these the- *4*
ses "manfully." The verbs and sometimes certain adverbs of dedication were expressed in single-letter abbreviations such as had been
used in the dedication of books in the sixteenth century. The simplest formula was D.D.D. (*Dant, Dicant, Dedicant*), but a number
of them were much more complicated than this. For instance, the

---

4. 1769–1774, 1786, 1788–1800, 1802–1805, 1808–1817.
5. Information from office of the secretary of the university.
6. 1761, 1762, 1763. That of 1762 is reproduced in George Bacon Wood,
   Early History of the University of Pennsylvania from Its Origin to the Year 1827,
   3rd ed. (Philadelphia: J. P. Lippincott, 1896).
7. Every year from 1718 to 1797 inclusive, except 1719, 1721, 1722, 1729,
   1731, 1732, 1735, 1737, 1741, 1748, 1761, 1775–1780 inclusive, 1791,
   1792, 1794, 1796. During some of the vacant years, no theses were issued.
   Yale has copies of most of her masters' *questiones* for 1740–1789. Information
   from Yale University reference librarian.

Yale thesis sheet of 1751 has the letters H.L.M.D.D.C.Q. (*Humil-lime, Libenter, Merito, Dant, Dicant, Consecrant Que*—Most Humbly, Joyfully, and Deservedly Give, Dedicate, and Consecrate).[8]

The method of using these theses on commencement day is best understood by quotations from Cotton Mather's *Magnalia*, in which he makes it very clear that the principal part of the exercises on Harvard commencement day consisted of the public act in which these theses were discussed and disputed:

> When the *Commencement* arrived ... they that were to proceed *Bachelors*, held their *Act* publickly in *Cambridge*; whither the *Magistrates* and *Ministers*, and other *Gentlemen* then came, to put Respect upon their Exercises: And these Exercises were besides an *Oration* usually made by the *President*, *Orations* both *Salutatory* and *Valedictory*, made by some or other of the Commencers. ... But the main Exercises were *Disputations* upon *Questions* wherein the *Respondents* first made their *Theses*. ...
>
> At the *Commencement*, it has been the Annual Custom for the *Bachelors* to publish a Sheet of *Theses, pro virili Defendendae*, upon all or most of the *Liberal Arts* among which they do, with a particular Character, distinguish those that are to be the Subjects of the Publick *Disputations* then before them; and those *Theses* they *dedicate* as handsomely as they can, to Persons of Quality, but especially the GOVERNOUR of the Province, whose PATRONAGE the Colledge would be recommended unto.
>
> The *Masters* do, in a half-sheet, without any *Dedication*, publish only the *Quaestiones pro Modulo discutiendae*, which they purpose either affirmatively or negatively to

5

---

8. *Publications of the Colonial Society of Massachusetts*, V.

maintain as *Respondents,* in the *Disputations*, which are by them to be managed.[9]

These broadsides are often erroneously presumed to have been commencement programs. That they very distinctly were not, although commencement programs grew out of them. Originally a thesis sheet was in effect an intellectual challenge to the learned community by the graduating bachelors. It was a set of propositions to be demonstrated, that is, proved syllogistically, by any of the candidates for the degree and then manfully defended (*viriliter* or *pro virili defendendae*) against any objections that might be urged in contradiction or impugnment of them. Certain theses were, as Cotton Mather states, distinguished by special type or an index. These were "on the program" so to speak; the proponents and opponents of these theses were already selected, the debate already arranged. The other theses on the sheet were the challenges to the learned public. Presumably every candidate was prepared to take up any thesis chosen by an objector in the audience and maintain it.[10]

6

---

9. Cotton Mather, *Magnalia Christi Americana: The Ecclesiastical History of New England from Its First Planting in 1620, until the Year of Our Lord 1698* (London: Thomas Parkhurst 1702), bk. IV. See Anonymous, *New England's First Fruits* (1643), Old South Leaflets, n. 51 (Boston: Directors of the Old South Work, 1896), which shows that this procedure had been followed since the first Harvard commencement in 1642. The masters' commencement, for which the *quaestiones* sheets mentioned by Mather were issued, was held in the afternoon, the bachelors' commencement in the morning. The *quaestiones* disputed by the MA candidates were of the same character as the bachelors' theses but treated more complex and important subjects. For a checklist of Harvard *quaestiones*, which have been more abundantly preserved than the theses, see Lane, "Early Harvard Broadsides."

10. This was the practice at Edinburgh, from which Harvard probably got the idea of thesis sheets. A. Grant, *History of the University of Edinburgh* (London, 1927).

Many ministers of the Gospel in colonial America were graduates of European universities, particularly of Oxford, Cambridge, Leyden, Dublin, and Edinburgh, in all of which an important method of education in the arts and philosophy courses, down to the nineteenth century, was the disputation. At Cambridge, for instance, every freshman was required to go through a series of public disputations before he became a junior sophister. The senior sophister was subjected to another such test before he became a bachelor, and the bachelor disputed again before he could take his master's degree. In addition, every college of the university had disputations among its members for practice. It is easy to understand, then, that some of the attending clergymen at early Harvard commencements would be ready to renew their college memories and take part once more in disputations, although I am told that there is no positive proof that they did so.

Even if the disputations were confined to degree candidates, there must have been some interesting intellectual tilts on the occasion of commencement. The public act, or *inceptio* (commencement), as this public performance was still termed in accordance with medieval custom, must have represented something of an ordeal for the commencers. It is probable that professors and tutors would come to the rescue of flustered students who were defending some dubious proposition and not making themselves quite so convincing as they should. This had always been the custom in such university exercises in Europe. It is probable that even those present who did not understand Latin were amused and interested in the element of contention which was thus brought into the commencement exercises.

When I was a student under Father Jouin, SJ, fifty years ago at St. John's College (now Fordham University)—his textbooks of philosophy are still in use—we held disputations every week and, toward the end of the academic year, our public act, as we still called it, in which certain of us were appointed to defend certain theses and others required to oppose them. After the formal disputation of the public act was over, some of the clergymen who were present and who had received their training in philosophy after the Scholastic method took occasion to offer certain objections to our theses. They argued syllogistically just as we were supposed to do, *8* making the proper distinctions. I well remember the Reverend Dr. McGlynn and the Reverend Dr. Burtsell taking part in our public act at Fordham. Monsignor Capell, a distinguished visitor from London, also took part in the discussion; but I recall that he asked the privilege of using English instead of Latin.

It is not merely as a survival of a medieval custom that these theses are interesting. They are chiefly significant as indicating the principal subjects of study in the colonial college curricula. Many have assumed that American college students of the eighteenth century devoted their undergraduate years principally to the study of the classics. These theses reveal that classical studies took up a comparatively small portion of their time. In New England, particularly, students entered college from Latin grammar schools where, from early childhood, they had devoted themselves almost exclusively to Latin with a modicum of Greek. They had mastered Latin grammar, read various Latin authors, and were acquainted with some of the simpler Greek classics or the New Testament. Latin, then, was an instrument which every freshman was supposed to be capable of using. College students were subject to a fine if they talked anything but Latin in college except during those hours set aside for recreation.

During their first two years, the collegians read certain Latin and Greek authors for the sake of their content rather than for linguistic training. Cicero, for example, was studied mainly because *9* he was a model of oratory, and really forceful public speaking was one of the facilities that a college man was supposed to acquire. Homer was read because of his knowledge of human nature. A favorite author was Longinus "On the Sublime" because of the value that his presentation of this subject was supposed to have for rhetoric. The definitely announced purposes of education at all the colonial colleges were the preparation of men for the ministry and the magistracy. Above all, the colonists wanted learned ministers capable of expounding the Scriptures. They also wished to have as judges and other government officials men who were learned in the law and capable of expressing themselves in such a way as to be leaders of the people and teachers of good citizenship. A somewhat slighter emphasis was placed on the study of *bonae litterae* (*belles lettres*); but that purpose is found as early as the Harvard charter of 1650 and was stressed in the eighteenth century. Every colonial college proposed to continue the English tradition of giving a good general education to gentlemen who did not intend to follow any particular profession.

Sometimes Horace and Virgil found a place in the curriculum of the first two years, but the principal subjects for freshmen and sophomores were grammar, logic, and rhetoric. Anyone familiar with the curriculum of the medieval universities will recognize these subjects as the old *trivium*, or first three of the seven liberal arts which came down through the Middle Ages. The *quadrivium*, modified by the advance of knowledge and consisting in medieval times of arithmetic, geometry, astronomy, and music, constituted another part of the seven liberal arts which made up the curriculum of the university studies for the degree of Master of Arts. And finally, the arts course was crowned by the three philosophies: natural (physics, etc.), mental (metaphysics), and moral (ethics).

It may be thought that this curriculum was stunted and conventional, little calculated to provide mental development, but that is not the opinion of authorities such as Denifle, Haskins, and Rashdall, who have given critical attention to medieval education. Nor is praise of the medieval curriculum confined to historians. When Huxley was elected rector of the University of Aberdeen, he made a study of what comprised the arts curriculum at the time when Aberdeen was founded some four centuries before. He found, however, quite contrary to his expectations, that the arts course had a precious value of its own. His inaugural address as

10

lord rector on the subject of "Universities: Actual and Ideal" must have quite taken the breath away from "progressive educators" in his audience: "The scholars (of the medieval universities) seem to have studied Grammar, Logic, Rhetoric; Arithmetic and Geometry, Astronomy, Theology, and Music." And he added in commentary, "Thus their work, however imperfect and faulty, judged by modern lights, it may have been, brought them face to face with all the leading aspects of the many-sided mind of man. For these studies did really contain, at any rate in embryo—and sometimes, it may be, in caricature—what we now call Philosophy, Mathematics and Physical Science, and Art." And in conclusion, a statement which must have seemed particularly strange in the mouth of Huxley: "*And I doubt if the curriculum of any modern University shows so clear and generous a comprehension of what is meant by culture, as this old Trivium and Quadrivium did*" (emphasis added).   *11*

Our colonial thesis sheets are, naturally, in Latin, as were the disputations as well as most of the textbooks and lectures in the colonial colleges. To most modern students, this would add a new and almost insuperable difficulty to study, but Latin was then the language of scholars and of textbooks, and as we have seen, no one was admitted to the colonial colleges who could not use Latin readily. After a certain familiarity with technical terms had been acquired, it is probable that the student found no difficulty in reciting in Latin. In that language, there is a very definite expression of philosophic knowledge in terms that do not vary and that bring out the inner and substantial meaning of things.

The mental and moral philosophy of these theses, the metaphysics and ethics as taught by the college presidents and tutors, were a direct heritage from the Scholastic philosophy of the medieval universities. Certain modifications had been made in the course of time, but these were far from enough to change their essential character. Scholasticism means simply the philosophy of the monastic *schools* during the early Middle Ages. The principal   *12*
object of the medieval study of philosophy was to furnish students

with a scientific basis for the Christian faith that all were presumed to have. This method of education began with the earliest medieval schools and was gradually developed under great teachers like Boethius in the sixth century, Alcuin in the ninth, and Anselm in the eleventh, until it came to its highest expression in the thirteenth century. William Turner, in his *History of Philosophy*,[11] says, "Scholastic philosophy had its origin in the foundation of the Carolingian schools, an event which was the beginning of an intellectual renaissance of Europe in no way inferior in importance to the humanistic renaissance of the fifteenth century." He adds, "The schoolmen were defenders of the rights of reason. ... Scholastic philosophy was eclectic in the truest sense of the word. While preserving a correct idea of systematic cohesiveness, it admitted elements of truth from whatever source they were derived."

The schoolmen contended that there could be no contradiction between philosophy and theology. The two subjects were complementary. Both were studied and taught for the same purpose: the rational defense and exposition of Christianity. If they were properly taught, it was certain that the more knowledge a student acquired, the better Christian he would be.

This conception of the proper relation between philosophy and theology was unshaken by the Reformation. Oxford, Cambridge, Edinburgh, and Dublin had exactly the same idea of it in 1650. The colonial colleges inherited the same conception, although in the later seventeenth century, natural philosophy began to split off from the other philosophies and to become an experimental discipline. Apart from that, philosophy was taught definitely for the defense of Christianity. Observe, for instance, a pair of linked theses presented at the College of Rhode Island (Brown): *Deus potest esse ergo est*, "God can be, therefore He exists."

11. William Turner, *History of Philosophy* (New York: Ginn, 1903) [pp. 417, 418 —ed.].

Any "clerke of Oxenforde" or of Paris would have been able to take part handsomely in this disputation, could he have been translated to eighteenth-century Providence. For this is one form of the ontological argument for the existence of God first called to the attention of the schoolmen by St. Anselm in the eleventh century. If the human mind has an idea of God, that can only be because the idea of God comes to us by our very nature, or since there is in the mind the idea of such a Being (greater than any that can be thought), such a Being must exist outside of the mind; therefore, God exists not only in the mind as an idea but also outside the mind as a reality.[12]

To most modern minds, this argument of St. Anselm's does not carry much weight. Aquinas called attention to what is really the fatal flaw in every ontological proof—the transition from the ideal to the real, from the world of thought to the world of things. Duns Scotus, nevertheless, took up this ontological argument with enthusiasm later in the thirteenth century and endeavored to give it greater strength. In modern times, the argument has been renewed in slightly different form by Descartes and Leibnitz and, I think, also by Hegel. Almost in the present generation, philosophers like Rosmini or our own Thomas Davidson and Orestes Brownson were taken by what is known as ontologism, or the ontological proof for the existence of a Supreme Being. The fact that such distinguished thinkers should have found satisfaction in this argument illustrates what an appeal it has to a certain lofty type of mind.

14

Certain features proper to Scholasticism have drawn down upon it no little obloquy in modern times because they have been presumed to demonstrate the metaphysical trivialities and the super refinements of logic which the Scholastic philosophy cultivated. These characteristic features of Scholasticism are (1) universals,

---

12. Turner, op. cit.

that is, the discussion of how the mind abstracts a universal idea from the concrete, (2) prime matter and form as the explanation of the constitution of matter, (3) the distinction between essence and existence, and (4) the syllogistic method of argumentation which presupposed the use of deduction rather than induction for the demonstration of truth. All these peculiar characteristics of Scholasticism are found in the theses of the colonial colleges down to the end of the eighteenth century and even beyond. Scholasticism, the philosophy of the medieval schools, formed the minds of the Fathers of the Republic.

15   The only way to illustrate the Scholasticism of these theses is to quote examples which show very clearly the medieval origin of the propositions. The Harvard theses for 1653 make it clear that the teaching as to the constitution of matter was the Aristotelian formula, matter and form:

- Quantity is derived from matter and quality chiefly from form.
- Prime matter is without form.

The Harvard students of 1653 were discussing space as we are in these Einsteinian days, but from the metaphysical standpoint. Their formula ran, "Space is not a being." They were also discussing the necessity for a medium if action was to take place: "No nature can operate *in distans*" (i.e., unless there is some medium to carry the activity). Under *theses theologicae* was the proposition "Even though the future life should be taken away there still remains an obligation to virtue."

Over a century later, the Harvard theses of 1767 included the following under *theses logicae*:

- Simple ideas are the foundation of every human cognition [the familiar fundamental proposition in epistemology].
- The conclusion of a categorical or hypothetical syllogism does not reveal any truth that was not included

12

in the premises; therefore, the purpose of syllogistic argumentation is not to investigate but to defend truth.

Under *metaphysics* that year (1767), the Harvard men defended the following propositions:

- There are no innate ideas [showing that they were followers of Aristotle, and not Plato].

- Necessary immortality is to be attributed to no spirit except God.

- Two created spirits cannot occupy the same place at the same time.

16

The next two theses are connected and represent an important truth in psychology, which is still the teaching of Scholastic philosophy: "The soul is not propagated from the fertilized *ovum* (*traduce*); therefore, it is created by God and breathed into the *foetus*." A very interesting proposition for modern times is number 9 among the metaphysical theses at Harvard in 1767: "The *foetus in utero* has ideas." Freud's teaching suggested that there were some ideas, especially with regard to sex life, which made their appearance in the mind of the foetus during its life in utero. I need scarcely say that this is not Scholastic teaching, although the idea underlying the proposition had been broached a number of times during the Middle Ages, and some of the mother's ideas were supposed to affect the mind of the foetus and produce something resembling mental operations in the unborn child.

Some of the ethical theses at Harvard in 1767 are of special interest: "Ethics is equally capable of demonstration as mathematics." In our time when morals are thought by so many to be lacking in firm foundation and when we have had a number of suggestions as to the "new morality," this declaration with regard to ethics takes on a very special significance. Other ethical theses are quite as positive:

- The obligation to virtue is eternal and immutable.

- The joy of sensitive pleasure is perceived in hope rather
17   than in possession.

- An object equal to human desire is necessarily Infinite.

This last represented one phase of the proof for the existence of God as desumed from man's desire for happiness.

The last two propositions in metaphysics at Harvard that year were extremely important and definitely Scholastic: "Spirits are as equally true and real as bodies" (i.e., spiritual substance is as real as matter). The twelfth proposition under metaphysics that year is quite as important and quite as Scholastic, although it has not the same appeal to the generality as to the Scholastically minded: "An infinite series implies a contradiction" (i.e., things that succeed each other must have a beginning; they cannot run on forever; there cannot be an infinite series of causes; there must have been a first cause).

The theological theses in these colonial colleges are all interesting, but many follow the particular tenets of the sect which controlled the college. For instance, at Harvard in 1767, number 3 among the theological theses ran, "There is no absolute necessity of baptism for salvation." But at the College of Rhode Island, where the Baptists were in charge, they were very emphatic about the necessity for baptism. Others showed the infiltration of rationalism as the "century of enlightenment" approached its tempestuous close. For instance, among the theological theses at Harvard in 1767: "'No religion is rational without liberty of conscience." But *18* the metaphysical theses at Brown in 1774 were the old-fashioned metaphysics of the medieval schools:

- The highest happiness of intelligent beings accrues from the pursuit of perfection.

- If matter existed of itself there would be a universal *plenum* [i.e., all space would be full of matter].[13]

---

13. A college song sung at Harvard at that time ridicules the *plus* and *plenum* of the Scholastic metaphysics. See *Publications of the Colonial Society of Massachusetts*, XXV.

14

Other propositions defended at Brown are similarly medieval:

- Being can effect nothing of higher dignity than itself.
- All the spiritual ideas which we possess are acquired from our own spirits.

The influence of modern philosophers was making itself felt; this last proposition is decidedly Cartesian. The Scholastic mode of expression for the same truth would be, I am told, "All the spiritual ideas which we possess are obtained by intellectual abstraction from sensuous representations." The two are perhaps not so distant in meaning that they might not be harmonized.

We find the Scholastic discussion of universal ideas illustrated at Brown in the *theses logicae* of 1774: "All universal ideas are entities of reason." Then there is that interesting question of time which we are still discussing: "The idea of duration accompanies every idea of the human mind."

The *theses metaphysicae* at Princeton in 1752 help us to understand the Harvard theses of about the same period:

- Whatever is made up of parts cannot be infinite.
- A simple being as such is prior to and more perfect than a composite being.
- Cyclogenesis [i.e., the birth of one thing from another in a closed series without any beginning] is impossible; therefore, the existence of God may be clearly proved by the argument from cause and effect.

Perhaps the most striking of all: "Moral evil does not take away the perfection of this world."

Among the *theses ethicae* at Calvinistic Princeton that year were these distinctively Scholastic propositions:

- God's foreknowledge does not at all impair the freedom of the human will.
- Whatever is opposed to the universal good of mankind is opposed to the law of nature.
- God in His decrees takes account of the whole universe.

The Princeton students emphatically defended freedom of the will, which they considered quite as important as the intelligence: "In beings that either absolutely or in their own kind are perfect the perfection of the will is equal to the perfection of the intellect" (i.e., the more developed in intelligence, the higher the responsibility, because the greater the power of the individual to regulate his actions). The following is printed in italics with an index in the margin to show that it was on the program to be actually debated: "All the actions of a moral agent do not proceed from self love." This was a most timely proposition for that time, when the utilitarian school of philosophy in England (Benthamism) was asserting the contrary: that man acted only from a striving after something that would be useful for himself.

20   In 1718 the Yale theses were entered under the rubrics *technology, logic, grammar, rhetoric, mathematics*, and *physics*, but there were many theses under *physics* which were really metaphysical. For instance,

- The will cannot be forced.
- All the predictions of the astrologers with regard to future contingent events are fallacious and vain.[14]
- The rational soul can act without being attached to the body. [This would have been called a psychological proposition in the Middle Ages.]

Besides these metaphysical and psychological theses, we have a number of strictly physical and chemical theses:

- Heat is produced by the transverse agitation very rapidly of very small particles.

---

14. Such events as were dependent on human free will and therefore could not be foretold by natural means. It is perhaps significant that Jonathan Edwards was a student at Yale at this time and probably heard this thesis debated.

- The *ignis fatuus* (or will-o'-the-wisp) is not due to the ignition of meteors.
- Earthquakes are caused by subterranean heat.
- There is such a thing as the transmutation of metals.

For many years during the nineteenth century, when the atomic theory was at the height of its influence, the question of the transmutation of metals seemed to be absurd, but we are now back to the teaching of the colonial colleges in the early eighteenth century in this respect.

There were a number of biological theses:

- Metamorphoses of insects occur.
- There is no such thing as spontaneous generation. [This was later denied by biologists but restored to science by Pasteur.]

21

A thesis in what we would now call physiological psychology, the truth of which is supposed to be a nineteenth-century discovery, runs, "The diversity of sensation depends on the diversity of the nerves which carry it."

The Yale *theses logicae* of 1770 furnish abundant evidence of the intimate relation between the colonial teaching of philosophy and that of the Middle Ages. Two of the twenty-five *theses logicae* run,

- The knowledge of particulars is prior to that of universals.
- Genus and species are the handiwork *(opificium)* of the intellect.

All of which goes to show that Yale men were still occupied with the two leading medieval problems of universals and particulars, genus and species, when such men as David Humphreys and Abraham Baldwin were in college. There were such other propositions as

- Intellectual cognition is more certain than sensory.
- The best method [of securing knowledge] is by proceeding from the simplest things by degrees to the most difficult.

Most of the *theses physicae* at Yale that year (1770) were definitely related to mechanics and physics. Others took up problems in astronomy, a few touched on biology, but some would now be considered metaphysical rather than physical. Two theses marked for actual debate are

- All matter is the same [in its underlying substratum. Scientists are back to that idea again].

- Privations [negative qualities] have no true and real entity.

22   The theses at the College of Philadelphia (University of Pennsylvania) were of the same general character as the others. The first provost, William Smith, had been recently connected with the University of Aberdeen and was, therefore, closer than other colonial college presidents to European traditions. This only made him insist on more theses and in greater variety. In 1763 over a hundred theses appeared under ten different rubrics. It might be expected that under the influence of Benjamin Franklin, the most prominent figure among the trustees, metaphysics would receive slight attention, but there are no less than sixteen propositions under this rubric, arranged in three divisions: on being in general, on God, and on the human mind. In other colonial colleges, these would have been classified as ontology, natural theology, and psychology or pneumatology. The University of Pennsylvania also had an important general rubric, *theses morales*, with three Aristotelian divisions: ethics, natural jurisprudence, and politics.

The three extant thesis sheets of the University of Pennsylvania give a major part of the space to metaphysics and ethics, the subjects taught by Provost Smith. Among the theses *de Deo* in 1761 are these:

- The existence of God can be demonstrated both *a priori* and *a posteriori.*

- The will of God is eternal and altogether immutable.

Philadelphia had decided ideas on the place of sin in the world and the punishment that it deserves:

- God cannot be the author of sin.
- Eternal punishment is in no way repugnant to the divine attributes.

Among the theses *de mente humana* in 1761 is this thesis: "Matter cannot, but mind can think; therefore, the mind is not material."   *23*

Under *theses mathematicae* are these:

- Mathematics is concerned with quantity and is an entirely necessary handmaid of natural philosophy.
- Mathematical truth can be demonstrated; therefore, to propose mathematical theses as if there could be any disputation over them is absurd.

This was a trenchant criticism of other colonial colleges, which were debating mathematical theses just as they did those in physics and metaphysics. They continued to do so, ignoring their critical colleagues in Philadelphia.

The distinctive Philadelphia theses were those on natural law and natural jurisprudence. There were not a few which seem to reflect the practical wisdom of Poor Richard:

- Every lie even in a joke or out of politeness is a sin.
- It is permitted to human kind by the laws of nature to slaughter brute animals and to eat their flesh.

It will be remembered that Benjamin Franklin once believed the contrary but took to the fleshpots after discovering that big fishes ate little ones!

The Brown theses of 1769 in pneumatology, a term almost the equivalent of our psychology, are interesting as representing a series of direct assertions as to the existence of spirits and the spirit world, which most psychologists of the present day are unwilling to accept:

- Pneumatology is the treatise in which there is discussion of spirits.
- Whether spirits exist not joined to bodies can be known only from revelation.

24

- For spirits considered in themselves there is no where [i.e., they do not exist in space].
- Angels have not by their own nature the power of moving matter.
- Liberty is an attribute of the will.
- Spirits do not consist of parts; therefore, by their very nature they are immortal.
- Matter cannot think.

These propositions come down from the Middle Ages. They were often defended in these exact words in the medieval universities, and most of them are still defended by the students in the Jesuit schools. It was their close similarity with the theses which we had at Fordham in my graduation year (1884), when we held our public act and defended our theses before a group of invited guests, that made me realize the continuity. Visitors who attended the public act at Fordham were supplied with lists of theses from which they might take up their argumentation, just as the printed broadsides were distributed at the colonial colleges.

I submitted a number of colonial college theses to Right Reverend John A. Ryan, professor of ethics in the Catholic University of Washington, and to the Reverend John X. Pyne, SJ, professor of philosophy in Fordham University and author of a treatise on Scholastic psychology. Monsignor Ryan commented as follows: "Many of these subjects are represented in the theses which our candidates offer for the degree of licentiate in theology at the examinations. As we should naturally expect, some of the theses falling under the head of theology and ethics in the colonial college lists

25   are not entirely orthodox but as a whole they show a considerable measure of agreement with those that a Catholic would undertake

to defend in this same field. *The observation that occurs to my mind most frequently on reading these is that scholastic requirements have considerably declined in the secular colleges since pre-Revolutionary days*" (emphasis added). He concludes, "I am speaking of course of the requirements for a genuine liberal education." Monsignor Ryan agrees with Huxley in his estimate of the cultural value of such theses in developing the many-sided mind of man.

Father Pyne's opinion is closely similar to that of Monsignor Ryan. He refers to Fordham teaching:

> The material contained in the theses which were submitted to the students of philosophy in the early American colleges is of the same generic character as those submitted to students of philosophy and religion here today. It is obvious, of course, that theses on religion will vary according to the theological tenets of the faculty. What is likely to strike any reader of the theses is that, while they undoubtedly do differ in many essential respects from the present day scholastic theses, there are yet ever so many points of resemblance between them. The strictly philosophical theses show a close approximation to the Aristotelian viewpoint, as do the present day theses in Scholastic philosophy. Here again there are differences. But the similarities are much more striking than the dissimilarities.

Reverend Lucian Johnston, professor of philosophy at the *26* College of Notre Dame of Maryland (Baltimore), wrote me in similar vein: "Verily the reading of the theses carried me back to my seminary days at the College of the Propaganda in Rome where practically the same sort of theses were the customary themes for our weekly disputation and examinations, as well as for the Public Acts."

Reverend William J. Lallou, professor of sacramental theology at St. Charles Seminary, Overbrook, which is one of the best-known of our Catholic seminaries, that is, institutions for the intellectual training of young men for the priesthood, said to me when I presented a copy of the theses to him, "These theses are just like those which are now presented in our own seminary and indeed are of the same kind as are used in the various seminaries in Rome." There is a collection of colleges in Rome representing the various countries in which young men from distant parts of the world receive their education for the priesthood and get in touch with the true spirit of Roman Catholic tradition and philosophy during the four or more years that they spend there. It is from among these graduates of Roman colleges that the hierarchy in various countries is to a great extent recruited. They are supposed to have been trained in all that is intellectually Catholic to the last degree.

27

It is extremely interesting, then, to find that the matter and manner of their teaching philosophy is very similar in Rome at the present time to that which constituted the curriculum of the colonial colleges in America during the last two years of the collegians' devotion to their studies. Rome still maintains the old tradition, and it is conceded by those who know whereof they speak that the Roman students trained in Rome, and especially those who have received their doctor's degree there, know how to think. The great complaint that lies against the students of the colleges which a hundred years ago abandoned Scholastic teaching is that their pupils can no longer think for themselves.

We have, thus, the testimony of the Catholic University as well as of the Jesuits and of the Roman colleges and seminaries as to the similarity amounting practically to identity of the teaching of philosophy in the American colleges before the revolution and the Catholic colleges of the modern time. There can be no doubt at all about the thoroughgoing Scholasticism of the philosophic curriculum in the American colonial colleges.

It remained, however, to get in touch with the other important department of Catholic education for an opinion on this subject. The French have often differed from the rest of the Catholic world on many thoughtful subjects and especially with regard to philosophy. I sent a copy of the theses, therefore, up to Ottawa

22

to the Institute of Medieval Studies at the university there. Father Chenu, the director of the institute, who is also professor of the history of medieval theology at the University of Ottawa, wrote me in reply, "Your study on Scholasticism in the colonial colleges [of English America] is a very curious document for the history of *28* education; all these theses are pure Scholastic formulas." We have confirmation, then, from all quarters, of the Scholasticism which continued to be taught in the colonial colleges until after the Revolution and, indeed, for nearly a generation after that. Scholasticism constituted the principal part of the curriculum in the culminating years of the college course.

The amplest proof of the identity of these colonial theses with the Scholastic propositions which are still defended in the Jesuit colleges is to be found in the Latin textbooks on logic, metaphysics, and moral philosophy by Father Jouin, SJ. These textbooks were written more than fifty years ago but are still in use in the classes in mental and moral philosophy, and their phraseology is almost exactly the same as that of the colonial theses. There is the same discussion of universals, of matter and form, of substance and accident, of freedom of the will, of the natural law, of conscience, of happiness as man's last end, of the necessity for revelation, of the occurrences of miracles, and of man's rights and duties—all of which were constantly recurring in the colonial colleges.

These theses had been in use in the Jesuit schools since the adoption of the Jesuit *ratio studiorum* in the early seventeenth century and by them were taken over from the medieval universities. With regard to these Scholastic theses and their significance, both as mental training and as a method for approaching ultimate truth, Professor Saintsbury of the University of Edinburgh has written, *29* "There have been in these latter days some graceless ones who have asked whether the science of the nineteenth century after an equal interval will be of any more positive value—whether it will not have even less comparative interest, than that which appertains to the Scholasticism of the thirteenth." Professor Saintsbury adds,

However this may be, the claim, modest and even meager as it may seem to some, which has here once more been put forward for this Scholasticism—the claim of a far reaching educative influence in mere language, in mere system of arrangement and expression—will remain valid. If at the outset of the career of modern languages, men had thought with the looseness of modern thought, had indulged in the haphazard slovenliness of modern logic, had popularized theology and vulgarized rhetoric as we have seen both popularized and vulgarized since, we should indeed have been in evil case. It used to be thought clever to moralize and to felicitate mankind over the rejection of the stays, the fetters and the prison in which its thought was medievally kept. The justice or the injustice, the taste or the vulgarity of these moralizings, of these felicitations, may not concern us here, but in expression as distinguished from thought the value of the discipline to which these youthful languages was subjected is not likely now to be denied by any scholar who has paid attention to the subject.[15]

30   So it was by medieval methods and largely through the study of medieval subjects that the men were educated who signed the Declaration of Independence—for the majority of the signers were college men—but also formed the minds of the men who gave us the constitutions of the United States and of the various states of the Union. No generation, either in this country or elsewhere, ever thought out more deeply and more thoroughly the problems of human life and their relation to the happiness of the many than this group of men who, between 1770 and 1790, laid the deep foundations of our republic.

---

15. George Saintsbury, *The Flourishing of Romance and the Rise of Allegory* (New York: Scribner, 1897).

Part I

1

The Education of the Founders

In his introduction to the revised edition of Sanderson's *Biogra-*   *33*
phies of the Signers of the Declaration of Independence,[1] Robert T.
Conrad said,

> It may be doubted whether any popular body has com-
> prised so large a proportion of highly educated members
> [as the Continental Congress who signed the Declaration
> of Independence]. The number of those who had regu-
> larly graduated in the colleges of Europe or America was
> twenty-seven or nearly one half the whole number, fifty-
> five. [There were] Twenty other members whose educa-
> tion though not regularly collegiate was either academic
> or by dint of unaided energy as in the case of Franklin was
> equal or superior to the ordinary course of the universities.
> Nine of the members only of that august body can be set
> down as of ordinary and plain education, though in that
> number are included men of extensive reading, enlight-
> ened views and enlarged sagacity.

---

1. John Sanders, *Biographies of the Signers of the Declaration of Independence*, rev.
and ed. R. T. Conrad (Philadelphia: William Brotherhead,1865).

He adds, "There is no movement on record in which so large an amount of political science, observation, wisdom and experience was brought to bear as in the American Revolution."

These facts are all the more noteworthy because there were almost no free schools in those days and of course nothing like compulsory education. In spite of that fact, all the signers of the Declaration were men of well-developed mentality. This is strikingly exemplified in the lives of all the signers. Even the one among the signers who is sometimes picked out as a noteworthy exception to the rule that these statesmen received the opportunity for a good preliminary education at least, George Walton of Georgia, succeeded, in spite of the handicap of never having been at school, in securing for himself a mental development that made him an important member of the bar in the colonies, and tradition declares him to have been in later life a man of wide reading and cultural attainments.

Most of the signers were members of what are called the learned professions. Twenty-four, or nearly one half the whole number, were lawyers; there were thirteen planters or farmers, but in those days, dwellers on plantations and farms, almost as a rule, found opportunities for cultivating their minds as well as the soil, and many of them were deeply interested in having their sons receive a good education. Besides, there were nine merchants, five physicians, two mechanics, one clergyman, one mariner, and one surveyor. Forty-two out of the fifty-five signers at the time of signing were between the ages of thirty and fifty, most of them between thirty and forty, just the period in life when men are still likely to be deeply influenced by the education which they have received.[2]

---

2. All of these men went through serious mental trials and deep solicitude, some of them suffered severe physical hardships for the nearly seven years of the Revolution, and yet their average age at death was sixty-eight years and four months, and this in spite of the fact that one of them (Button Gwinnett) was killed in a duel within the year after signing the Declaration of Independence,

It is a never-ending source of surprise to note how many of   *35*
the signers had the full benefit of the college education of that day,
which required a preparatory school training of some four or five
years in the classics and then four years of college work. These men
who received their degree of Bachelor of Arts had had an excellent introduction to the classics in Latin but also in Greek, knew
more than a little about Hebrew, and had been trained in the college curriculum of those days in rhetoric, grammar, logic, and the
three philosophies—mental (metaphysics), natural (physics) which
included some physiology, and moral (ethics)—as well as in natural
theology, with mathematics which included some astronomy.

When as students they came up from the Latin schools to
college or from their private tutors, they were expected to be able
to talk Latin. Indeed, their collegiate exercises in logic the first year
and in metaphysics and ethics but also in natural philosophy in the
concluding years were conducted in Latin. They even knew their
mathematics in Latin terms and were thus closer to the great math-   *36*
ematical classics than are our students. There was a fine for talking
anything but Latin except in recreation, and the tradition is that
the statute in that regard was enforced and the fine was substantial
and money was very precious in those days. They were expected to
be able to read at least the New Testament in Greek, and it must
not be forgotten that when the *Massachusetts Bay Psalm Book* was
printed (1638), it was translated from the original Hebrew by clergymen in the colonies who had been educated in the English and
Scotch colleges after the same method and in accordance with the
curriculum that was introduced into the colonial colleges.

---

and another one (Thomas Lynch Jr.) was lost at sea (not a trace of the vessel on
which he and his wife sailed ever having been found) within three years after
the signing. John Adams and Thomas Jefferson lived until July 4, 1826, the
semicentennial of the day on which the signing is usually said to have taken
place. Charles Carroll of Carrollton, the oldest and latest survivor who had
put most to the hazard of revolution, died at the age of ninety-five in 1832.

The first signer of the Declaration of Independence, John Hancock, is a typical example of the sort of man to be found among these signers. The president of the Congress received his preliminary education under the care of his uncle, a rich Boston merchant who was also, strange as it may seem in colonial America some two hundred years ago, a distinguished patron of science and literature. His uncle saw to it that his nephew, John, received a good preparatory education and then sent him to Harvard, where he received his Bachelor of Arts degree. This meant that he had successfully pursued the course known as the seven liberal arts, the *trivium* and *quadrivium*, which constituted the college curriculum of those days as it had been pursued in the English universities as an inheritance from the medieval universities.

37   What is true for John Hancock is quite as true for the other signers from Massachusetts. Samuel Adams made his preparatory studies at the well-known Latin grammar school of Mr. Lovell and received the degree of AB from Harvard in 1740. Not satisfied with this collegiate distinction, he pursued his studies further and three years later was granted the degree of Master of Arts. His cousin, John Adams, made his preparatory studies at Braintree and received the bachelor's degree from Harvard in 1755. Both of these men continued to be students all their lives.

Robert Treat Paine, like Samuel Adams and a number of the other men who reached prominence in Massachusetts about this time, was prepared at the Lovell School for Harvard, which he entered at the age of fourteen and from which he was graduated with the degree of AB four years later. Elbridge Gerry, who was to be so prominent in political life and later to be vice president of the United States, received his degree of AB from Harvard in 1762. All of the Massachusetts signers, then, were college men, but all of them were men who did not think that their studies begun in college were ended when they took their degrees. All of them continued their interest in their classical studies and reviewed their philosophy during the subsequent years. A Latin quotation would never go over their heads, and their philosophy of life was always molded by their knowledge of the significant events that had occurred in the past and the works of the classical writers who had contemplated the human scene and made reflections on human life that threw interesting side lights on existence at all times.   *38*

What was true in this regard in Massachusetts was almost as true in Virginia. George Wythe, the first of the Virginia signers, had no college experience, but he was fortunate in a mother who was herself learned in Latin and who pursued her studies with her son, encouraging him in Greek, as well as in Latin, so that she made of him one of the leading classical scholars in the country. We know the scholarliness of George Wythe because he had among his law students three of the most distinguished men of that time: Thomas Jefferson, John Marshall, and Henry Clay. We have no greater intellectual trio in our history than these, and since they agreed in proclaiming the scholarship of their preceptor, there can be no doubt at all of the fact.

Virginians usually obtained their preliminary education from private tutors in their homes. Their fathers lived on plantations, as a rule somewhat as medieval seigneurs on their estates, but they were deeply intent on their boys' receiving a thorough education. They had the leisure to continue their studies after graduating at college, and the surprise is how many of them, or at least, strange as it may seem, of those who interested themselves in politics, occupied their leisure very profitably with cultural subjects.

Richard Henry Lee, the second of the Virginia signers, after having had the benefit of private tutors, was sent for further education to Wakefield in Yorkshire, England. They seem to have imbued him there with a love for learning so that when, at the age of nineteen, he returned to Virginia, he devoted his leisure to a great extent to his books. He was interested particularly in the study of ethics and in the philosophy of history, the story of events not for themselves but for their causes and effects. Lee's copybooks   *39* have been preserved, and they furnish an excellent idea of the extent of his intellectual interests and his use of his leisure for study.

Thomas Jefferson, the author of the Declaration as well as one of its signers, is one of the world's greatest thinkers in the realm of politics. In our own day, Mr. John W. Davis, the well-known American lawyer, at the unveiling of a bust of Jefferson in Richmond, Virginia, September 22, 1931, hailed him as "first among American political philosophers, the great apostle of freedom, the foremost liberal in the modern world." Under private teaching and through the influence of his father, Jefferson received an excellent preparatory education and entered the College of William and Mary at sixteen. He had been so well trained that two years later he was given the degree of Bachelor of Arts at eighteen. He was quite willing to confess that his years in college exerted a deep influence on him all through life. He said in his *Autobiography*, "It was my great good fortune and what *probably fixed the destinies of my life* that Dr. William Small of Scotland was then professor of mathematics at William and Mary" (emphasis added). Dr. Small was made president and took over the teaching of ethics, "and from his conversation," Jefferson says, "I got my first views of the expansion of science and of the system of things in which we are placed." As we shall see in the chapter on William and Mary, Jefferson was quite willing to attribute the success of his career to the influence exerted over him in his impressionable youth by President Small.

40

The next of the Virginia signers, Benjamin Harrison, was the father and great grandfather of presidents of the United States. He was governor of Virginia just after the Revolution. He entered as a student at William and Mary but, owing to friction with the faculty, did not take his degree there, though he continued all his life to be interested in the studies begun there. Thomas Nelson Jr., his colleague, was another one of these Virginians who was sent to England to have the opportunity for education afforded by the mother country. He received his preparatory training at the school at Hackney near London and was prepared for entrance to

Cambridge. He was very proud of the fact that his college at Cambridge was Trinity, where he had the advantage of the teaching of such well-known scholars as Dr. Porteus, afterwards bishop of London. At "Trin. Coll. Cam.," as might well have been expected, he acquired a taste for literature, which continued to occupy him for the rest of his life. He was looked up to as an educated gentleman well grounded in the knowledge of his time.

The next of the Virginia signers is another example of what might be secured by private education at this time in Virginia. This was Francis Lightfoot Lee, who was trained in classical *41* knowledge and received his taste for literature, which remained with him all his life, from the Reverend Mr. Craig, a Scotch clergyman. The last of the Virginia signers, Carter Braxton, was another college graduate, receiving his degree of AB at William and Mary, but so far from considering that his education was finished, he went over to England where he spent some three years mainly in securing such cultivation of mind as would enable him to use his leisure properly.

The more one knows of the lives of these men, the more one realizes how successful their college educations were in arousing them to such interest in culture as made their education a living force during all their subsequent lives. Their education was not taken up with the idea that it would help them to get on in the world, but that it would broaden and deepen their intellectual lives and give them a real interest for ever afterwards in the things of the mind.

We have been accustomed to think of these gentlemen of leisure of the South as fox-hunting squires mainly occupied with the country life of their day and inclined to indulge their appetite for strong drink and gambling to an unfortunate degree, but the fathers of the signers of the Declaration of Independence were all intent on seeing that their sons secured a real education that would be a support to them in all their subsequent lives, with such cultivation of taste and judgment as made life really worthwhile.

42   South Carolina is not always thought of as one of the important centers of culture and intellectual life in this country, but such it was in the period before the Revolution. It is not surprising to find, then, that the signers of the Declaration of Independence from South Carolina are typical illustrations of the sort of scholarly men who risked their lives, their fortunes, and their sacred honor by signing the Declaration of Independence and then devoting themselves to the task of securing freedom from the mother country and making the united colonies a government of the people, by the people, and for the people so far as that was possible.

The first of the signers from South Carolina, Edward Rutledge, received his preliminary education from private teachers and then was placed under the tutelage of his elder brother, who was at that time probably the leading lawyer of Charleston. Instead of considering that a legal education secured in this way was sufficient and would, surely with his brother's influence, enable him to make a good living, Edward Rutledge on his brother's advice went to London to make special studies in law at the Temple there and was called to the English bar. He returned home, however, shortly before the Revolution to take up the practice of his profession at home.

What has been said of Rutledge can be repeated almost exactly for his cosigner, Thomas Heyward who, from private tutors, for his father was one of the wealthiest men in the colony, received

43   an excellent classical education and then, as was the custom, read law in the office of one of the best-known attorneys of the time. Like Rutledge, he did not consider that this was sufficient preparation for his life work, and so he went for some years to the Inns of Court in London. After admission to the bar, he made the grand tour of Europe, taking several years to gather all the information that he could with regard to European countries and peoples and make his knowledge of the foreign languages practical. It was only after this that he returned to America to settle down to the practice of law. Within three years, he put everything that he had and was to the hazard by signing the Declaration of Independence.

34

The third of these signers from South Carolina was Thomas Lynch Jr. who, like the other South Carolinians, received his early education from private tutors and then was sent to Eton in England. He entered the University of Cambridge as a gentleman commoner and received his degree of Bachelor of Arts. On the urging of his father, he then proceeded to the Temple in London to take up the study of law. Altogether he spent nearly ten years in educational work in Europe. Only a year or two after his return, he was actually engaged as an officer of the South Carolina colonial troops in the Revolution, having risked all by his signature to the Declaration of Independence.

The fourth of the signers from South Carolina was Arthur Middleton. At the early age of twelve, he was sent on the long and hazardous voyage across the Atlantic to enter the school at Hackney near London. Some two years later he was transferred from Hackney to the well-known Westminster School. From here, after four years of preparation, he entered Cambridge University, from which he received the degree of Bachelor of Arts at the age of twenty-two. Already by this time, he knew much of England, but he spent the next two years traveling on the continent for the sake of the educational influence that would thus be exerted on his mind. He passed altogether some four months in Rome and corresponding intervals of time in other important cities and countries of the continent. He returned to South Carolina and married shortly afterward and took his bride on a wedding tour through Europe and then came home to take his part and chance in the Revolution that would surely have led, had it failed, to the execution of all the signers. What Benjamin Franklin said while they were signing—if this, like so many other apt sayings attributed to him, is not apocryphal—"Now gentlemen, we must all hang together or we shall hang separately," would surely have come true if England had conquered the colonists.

Pennsylvania had the largest number of signers, nine, as it had the largest population of the colonies, and practically all of them were distinguished intellectually. Benjamin Franklin was

44

35

probably the most progressive thinker in this country, looked up to by the English before the Revolution and by the French during it as a distinguished scientific investigator. His formal education was limited enough, but he had an introduction to Latin for a year at the age of eight at the Boston Latin School. He tells us in his *Autobiography* that after this year of Latin, he neglected the language entirely. It is a striking tribute to the thoroughness of the teaching that years afterwards when he had attained an acquaintance with French, Italian, and Spanish, he was surprised to find on looking over a Latin Testament that he understood more of that language than he had imagined he would. This encouraged him to apply himself again to the study of it, and almost needless to say, with his mental energy and persistence he met with success. How utterly lost a single year of Latin study at the age of eight would be thirty years later by our modes of education, I need scarcely say.

45

Franklin had to get to work as a boy, because the large family had to be supported—he was one of fifteen children—but in spite of this educational handicap, he succeeded in making himself a leader not only in the political but also in the intellectual life of the country. He probably must be considered one of the most all-around men of his day in scholarly attainments and intellectual power. His foundation of the American Philosophical Society meant a distinct step forward for scientific culture in this country. He must also be considered the founder of the University of Pennsylvania, a distinguished philosopher, statesman, diplomatist, and author.

Robert Morris, another of the Pennsylvania signers, is better known for his financial ability than for his scholarship. He received his early education in England and was looked upon by those who knew him best as a man of parts. His political career stamps him as one of our greatest citizens. He established the Bank of North America, was superintendent of finance and a member of the Constitutional Convention, besides being United States Senator from Pennsylvania (1789–95). His cosigner Benjamin Rush, a member of the medical profession, was a thoroughly educated man

46

who made his studies preparatory to Princeton at the Nottingham School in Maryland. After four years at Princeton, he received his degree of Bachelor of Arts just ten years before he set all to the hazard by his signature to the Declaration of Independence. In the meantime, he had made his medical studies overseas at the great medical school of the University of Edinburgh, at the moment one of the most progressive in the world, and was brought in touch with some of the most distinguished physicians in Europe. Dr. Garrison, in his *History of Medicine*,[3] says that "Rush's writings won him golden opinions abroad." He adds that "Rush was easily the ablest American clinician of his time." Lettsom, the distinguished English physician, called Rush "the American Sydenham," and others gave him the title of "the Hippocrates of Pennsylvania." He was undoubtedly the most scholarly physician in American medical circles. His scholarship made him an important factor not only in the medical world and in education but also in the politics of that day. He was ready to devote time and intellectual energy to securing opportunities for life, liberty, and the pursuit of happiness for his brother colonials here in America. He was willing, moreover, to risk all for the independence of the country.   *47*

James Smith, another of the signers from Pennsylvania, had the precious advantage of being placed under the tutelage of Rev. Dr. Francis Allison, afterwards the vice provost of the Academy and College of Philadelphia and a distinguished teacher. Smith made his living during his adolescent years as a surveyor but continued to study Latin and Greek and devoted himself to law and settled down as a successful lawyer in Lancaster, Pennsylvania. Another Pennsylvania signer, George Taylor, was born in Ireland the son of a clergyman who, in those days when it was considered

---

3. Fielding H. Garrison, *An Introduction to the History of Medicine, with Medical Chronology, Bibliographic Data and Test Questions* (Philadelphia: W. B. Saunders, 1913), 310.

essential for a physician to have a thorough intellectual training before taking up the study of medicine, devoted himself to tutoring his son so as to prepare him for his medical studies. Instead of studying medicine, however, the boy came to America where he took up business as a profession with great success. The studies of his early years, however, proved an incentive all during his life to keep in touch with culture, and so he was an important factor in the intellectual life of the time.

James Wilson of the Pennsylvania signers was a native of Scotland, and after his classical education, he studied at Edinburgh and Glasgow as well as at St. Andrew's and Aberdeen. He deliberately set out to make himself as good a teacher as possible, and after coming to this country, he taught Latin in the College of Philadelphia (since the University of Pennsylvania) and afterwards read law in the office of John Dickinson. He continued his studies and deservedly came to be looked upon as one of the most intellectual of the signers, no mean distinction under the circumstances.

John Morton, George Clymer, and George Ross did not have the advantage of collegiate training. John Morton was educated by his stepfather, well known for his knowledge of mathematics and surveying at that time. Clymer was educated by his uncle, who had a reputation for scholarship, and George Ross, the son of a pastor of the Anglican Church at Newcastle, Delaware, received his instruction in the classics from his father. After this he entered the office of his brother in Philadelphia and was admitted to the bar.

The little colony of Delaware was represented in the Colonial Congress by men who were worthy colleagues of the other signers so far as intellectual training went. George Read received his classical training from Dr. Francis Allison in his grammar school at New London, Pennsylvania, and so also did Thomas McKean. Both of them went on from their classical education to the study of law, and both of them were successful lawyers. Of Caesar Rodney, a third signer from Delaware, we have comparatively few details, but the tradition is that he was well born and well bred and that he took his place appropriately beside the educated men who made up the Continental Congress.

At least one of the two representatives from Rhode Island, William Ellery, was prepared for college by his father, who had been elected to the office of lieutenant governor of the colony, and entered Harvard in 1743. He received his degree of AB there four years later. *49*

Of the four Connecticut signers, two were college graduates, Oliver Wolcott of Yale and William Williams of Harvard. Mr. Williams had been prepared for college by his father, a minister of the Gospel, and was successful in his college career. Samuel Huntington attended one of the many preparatory schools in Connecticut and came to be considered an excellent Latin scholar. He went on to study law and became a successful lawyer. Roger Sherman, like Benjamin Franklin, had to carve out his own education for himself. He came to be looked upon as one of the leaders of thought in this country, and his missing the opportunity for regular college work did not prove a handicap.

The Maryland signers were all of them classically educated. The first of the signers was Samuel Chase of the Eastern Shore. He was the son of an Anglican clergyman who had a wide reputation for scholarship. He gave his son a classical education and then secured an opportunity for him to study law at Annapolis. All during his life, Chase continued to be a widely read, deeply thoughtful man, so that it is not surprising to find him at the end of his life occupying a place on the bench of the United States Supreme Court. William Paca, the next of the Maryland signers, after preliminary training at home, was sent to the College of Philadelphia and put in special charge of Dr. William Smith, the provost of that institution. Smith was undoubtedly the most serious student of *50* education that we had in this country at that time. Paca received the degree of Bachelor of Arts in June 1759 and, as a favorite pupil of Dr. Smith, was considered a typical scholarly product of the university. He studied law in Annapolis and was admitted to the bar, but only after devoting five years to serious studies in the theory and practice of law. They were not in haste to get to money-making at that time. Thomas Stone, the third of the Maryland signers, rode daily ten miles back and forth to a school in Maryland at which he obtained a thorough knowledge of Latin and Greek. The classics were the favorite set of preparatory studies for law, and he devoted himself to that profession.

Charles Carroll of Carrollton, the fourth signer from Maryland, was the son of a very wealthy father who afforded him ample opportunity and provided strong incentive for education. At the age of ten, he was sent to the school at Bohemia Manor, Maryland, which had been founded by the Jesuit priests who came over with the proprietor, Lord Baltimore, at the foundation of Maryland. Here he secured a good grounding in the classics and then, after some two years, was sent to the Jesuit college of St. Omer in France some twenty miles from Calais. Afterwards he was at Rheims, another one of the colleges founded on the continent to enable the sons of English-speaking Catholics to secure the university education which they could not obtain in England or America because of religious intolerance and the administration of test oaths calculated to prevent their securing any higher education. After this, Carroll went to the college of Louis-le-Grand in Paris, where he came to be looked upon as one of the most talented of the scholars in this extremely intellectual institution. He was selected to make the public act, that is, to demonstrate the truth of a set of theses and answer all objections to them at a public session of the college. He succeeded so admirably in this that his name came to be known all over the academic world of France, and when later the French Revolution caused many of the French nobility and clergy and the educated people generally to emigrate, and some of them came to America, they recalled the name of this champion of Scholastic philosophy and were eager to meet him.

The course studied at Louis-le-Grand, or for that matter at St. Omer's, was not different from that pursued in the colonial

51

colleges here in America, for as we shall see, Scholasticism was the basis of college work, and the *trivium* and *quadrivium*, the seven liberal arts so called, furnished forth the materials for study in this country just as they did at the European universities, not only in England and Scotland but also over on the continent. Altogether Charles Carroll spent some sixteen years in Europe securing a broad and deep education. All during his extremely long life (he lived to be ninety-five), he continued his interest in the intellectual life, and his example of mental industry and scholarly culture exerted a strong influence all over the country during and after the Revolution.

Of the five signers of the Declaration from New Jersey, three 52 were college graduates. Reverend John Witherspoon made his preparatory studies at Hadington for the University of Edinburgh, where he was in residence for some seven years and received his degrees and his license to preach. In 1768 he was invited by the College of New Jersey to become its president, and by the time the Revolution began some seven years later, he was an American of the Americans and one of the most prominent factors in the securing of independence. During the quarter of a century while he was president of what is now Princeton, he had in his classes altogether some thirteen men who afterwards became the presidents of various colleges throughout the country. It is easy to understand, then, what a deep influence he exerted in this country over the men of his time and the succeeding generation. He is more responsible than any other for the rescue of Princeton from what seemed impending dissolution before the Revolution at the beginning of his presidency, and again for lifting the college up out of what was almost chaos after the Revolution was over. During some seven years, there had been no classes, and very special efforts were required to enable the institution to carry on. Witherspoon proved equal to the task.

Richard Stockton, the next of the signers from New Jersey, made his preparatory studies at Nottingham, Maryland, and with a talking knowledge of Latin and a reading knowledge of the New Testament in Greek, as the statutes required, he entered the 53

41

College of New Jersey. He graduated with the degree of AB at the first annual commencement in what was then known as Nassau Hall. The third New Jersey signer was Francis Hopkinson, who had been educated by his bluestocking mother to the point where he was accepted as a matriculant at the College of Philadelphia and received his degree there. He became very prominent in the civic life of the time and must be considered one of the founders of the Republic. Their two cosigners from New Jersey, John Hart and Abraham Clark, were not college graduates but just men of common sense whose intelligence and initiative had appealed to their neighbors as making them worthy to be sent as representatives to the Continental Congress.

Georgia was the farthest away of the colonies from the center of the movement for independence. The colony's representatives among the signers measure up in education and intellectual influence to those from the other colonies. Button Gwinnett, whose name is probably more familiar in our time than those of most of the signers of the Declaration, because he left such rare autographs that they command a high price in the autograph market, was a native of England and is said to have received a liberal education before making his home in America. His cosigner Lyman Hall, born in Connecticut, received a good classical education before studying medicine and took up the practice of his profession, at which he was successful. George Walton, as we have said, the third of the Georgia signers, had no opportunity for schooling but succeeded, nevertheless, in making of himself an educated man and became a lawyer of distinction.

54

The first of the North Carolina signers, William Hooper, was born in Boston and, like his Massachusetts brethren in the Continental Congress, had received his early education in the Lovell School and then entered Harvard, where he received the bachelor's degree in 1760. John Penn was afforded no opportunity for schooling by his father but came under the patronage of Edmond Pendleton, a well-known, scholarly kinsman of his, and secured an education for himself. He, like many of the others, took up the study of law after a reading course taken in Pendleton's library which broadened his mind, and he became a successful lawyer. Joseph Hewes was one of the signers with but very little education, chosen by his neighbors for his common sense.

There remain only New Hampshire and New York. The first of the New Hampshire signers, Josiah Bartlett, had made sufficient advance in knowledge of the classics that he was allowed to take up the study of medicine at the age of sixteen. William Whipple of Kittery, Maine, received his education so far as it went in the public schools of that time. Matthew Thornton, the third of the New Hampshire signers, an Irishman by birth, received a classical education at Worcester, Massachusetts, and then devoted himself to the practice of medicine in Londonderry, New Hampshire.

Of the four signers from New York—the smallness of the number of her representatives showing the comparative unimportance of the colony at that time, fifth in population among the colonists—two were college graduates, Philip Livingston and Lewis Morris, having received their degrees from Yale. A third of the signers, Francis Lewis, was trained by a maternal uncle, the dean of St. Paul's, London, who sent him after a time to the well-known Westminster School, where he received a good education in the classics. Mr. Lewis knew both the Welsh, or Cymric, language and the Irish, or Gaelic, and was probably the only one of the signers who understood these Celtic tongues. He was looked upon as one of the well-educated men of the period. *55*

If we are to attribute the successful efforts of these men as leaders of the colonists in securing independence and stable government for the colonies to their education and what it meant for them, and this seems a reasonable inference, it cannot but be extremely interesting to bring out what was the manner of education which these men received in the academies, Latin schools, preparatory schools, and colleges during the twenty-five years immediately preceding the outbreak of the Revolution. They began their serious study rather early, for we hear of their taking up work in the Latin schools at the age of eight or nine and spending five or six years or more in the acquisition of Latin and of a certain amount of Greek. By the age of fourteen or fifteen when as a rule they entered college—not a few of them were younger—they were capable of talking Latin, though such attainment may seem almost 56 impossible to teachers in our time, and they were able to read the New Testament in Greek. These constituted the principal requirements for admission to college in those days. As we have said, they were fined substantially if they talked anything but Latin at any time during the day except at recreation.

They studied the Latin classics very faithfully and continued them during the first two years of college work, and they took up at this same time grammar, rhetoric, and logic and then devoted themselves almost exclusively during the last two years of college work to mental, moral, and natural philosophy, which they called metaphysics, ethics, and physics, as well as mathematics. That is to say, they followed very closely the medieval *trivium* and *quadrivium*, the so-called seven liberal arts of the medieval universities, with such modifications as were introduced into these as a consequence of the development of knowledge down the centuries.

What is most important to realize is that these intellectual leaders among the colonists had been educated according to a university or academic tradition that had been in existence for more than a thousand years and that had been thoroughly formulated for over six hundred years before their time.

What they studied principally, as we have seen in the introduction, was Scholasticism, or Scholastic philosophy. The demonstration of this fact is to be found in the theses which were printed at all the colonial colleges on commencement day on large sheets of paper called broadsides and which were distributed to those of the 57 audience who might care to take part in the disputation over the propositions listed among the theses. They called this ceremony, which took place in the morning of commencement day, a public act or public (or syllogistic) disputation. These terms come from the Middle Ages and were originally invented by the medieval philosophers and were commonly used in the medieval universities. The terms are as typically medieval as are the academic costumes worn at commencements in our day.

The principal part of their teaching concerned the ethical sciences. Usually the number of theses listed under the heading of ethics was larger than that under any other except occasionally physics. Ethics was taught by the president of the college as a rule and represented the most important course in the last year at college. These ethical propositions represented definite moral principles for the guidance of conduct in life, not only for personal but also for political conduct. In practically all of the colleges from which we have commencement theses, as the Revolution approached and the question of demanding independence brought anxiety to a great many minds, there were groups of theses printed under the title of politics and others on natural jurisprudence, though as a rule the important moral principles were included under the term ethics. Only a little study of the theses is needed to reveal that they constituted the fundamental principles on the strength of which the colonies set forth the rights they thought themselves entitled to and the grievances which violated those rights.

This was the education received by the men to whom we are *58* indebted for the securing of independence which has meant so much for the opportunity for the United States to develop apart from European reactionary influences, and which has secured the opportunity for life, liberty, and the pursuit of happiness for a whole people better than that purpose has ever been accomplished before in history. They were deeply influenced by the old-fashioned philosophy which it had taken some five hundred years to develop and which had then been in use as an instrument of education for some five hundred further years at the time that it proved so efficient in molding the minds and hearts of the men who were to be members of the Continental Congress and who, after the Revolution was over, were to demonstrate their intellectual caliber further in the writing of the Constitution of the United States and of the constitutions of the various states which made up the American republic.

Manifestly their education had been a precious boon to them. Even in the inchoate state in which our generation is inclined to think of education at that time, there was something in it effective for making men capable of deep thinking not for self but for others. We are very much disturbed about our education at the present time and have come to recognize that there is something sadly lacking in it. It would seem well worthwhile to look thoroughly into the education which accomplished so much for the fathers of the country. A system that had been in existence for over a thousand years, including some periods of human culture when men had accomplished marvelous results in artistic, intellectual, and social endeavor, deserves such study as would enable us to appreciate what its fundamental elements were and what the secret of its influence over men's minds actually was.

The personnel of the Constitutional Convention are as striking as the signers of the Declaration. Thomas Jefferson, himself not a member, because he was at the moment minister to France, was thoroughly appreciative of the character of the men who had been chosen for the great purpose of making a new constitution for the country. He wrote that it was "an assembly of demigods." Most of the delegates to the convention had filled high positions before, and many were destined to fill still-higher positions afterwards. Two later became presidents of the United States, one vice president, and many others were chosen as cabinet officers by successive presidents, and above all it was out of this group of the members of the Constitutional Convention that ministers to represent this country in Europe were chosen. No less than seven of them were governors of states, and twenty-eight of them served as members of Congress. They were distinguished for long service in the cause of their country. Eight had signed the Declaration of Independence a dozen years before, and some of them had been members of the Congress assembled to debate the question of the Stamp Act twenty years before.

Among the members of the Constitutional Convention were, besides Washington and Franklin (who was still, at the age of eighty-one, of the greatest possible service), many others famous in the history of the country: Robert Morris, the financier who saved the country during the Revolution; Roger Sherman; Elbridge Gerry; James Wilson; Gouverneur Morris, who was to be so useful in the organization of our currency; Edmund Randolph, the young governor of Virginia, who was one of the best-known men in the country, later to be governor of his state and a member of Washington's cabinet; and of course Rutledge from South Carolina; and Rufus King; and Pinkney, who went on the famous mission to France; and perhaps the greatest of them all, two young men in their twenties, one of them James Madison, of Virginia but a Princeton graduate, and Hamilton, who left King's College, now Columbia, in order to join the Revolutionary Army and came to be so close to Washington all during the struggle for independence. *60*

Perhaps the most interesting feature of the attitude of the Founding Fathers toward the Constitution which they drew up and offered for adoption by the people is that they had the good sense not to think it a final document. Recent historical research shows that the Constitution was not put forward as anything more than a charter of government suited to the needs of the moment. They appreciated how little they knew of what was necessary to set forth definite formulas for the ruling of a nation. The Articles of Confederation had failed egregiously and had given rise to what constituted almost organized anarchy. The Articles had produced a critical emergency which had to be met. Owing to the jealousies and rivalries among the colonies, that first formulation of a scheme of government for the emancipated colonies led to the collapse of federal authority. Most of these rivalries and jealousies still existed, and they influenced the wording of many of the clauses of the Constitution. *61*

The Constitution drawn up to replace the Articles of Confederation was presented only as a hopeful document that might be helpful for the time being for the government of the country. They did not look upon it as a perpetual charter, and Thomas Jefferson, the deepest political philosopher of the time in this country, did not hesitate to suggest that it would be an advantage to the people of the United States if the Constitution were to be rewritten every generation. The most surprising thing, then, about these Founding Fathers is the modesty with which they approached their great task and the scholarly humility with which they contemplated their frankly acknowledged experiment in charter making, and yet it has proved to be one of the greatest documents of human history.

Men who looked at their work thus impersonally and objectively were scholars in the best sense of that term. They knew how little they knew about human beings and possible future developments of humanity and its needs in this young, growing country. That is after all the highest mark of a scholar, that he appreciates how little he knows. From this standpoint, the Founding Fathers must be considered as really educated men. They had learned to think and not merely to remember. They were occupied with finding a solution of human problems, but not absorbed in the idea that all wisdom was born with them and might die with them and that no one else could possibly solve the problems presented to them better than they could.

This proper appreciation of their lack of ultimate knowledge is characteristic of the Socratic method and philosophy with which they had been so much occupied during the time they were attending college. As de Tocqueville said, "The Federal government condemned to impotence by its constitution [the Articles of Confederation] ... was on the verge of destruction when it officially proclaimed its inability to conduct the government and appealed to the constituent authority of the nation. ... It is a novelty in the history of a society to see a calm scrutinizing eye turned upon itself when apprised by the legislature that the wheels of government are stopped; to see it

62

carefully examine the field and wait patiently for two years until the remedy is discovered which is voluntarily adopted."

Their contemporaries appreciated these Founding Fathers of the republic at their real worth. Robert Walsh, who was one of the prominent literary men in the United States, the editor of a series of magazines during the first quarter of the nineteenth century, in his collected essays under the title *Didactics*,[4] pays a tribute to the signers of the Declaration of Independence which enables us to understand 　*63* something of the feeling of appreciation that the men of the time had for their statesmen. Walsh's declaration makes it very clear that there was definite recognition of the fact that the Founding Fathers were guided by philosophic principles and that they were men who thoroughly understood what their purpose was and what were the guiding stars of political philosophy which they had to follow:

> If the Declaration of Independence be, of itself, excellent and glorious, it is rendered more so by the characters of the signers; not such as they are lauded by chosen encomiasts, but as they are proved to have been by their performances, their sacrifices, and those remains, originally of a private nature but now divulged, which lay bare their secret feelings, thoughts and designs, unsusceptible of doubt or misconstruction. The degree in which they acted, so perilously and strenuously, upon principle, not less than sentiment, and with reference to probable future, rather than present or personal ills, is unparalleled in the examples of collective public virtue. They pledged their lives and property, made prodigious efforts, underwent the sharpest trials, voluntarily and mainly for abstract right; for the mere sense of regulated liberty, and for the political dignity, more than the vulgar welfare, of their descendants. *All their political speculation, too, had a sure anchorage in religion, morals, law and order* [emphasis added].

---

4. Robert Walsh, *Didactics, Social, Literary, and Political* (Philadelphia: Carey, Lea, and Blanchard, 1836).

2

HARVARD COLLEGE

The first college founded in the English colonies was Harvard. Six   *64*
years after the foundation of the Colony of Massachusetts Bay,
October 28, 1636, the General Court (the legislature) voted four
hundred pounds "towards a schoale or colledge." The next year,
the General Court appointed a board of overseers "to take order
for ,a colledge at Newetowne," a village on the Charles River whose
name was in 1638 changed to Cambridge. Cotton Mather, in *The
History of Harvard College*,[1] says, "The name of the town was for
the sake of somewhat new founding here, which might hereafter
grow into an university, changed into Cambridge." That summer
a college was opened in a dwelling house on property which is still
part of Harvard College Yard. A few weeks after its opening, John
Harvard, a young graduate of Emmanuel College, Cambridge,
who was preaching at Charlestown, died, leaving his library and
estate of some £750 to the college, which by act of the General
Court took his name.

---

1.   Cotton Mather, *The History of Harvard College*, Old South Leaflets, n. 184.

65

The first master, Nathaniel Eaton, an alumnus of the universities of Cambridge in England and of Franeker in Holland (this closed in 1811), was soon discharged for cruelty to an assistant, and for one year (1639–40), the students dispersed to study with individual ministers. Under Henry Dunster, a young minister who was a graduate of Magdalene College, Cambridge, and became president of Harvard in 1640, the standards and discipline of Oxford and Cambridge were adopted. The first class graduated BA 1642. Only three years study for the bachelor's and three more for the master's degree were required until 1654, when the tradition of a seven years art course was adopted.

The legislature in 1650 incorporated the president, treasurer, and tutors as the President and Fellows of Harvard College; this corporation, which was self-perpetuating and still exists, was given full control over college property and discipline, subject to a veto of the Board of Overseers composed of magistrates and ministers. None but art degrees were granted until 1692, and only a few divinity degrees after that until the nineteenth century. Harvard was an arts college of English university standards.

The seven liberal arts, the old *trivium* and *quadrivium*, somewhat modified because of the development of knowledge, formed the basis of the curriculum. During the first two years, the principal subjects were logic, rhetoric, and grammar, though a certain limited amount of the classics was added. During the last two years, the three philosophies—mental, moral, and natural—with mathematics constituted the principal occupation of the students.

66

The college was founded principally for the education of ministers of the Gospel and magistrates, or political officials, and an even more important element in education than the seven liberal arts as outlined above was the cultivation of religion. This first colonial college in America affords a striking picture of the educational influences that were at work for the training of mind and character during the colonial period. The education afforded for students was well-calculated to bring out the best that was in them, and it is to that education, enforced as it was by strict discipline, that we owe the development of the principles of civic conduct on which our republic is founded. Harvard was a leader not only in time but in prestige, and her graduates of those early days meant very much for the development of thought not only in Massachusetts and throughout New England but all over the English colonies.

The attraction of the colonies for college men at this time, in spite of the difficulties that they had to face in a country where pioneering was still the order of the day, will be best understood from the fact that one hundred thirty men, representatives of almost every college at Cambridge as well as the Oxford colleges and Trinity College, Dublin, emigrated to Massachusetts before the middle of the seventeenth century. These men were zealous that the education of the mother country should be continued in the colonies, and undoubtedly their presence at the commencements and their personal participation in the disputations, or public acts, served to preserve and consecrate the old traditions in education. Some of them undoubtedly had studied under professors who disagreed at least in minor points with some of the propositions that were presented for argumentation, and for the honor of their colleges at home in the mother country and their teachers, they would be anxious to bring out these points in the disputations. Most of them were definitely determined to continue in the New World the customs and traditions so firmly fixed in the colleges of the Old World.   *67*

That was the principal reason why from the very beginning, though paper was expensive and printing costly, these broadsides with the theses printed in Latin were issued and indeed continued to be issued until well on in the nineteenth century. The expense involved—for they were paid for by the graduates—made the number printed for each occasion very limited, and probably most of those distributed were taken home with them by the college graduates and the visiting clergy, so that comparatively few were left for the archives of the colleges—hence their rarity at the present time.

It is only in recent years by the help of photostats—Dr. Osler in his own very thoughtful way sent a dozen of the Harvard theses for the earlier years from the Hunter Museum in Glasgow where they had been preserved by that faithful collector of things educational, William Hunter—that Harvard's supply of extant theses has reached a respectable number, and even yet only very few are known from the seventeenth century, though after that, examples of most of the theses have been preserved.

In spite of the comparatively large number of clergymen who were graduates of English universities, it would seem as though the printing of the thesis broadsides for distribution would be scarcely more than a conventional gesture, since so few among them would be likely to think of taking part in a disputation in Latin. That would certainly be the case in our time, and only a very rare academic visitor would be likely to intervene in the disputation. It must not be forgotten, however, that all of these many clergymen had been trained in the disputation method, they had taken part in them dozens of times, the formularies were always the same, the terms employed thoroughly understood, so that taking part in the disputation would be a pleasant reminiscence of college life not so very different from the experience of returned alumni taking part in various games in memory of their sports at college.

Professor Arthur O. Norton, in his article on Harvard College in *The Commonwealth History of Massachusetts*, points out that out of fifteen clergymen of five towns in Massachusetts, thirteen were graduates of Cambridge and two of Oxford. About the time of the foundation of Harvard College, actually one person in every two hundred in Massachusetts was a college graduate. Some of these men at least would surely welcome the opportunity to revive college memories by taking part in the disputation.

Fortunately, there has been preserved for us, in a little volume with the title *New England's First Fruits*, an exact account of the college curriculum from the very beginning. This little work was published as a sort of advertising booklet with regard to the

54

settlement in New England: the colony sadly needed aid from the   *69*
mother country, and this means of providing information for those
who were interested or might be interested in Massachusetts was
chosen very much as would be the issue of a promoter's prospectus
in our day. The colonial authorities wanted to tell English people,
benefactors past or prospective, how much of good their benefac-
tions actually accomplished, either through the conversion and
civilization of the Indians or through the great good work that was
being accomplished in the college which had been founded some
four years before and had already graduated its first group of Bachelors of Arts.[2]

The writer or writers of *New England's First Fruits* endeavored to give just as roseate a picture as possible of conditions as they
existed in the colony and especially of the successful initiation of the
college. Some of the realities probably did not approach the ideals
that they were striving to secure. However this may be, the account   *70*
of the early days of the college enables us to understand what they
were aiming at and what they hoped to accomplish. Their one idea
was to have a college in New England as nearly like the colleges in

---

2. The title page of the book serves to shows its purpose:

NEW ENGLAND'S
FIRST FRUITS
in Respect

First of the { Conversion of some
Conviction of divers } of the Indians
Preparation of Sundry

Of the progresse of Learning in the Colledge at Cambridge in
Massachusetts Bay
With Divers other special Matters concerning that Countrey
Published by the insant request of sundry friends who desire to be satisfied
in these points by many New England Men who are here present and were
eye or eare witnesses of the same.

London, 1643.

the mother country as possible. They were manifestly endeavoring to create the impression that already the students at the college in New England were being afforded opportunities for education equivalent or very nearly so to those which they might be securing in the English colleges and universities. The success of their efforts was recognized by the European sister institutions, for no less than nine Harvard graduates were incorporated *ad eundem gradum* in the universities of Oxford and Cambridge 1648–1669, and several others who did not graduate were granted advanced standing at the same university.

The *First Fruits* chronicles the first commencement at length in a document which was quasi-official:

> The manner of the late Commencement in a letter sent over from the Governor and diverse of the Ministers, their own words these:
>
> The Students of the first Classes that have been these four years trained up in University Learning (for their ripening in the knowledge of the Tongues and Arts) and are approved for their manners as they have kept their publick Acts in former years, ourselves being present at them; so have they lately kept two solemne Acts for their Commencement, when the Governor, Magistrates and the Ministers from all parts with all sorts of Scholars and others in great numbers were present and did heer their Exercises; which were Latine and Greeke orations and declamations and Hebrew Analysis, grammatical, logical and rhetorical of the Psalms. And their Answers and Disputations in Logicall, Ethicall, Physicall and Metaphysicall Questions; and were found worthy of the first degree (commonly called Bachelour) *pro more academiarum in Anglia* [after the fashion of colleges in England]; Being first presented by the President to the Magistrates and Ministers and by him upon their approbation solemnly admitted into the same degree and a Booke of Arts delivered unto each of their hands and power given them to read Lectures in the Hall upon any of the Arts when they shall be thereunto called and at liberty of studying in the library.

71

> All things in the college are at present like to proceed
> even as we can wish, may it but please the Lord to go on
> with his blessing in Christ and stir up the hearts of his
> faithful and Able Servants in our own Native Country and
> here (as he hath graciously begun) to advance this Hon-
> ourable and most hopeful worke the beginning whereof
> and progress hitherto (generally) doe fill our hearts with
> comfort and raise them up to such expectations of the
> Lord's goodness for hereafter for the good of posterity and
> the Churches of Christ Jesus.

The only contemporary copy extant of the theses broadsides
of this first commencement is preserved for us in *New England's
First Fruits.* The formal dedication of the theses to the governor
and all the prominent officials of the colony as well as to the most
prominent ministers of the churches precedes the theses, and the
general makeup of the thesis sheets was to continue in very much
the same form for over a hundred and fifty years. The theses were
divided under two general heads, the philological and the philosophical theses. Under the philological were the three groups of
grammatical, rhetorical, and logical theses. Under the philosophical theses came ethics, physics, and metaphysics. Only a glance at
these theses is needed for anyone familiar with the subject to realize
that they are exactly the old Scholastic theses. Here in the first thesis under logic is to be found: *Universalia non sunt extra intellectum,*
"Universals [universal ideas] have no existence outside the mind."
The old medieval problem of universals was still being discussed.
Number 7 under logic is typically Scholastic in mode and content:
Sublato relato tollitur correlatum, "When one of two correlatives is
taken away, the other correlative falls out." It takes a good many
words in English to say as much as the four Latin words of the thesis. No wonder the Scholastic Latin is sometimes said to have been
a sort of shorthand in its power to express much with few sounds.

Curiously enough, under the rubric *physicas* there are some
theses which serve to indicate that the old Scholastic metaphysics was
still in honor. Number 5 runs, *Forma est principium individuationis,*

74

Spectatiffimis Pietate, et Illuftrisfimis Eximia
Virtute Viris, D. *Iohanni Wintbropo*, inclytæ Maffachu-
fetti Coloniæ Gubernatori, D. *Iohanni Endicotto* Vice-
Gubernatori, D. *Thom. Dudlæ*, D. *Rich. Bellinghamo*,
D. *Ioan. Humphrydo*, D. *Ifrael, Stoughtono*.

Nec non Reverendis pientiffimifque viris *Ioanni Cottono, Ioan. Wilfono,*
Ioan. Davenport, Tho. Weldæ. Hugoni Petro, Tho. Sheparde, Collegij
Harvardenfi nov. *Cantab.* infpectoribus fidelißimis, cæterifq;
Magiftratibus, & Ecclefiarum ejufdem Coloniæ Pref-
byteris vigilantiffimis.

Has Thefes Philofophicas, & Philofophicas:quas Deo duce. Præfide
Henrico Dunftero palam pro virili propugnare conabuntur, (honoris & obfervantiæ gratia) ducant convecniæmque in artibus
liberalibus initiati Adolefcentes.

Benjamin Woodbridgin.	*Henricus Saltonftall.*	*Nathaniel Brewfteru.*
Georgius Downing.	*Iohannes Bulkleius.*	*Samuel Belinghamus.*
Galielmus Hubbardus.	*Iohannes Wilfonus.*	*Tobias Bernardus.*

Thefes Philologicas.

GRAMMATICAS.

1. nguarum Scientia eft utiliffima.
2. Literæ non exprimunt quantum vocis Organa efferunt.
3. Hæbrea eft Linguarum Mater.
4. Confonantes & vocales Hæbreorum funt coætaneæ.
5. Punctuationes chatephatæ fyllabam proprie non efficiunt.
6. Linguarum Græca eft copiofiffima.
7. Lingua Græca eft ad accentus pronuntianda.
8. Lingua Latina eft eloquentiffima.

RHETO.

RHETORICAS.

R Hetorica specie differt a Logica.
2. In elocutione perfpicuitati cedit ornatus, ornatui copia.
3. Actio primas tenet in pronuntiatione.
4. Oratoris eft clare Artem.

LOGICAS.

U Niverfalia non funt extra intellectum.
2. Omnia Argumenta funt relata.
3. Caufa *fine qua non* eft peculiari caufâ a quatuor reliquii gene-
ralibus,
4. Caufa & Effectus funt fimul tempore.
5. Diffentanea funt æque nota.
6. Contrarietas eft tantum inter duo.
7. Sublato relato tollitur correlativu.
8. Genus perfectum æqualiter communicatur fpeciebus.
9. Teftimonium valet quantum teftis.
10. Elenchorum doctrina in Logica non eft neceffaria.
11. Axioma contingens eft, quod ita verum eft, ut aliquando falfum effe poffit.
12. Præcepta Artium debent effe κατὰ παντὸς, καθ᾽ αὑτὸ, καὶ καθόλου πρῶτον.

Thefes Philofophicas.

ETHICAS.

P Hilofophia practica eft eruditionis meta.
2. Actio virtutis habitum antecellit.
3. Voluntas eft virtutis moralis fubjectum.
4. Voluntas eft formaliter libera.
5. Prudentia virtutum difficillima.
6. Prudentia eft virtus intellectualis, & moralis.
7. Juftitia mater omnium virtutum.
8. Mors potius fubeunda, uam aliquid culpæ perpetrandum.
9. Non impulfe agit nifi qui libens agit.
10. Menuri poteft qui verum dicit.
11. Juveni modeftia fummum Ornamentum.

PHYSI.

PHYSICAS,

Corpus naturale mobile est subjectum Phisicae.
2. Materia secunda non potest existere sine forma.
3. Forma est accidens.
4. Unius rei non est nisi unica forma constitutiva.
5. Forma est principium individuationis.
6. Privatio non est principium internum.
7. Ex meris accidentibus non fit substantia.
8. Quicquid movetur ab alio movetur.
9. In omni motu movens simul est cum mobili.
10. Coelum non movetur ab intelligentijs.
11. Non dantur orbes in coelo.
12. Quodlibet Elementum habet unam ex primis qualitatibus sibi maximé propriam.
13. Putredo in humido fit a calore externo.
14. Anima non fit ex traduce.
15. Vehemens sensibile destruit sensum.

METAPHISICAS.

Omne ens est bonum.
2. Omne creatum est concretum.
3. Quicquid aeternum idem & immensum.
4. Bonum Metaphysicum non suscipit gradus.

HARVARD'S FIRST THESES, 1642 (FROM *NEW ENGLAND'S FIRST FRUITS*)

"Form is the principle of individuation." This harks back to the
75   Scholastic teaching that matter and form is the explanation of
the composition of matter. This proposition was a direct heritage
from the Middle Ages. Number 7 ran, *Ex meris accidentibus non fit
substantia*, "Out of mere accidents substance is not constituted."
Number 14: *Anima non fit ex traduce*, "The soul does not come
into existence from the physical contribution of the parents."

Under the rubric *metaphysicas*, there are the four Scholastic propositions: 1, *Omne ens est bonum*, "Every being is good";
2, *Omne creatum est concretum*, "Every thing created is concrete";
3, *Quicquid aeternum idem et immensum*, "Whatever is eternal, the
same is also incommensurable"; 4, *Bonum metaphysicum non suscipit gradus*, "Metaphysical good does not admit of degrees."

This represents the introduction of Scholastic philosophy
in the curriculum of the first college in this country. Only a little
consultation of historical documents that are now easy to reach is
needed to demonstrate that all the other colonial colleges followed
the lead of Harvard in this regard, as Harvard had followed the
English, Scotch, and Irish universities.

The conditions for admission to Harvard as outlined in
New England's First Fruits indicate what we would consider rather
advanced scholarship for boys of sixteen or less, and there are
many who are inclined to think that the standards suggested represented ideals rather than actualities. There is no lack of defi-
76   niteness as to the conditions required: "When any Scholar is able
to understand Tully [Marcus Tullius Cicero] or such like Classical Latine Author *ex tempore* and make and speake true Latine in
Verse and Prose *suo ut aiunt Marte* [on his own hook, as they say];
And decline perfectly the Paradigms of Nounes and Verbes in the
Greek tongue: Let him then and not before be capable of admission into the college."

That this set of requirements was not merely the unofficial
announcement of an enthusiastic advocate of colony scholarship
made for advertising purposes is clear from the Reverend Cotton

Mather's setting forth of the admission requirements to the college: "When scholars had so far profited at the grammar school that they could read any classical author into English and readily make and speak true Latin and write it in verse as well as prose and perfectly decline the paradigms of nouns and verbs in the Greek tongue, they were judged capable of admission to Harvard College."

New England's First Fruits tells the arrangement of studies at Harvard when the course was completed to the point of graduating the first class. This makes it clear that the disputations were considered to be of primary importance:

> The times and order of their studies unless experience shall show cause to alter.
>
> The second and third day of the week (Monday and Tuesday) read lectures as followeth [the word *read* is used in the old-fashioned sense of an actor reading his lines or a Reader at an English university teaching his class]:
>
> To the first Yeare at eight of the clock in the morning Logick the first three quarters, Physicks the last quarter.
>
> To the second yeare at the ninth hour Ethicks and Politicks at convenient distance of time.
>
> To the third yeare at the tenth hour Arithmetick and Geometry the three first quarters, Astronomy the last.
>
> After noone.
>
> The first yeare disputes at the second hour.
>
> The second yeare at the third hour.
>
> The third yeare at the fourth every one in his Art.

77

How intent the Puritan fathers of the early days were on securing advanced up-to-date education for the first rising generations here in America in their new college is very well illustrated by one well-known incident. Cotton Mather, in *The History of Harvard College*, which is one of the Old South Leaflets (n. 184), tells that Comenius was invited by Governor Winthrop (second) "to illuminate the college and country in the quality of president of Harvard." At this time, Comenius was looked upon as one of the greatest educational reformers of the day, a man whose work for education in Protestant countries was considered to be the most outstanding of the time. This was in the early 40s of the seventeenth century, and about the same time, Comenius received an invitation from the chancellor of Sweden, Axel Oxenstjern, to suggest reforms in the educational system of that country. It is easy to understand that Comenius preferred to accept this invitation, for Sweden was then one of the important countries in Europe, rather than the one from the authorities in New England, which would have required him to take the long and dangerous journey across the Atlantic. The issuance of the invitation, however, shows that the Puritans were resolved to secure the best or at least the best known of the educators of that day for their college.

78

Harvard's experience with its first two presidents was not happy. The first one, as was said, to occupy the position was Mr. Nathaniel Eaton, who began the erection of the first building and was asked to resign before its completion. Cotton Mather said of him that he was "a blade who marvelously deceived the expectations of good men concerning him," though he frankly confesses that "he was a rare scholar himself and he made many more such." He had been the head of a school noted for the success of its pupils.

He was succeeded August 27, 1640, by Reverend Henry Dunster, who came over from England by invitation to take the presidency, which he occupied for some fifteen years to the satisfaction of all until he began to dabble in theology. He was removed for teaching that infant baptism was not necessary to salvation. This doctrine offended the Calvinists. The incident serves to show how important religious teaching was considered to be at that time and how strict the General Court was with regard to doctrinal questions in the teaching of professors whenever they touched upon religious subjects.

79

The curriculum at Harvard itself is amply revealed by the theses which the students, in Cotton Mather's phrase, "had to defend manfully" on commencement day before their degree of Bachelor of Arts would be conferred on them. These theses had been the subject of demonstration by the various professors during the year and had been seriously discussed, demonstrated, and objected to or defended by the students during their weekly disputations, presided over, as a rule, by the president. It is easy to understand that, under the circumstances, the definite significance of these propositions was brought home profoundly, at least to the more intellectual students in the class. Even the laggards, however, must have had these moral truths deeply engraved on mind and memory as the result of the repetition of them under varying conditions. Everything contributed to make the old Scholastic philosophy, and especially its metaphysics and ethics, the most important element in educational life during the last two years of their college course. Those of us who were subjected to this training at the Catholic colleges in the latter part of the nineteenth century know what a profound impression we received of the propositions with which we had been occupied during the last college year.

Fifty years later (1693), the Harvard theses were substantially the same in form and content, though there were more categories in which they were assembled and twice as many theses were listed. *80* The propositions were gathered by the dozen or score under seven different categories. They were *technologicae, logicae, grammaticae, rhetoricae, mathematicae, physicae, ethicae.* The category *technologicae* is of special interest because it replaces *metaphysicae* of the earlier sets of theses. Perhaps the word *metaphysicae* was coming somewhat into disrepute. The title made very little change in the content of the category and the significance of the theses. Among the *theses technologicae* is to be found *Quicquid est est positive bonum,* "Whatever is, is positively good." This is only a modification in words of the proposition *Omne ens est bonum,* "Every being is good." Some of the metaphysical theses were distributed under other categories. Under *theses logicae* in 1693, I note the old Scholastic aphorism *Forma non informat materiam sed totum compositum,* "Form does not inform matter but the whole compound." This particular proposition was printed in capitals with an index to indicate that it is one of the important theses which was to be demonstrated by one of the "commencers" and which he was to defend, a warning perhaps to others to be prepared particularly with regard to this proposition.

The ethical theses are particularly interesting, and all of them date back to the Scholastics. Some of them seem very old-fashioned at the present time. Number 2 runs, *Actio virtutis habitum antecellit*, "The action of virtue surpasses habit" (what is done from a virtuous motive deserves more merit than an action that is the result of habit). Number 4 runs, *Voluntas est formaliter libera*, "The will is formally free."[3] Number 5 is *Prudentia virtutum difficilima*, "Prudence is the most difficult of virtues." Number 7 runs, *Justia mater omnium virtutum*, "Justice is the mother of all virtues." Number 8 is a very surprising proposition from the point of view of our day at least: *Mors potius subeunda quam aliquid culpae perpetrandum*, "Death is rather to be undergone than any sin perpetrated." Number 9 is medievally casuistical: *Non injuste agit nisi qui libens agit*, "No one acts unjustly unless he acts willingly." Number 10 is *Mentiri potest qui verum dicit*, "A man may lie and yet tell the truth." According to the old Scholastics, a lie was a disagreement not between speech and the actuality, but speech and

81

---

3. Our secular colleges almost if not quite without exception rejected this teaching of free will in our generation and substituted for it determinism, but there has been a strong reaction against this teaching in recent years, and surprisingly enough it has come most emphatically from the physicists. Sir James Jeans in *The Mysterious Universe* (New York: Macmillan, 1930): "The picture of the universe presented by the new physics contains more room than did the old mechanical picture, for life and consciousness to exist within the picture itself, together with the attributes which we commonly associate with them, such as free will and the capacity to make the universe in some small degree different by our presence. ... Today science has no longer any unanswerable arguments to bring against our innate conviction of free will" (31).

the persuasion of the speaker. You might tell the truth, but if you thought you were deceiving thereby, you were actually telling a lie.

During the next hundred years (the eighteenth century), the theses at Harvard do not change materially, and the method *82* of teaching philosophy syllogistically and by disputation continues faithfully to be maintained. As we shall see in the story of each of the colonial colleges, very special emphasis was placed on the necessity for carrying on the disputations so that they would prove as valuable as possible for the students. The president himself was supposed to preside at them as a rule, and usually he taught the subjects, meta-physics and ethics, which constituted the principal sources of the theses which had to be defended. Harvard continued to present these theses every year—except certain years when there were no graduates or during the early years of the Revolution, when the col-lege was not functioning—until well on in the nineteenth century.

These theses, then, constitute an extremely important index of the education of the college graduates of that time. During the twenty-five years immediately preceding the Declaration of Inde-pendence, the men who were to play the largest role in the securing of freedom from the mother country in the organization of gov-ernment of the people, by the people, and for the people after the Revolution were being educated to powers of thinking by means of these theses as they were brought home to the minds of young collegians through the disputations.

When the Revolution was actually in progress, the teaching of politics at Harvard took on a very decided character of opposi-tion to monarchy and an insistence on the principles of democracy. For instance, under the rubric *theses politicae* in 1778, we have the *83* following definition and theses:

1. Politics treats of the external but above all the internal administration of government.

2. The right or authority of the highest civil magistrate always springs from the people; therefore

65

3. The highest civil magistrate has not the right of exercising any authority which is not given to him by the people.

4. Man having no right to end his own life cannot confer that right on the legislature; therefore

5. No civil magistrate has the authority unless for nefarious homicide of taking away a man's life.

6. A sure penalty that is less severe is to be preferred to an uncertain penalty which may be more severe.

7. The highest civil authority invading the right of the people destroys the bonds of faith in government.

8. The loyalty owed to the highest authority can be lawfully alienated; therefore

9. Democracy can be maintained only by the courage of the people.

10. Only by the bravery of the patricians can an aristocracy be maintained.

11. In a monarchy honor is the chief source from which forces are to be secured.

12. The state of man under despotic government is like to the state of the beasts and consists of an instinct, obsequiousness, and submission to punishment.

84

13. Luxury by reason of the inequality of possessions is increased in a kingdom, and when luxury gains ground in a kingdom, its military potency is diminished.

How well Harvard was thought to be fulfilling the purposes of its foundation is to be found expressed in some of the pronouncements made by the educational authorities in recalling the achievements of which they felt most proud. In the new articles issued in 1780, at a time when the approaching independence of the colonies was probably felt to be the most important event in the future of America, the board of overseers said of their *university*, using that word for the first time, "Many persons of great eminence have by the blessing of God been initiated in those arts and sciences which qualify them for public employment both in Church and State." This was what Harvard was particularly proud of, and the authorities did not hesitate to express their pride yet humbly attributed their success to the blessing of God. The charter of the original Harvard College proclaims the aim of the institution to be "for the advancement of all good literature, arts and sciences," but even above these was placed, for nearly a hundred and fifty years after the original foundation, the cultivation of religion.

The *theses theologicae*, as is illustrated very well by the propositions that come under this rubric at Harvard in various years, were not merely for theological students but represented natural theology, that is, the knowledge of the Deity which every Christian was supposed to have in order to know the reasons for the faith that was in him. For instance, in 1769 there were these theses and definitions: *85*

1. Theology treats of the knowledge of God and of all things pertaining to eternal felicity.

2. The authority of the evangelical revelations is supported by the testimonies of pagan writers.

3. A miracle in itself is credible.

4. The apostles in propagating the Gospel were not at all influenced by the expectation of the goods of this life; therefore

5. They were not impostors.

6. In all matters reasonableness marked the apostles; therefore

7. They were not fanatics.

8. Human reason alone does not suffice to explain how the true religion was introduced and built up so firmly in the world; therefore

9. There was need of divine revelation for Christianity.

10. The principles of religion are in harmony with human nature and with reason alone as a leader would never have been accepted; therefore

11. The clarity of method of the writers of today and the rightness of their sentiments in treating of natural religion arises to the greatest extent from divine revelation.

12. There are no relatives in the world to come [that is, "in heaven we shall not know our own," a proposition that was much disputed among the Scholastic philosophers and theologians].

86

The last set of theses at Harvard which are definitely Scholastic in character, for after that date there was a modification in the public act and the disputation ceased to have the place it had before, is that for 1810. There were sixty-three graduates that year. The name of a graduate is placed below each set of theses as if he were particularly expected to defend this series of propositions. Altogether, the thesis broadsheet has six *theses technologicae*, seventeen *theses grammaticae*, seventeen *theses rhetoricae*, thirteen *theses logicae*, twenty-six *theses metaphysicae*, twenty-three *theses ethicae*, twenty-one *theses politicae*, twenty *theses theologicae*, twenty-two *theses mathematicae*, and twenty-seven *theses physicae et astronomicae*. The old *trivium* and *quadrivium* went out in a blaze of glory, then. The *theses ethicae* of that year (1810) are perhaps the most interesting. They begin with the definition:

Ethics is the science which treats everything pertaining to (*mores*) manners and morals.

1. Moral precepts are deduced only from the will of God.

2. The precepts which are called the laws of nature reason unfolds to mankind.

3. Wisdom consists in the recognition of the precepts pertaining to morals; virtue consists in their assiduous observation.

4. The difference between good and evil, virtue and vice, set up by God is immutable, because it is founded on the nature of things.

5. The expectation of reward or punishment connected with the command of God is absolutely necessary for moral obligation.

6. God demands the actions which beget happiness; He prohibits those which bring misery.

7. Therefore when concerning any action there is question of knowing the will of God by the light of nature the investigation must determine whether that action seems to be connected with the increasing of general happiness or the lessening of it.

8. It is necessary that the will of God as a criterion be the test of the happiness of our actions.

9. The divine laws concern especially thought; because on them our actions depend.

10. An action done for the sake of praise or reward ought not only to be good in itself but ought to be done from a just motive and out of reverence for the divine will.

11. Anyone who omits a duty equally with one who violates a clear obligation is to be considered a criminal [omission is as bad as commission].

12. Men are accustomed to act more from habit than from thought.

13. Therefore care must be taken that we mould ourselves to good morals by habit.

14. The chief sources of virtue and happiness are the worship of God and the exercise of social feelings.

15. The divine laws for the most part regard the actions which spring from the affections of the soul; therefore care must be taken that we make these affections obedient to reason.

16. In the accomplishment of all duties of benevolence this must be particularly cared for that everyone whose need is the greatest shall receive the most help.

87

88

69

17. Those crimes are less serious which happen suddenly through some perturbation of mind than those which are premeditated and deliberated upon.

18. Loyalty in the keeping of promises and pacts is particularly necessary in commerce and in social life.

19. Promises and pacts which agree with the laws of nature are always to be observed and fulfilled.

20. Promises which are forced from one by unjust violence or which were made because of deception need not be kept.

21. Even if advantages should accrue to us from violating the law, greater disadvantages will surely come from the same source.

22. Therefore it is not allowed to do evil that good may come from it. [Here is the thesis that was so much discussed during the Middle Ages and subsequently, "The end does not justify the means," which the Jesuits were accused of teaching without the negative, though as a matter of fact Harvard's teaching was also that of all the Jesuit schools.]

23. To neglect the laws of nature is a crime that must be recognized; those who do this are worthy of punishment.

The *theses metaphysicae* that year at Harvard (1810) were mainly devoted to what we would call psychology. This the definition shows very clearly:

89

Metaphysics is the science which unfolds the laws and principles of the mind [or soul].

1. The soul (*anima*) is one and simple and all its operations are modes of existence.

2. In the soul are the intellect and the will of which the former judges and the latter impels to action.

3. When external things are presented to our senses, we perceive the things themselves, not images nor forms of them.

4. How external things are perceived we do not at all understand. [Nor do we yet.]

5. Perception does not depend on the will.

6. Between perception and memory this especially interests us, that when we perceive anything we cannot doubt that that thing then existed and that the same thing was called back into the mind afterwards by memory as having once existed.

7. Whatever we have seen or felt we can afterwards contemplate in the idea or conception of it.

A little farther on among these *theses metaphysicae* at Harvard in 1810, there is a discussion of sleep as well as of dreams and certain very interesting reflections with regard to memory. The theses run,

24. Voluntary actions from frequent repetition seem not to be voluntary, for we are not conscious that we are willing.

25. That we ourselves exist we know by intuition, demonstration shows us the existence of God, and the senses bear testimony to the existence of everything else.

90

The twenty-one *theses politicae* at Harvard in 1810 discuss a great many political problems. Most of these are concerned with broad general principles meant to enable students later on in life to judge for themselves in difficult cases. The first proposition runs, "In this science wise men have very different modes of reasoning; some found the science on the rights of men, others make utility the rule." Utilitarianism under the influence of Bentham was invading English philosophy.

The last of the theses in politics shows that the Fathers had no delusions as to immediate human perfectibility by mere law: "Therefore, as long as envy, ambition and pride remain in the human race and are combined with its very nature, so long there will be need, in spite of the weaknesses of men, of authority to suppress them; until that can be accomplished, the golden age pictured for us by the politicians in a republic will only be found in dreams."

The students of the seventeenth century were required to keep a commonplace book, which was often examined by their tutor or the dean of the college. This commonplace book was supposed to contain four kinds of exercises: first, there were notes of important passages in the student's general reading; second, notes on sermons which they had heard particularly in the college chapel; third, notes with regard to disputations that they took part in; fourth, there was a disquisition which had to be written by those who had the degree of Bachelor of Arts in preparation for their Master of Arts promotion. The commonplace book of the poet Milton has been published to show how seriously he took his academic obligation. All four types of notes in the commonplace book were required at Harvard, so that the old tradition in the matter was transferred to the colonies in the seventeenth century and continued to be maintained as a method of education until well after the Revolution at least.

If required hours of study were sufficient to effect rapid and sure advance in education, then surely the Harvard students must have attained that purpose. Harvard followed closely the discipline and curriculum of Emmanuel College, Cambridge, the *alma mater* of John Harvard, and that schedule was rather demanding. More than twelve hours every day were given to intellectual work. Abbé Dimnet, in his *Art of Thinking*,[4] calls attention to the fact that French schoolboys are expected to give nearly as much time as that even yet to their class work and studies, and that the daily schedule of an American schoolboy would seem almost a holiday for the French.

College discipline was maintained very rigorously until well on toward the middle of the nineteenth century. Here is a striking example from the Harvard revised code of 1734 of the disciplinary regulations for the observance of the Sabbath: "All the scholars shall at sunset on the evening preceding the Lord's Day retire to their chambers and not unnecessarily leave them and all disorders of the

---

4. Ernest Dimnet, *The Art of Thinking* (New York: Simon and Schuster, 1928).

said evening shall be punished as violations of the Sabbath hour and every scholar on the Lord's Day shall carefully apply himself to the duties of religion and piety."

According to the older code there was a fine of ten shillings (that would be at least the equivalent of $10.00 in our values) "for walking abroad idly on the Sabbath."

They were very emphatic in their insistence on piety among the students and particularly on the recognition of the fact that, while they were cultivating knowledge during their college course, it was extremely important to realize that the knowledge of God was more valuable than anything else: "Let every student be plainly instructed and earnestly pressed to consider well that the main end of his life and studies is to know God and Jesus Christ which is eternal life. (John xvii, 3). And therefore lay Christ in the bottome as the only foundation of all sound Knowledge and Learning." With this before us it is easier to understand Harvard's motto, *Christo et ecclesiae*, "For Christ and the Church."

Discipline was looked upon as an extremely important feature of college life in those early days. Physical punishment was not only in vogue but was invoked rather frequently. Indeed, the man who as we have said was elected the first president of Harvard was deposed before fulfilling many of the executive duties, because he inflicted exaggerated physical punishment on one of his ushers. That did not lead to the abrogation of the tradition of physical punishment, however, and it must not be forgotten that this tradition still obtains in the English public schools and that though it is in the hands of the alumni of those schools to ask for its elimination, they have never done so. The reason is because they have the feeling that, under certain circumstances, physical punishment is the only thing that would bring a boy in his adolescent years to his senses and make him realize that he is violating statutes that must be kept inviolate.

The Harvard statute with regard to discipline ran, "If any Schollar should be found to transgresse any of the Lawes of God or

93

the Schoole after twice Admonition he shall be lyable if not *adultus* (grown up) to correction. If *adultus* his name shall be given up to the Overseers of the College that he may be admonished at the public monethly Act."

Some idea of the very careful solicitude with which the students were regarded so as to be sure that they would be the seed of a godly ministry and not be guilty of giving bad example in any way may be obtained from a petition signed by a number of prominent Puritans asking the Harvard college authorities to put an end to what seemed to the petitioners a serious abuse among the students. A letter of solicitation for funds for the university, but with the postscript that the college authorities would be very glad to have suggestions or criticisms with regard to the carrying on of the school and the behavior of the students, was sent out rather widely. Some of the recipients took the letter quite seriously and proceeded to suggest one change at least that they thought ought to be made in the *mores* or customs of the students.

They called attention to "an evyl (as it appeareth to us) in the education of youth at the college and that is that they are brought up in such pride as doth in no wayes become such as are brought up for the holy service of the Lord either in the magistracy or ministry especially, and in particular in their long haire which lust first took head and break out at the colledg so far as we understand and remember and now it is got into our pulpets to be the great grief and offense of many godly hearts in the country."

Among the signers to the petition was John Eliot, the Indian missionary, to whom we owe the translation of the Bible into one of the Indian languages. This was one of the earliest books printed in this country and is a striking testimony to the zeal and ardor of the missionary spirit of the time. Eliot, while a zealous scholarly man, seems to have had very little tact, for he is said to have preached this doctrine of the sinfulness of long hair to his Indian converts.

The attitude of Harvard toward the Revolution and the fervent patriotism which animated the executive department of the college is strikingly illustrated by the method employed for dating the theses for the first year of the Revolution after the Declaration of Independence. The theses for 1776 at Harvard are dated, *Anno Salutis 1776 annoque rei publicae Americae primo*, "The year of salvation 1776 and the first year of the American republic." This was nearly a score of years before the French Republic established the custom of dating from its foundation, and there seems to be no doubt that the French modification of the calendar year was made in imitation of what had been done in this country and especially at Harvard. The preceding years, 1774 and 1775, no commencements were held, because Cambridge was the principal seat of the Revolutionary disturbances so far as the Americans were concerned, and until the evacuation of Boston by the British, March 17, 1776, there was too much civic unrest to permit of carrying on academic work successfully. Within a few months after the British evacuation, the college authorities went on with their educational work, and the commencement was held that year, and the high hopes of the patriots proclaimed on the thesis broadside that this was the beginning of a new era in human history in a new country based on new principles. *95*

It is surprising to look back now and note how few were the students who went to Harvard until after the Revolution. In spite of this, or perhaps because of it, Harvard graduates had a deep and lasting influence not only in New England but all over the country. They were leaders in the movement for democratic government that would provide rule of the people, by the people, and for the people. Comparatively few in numbers, they were not meager in the influence which they exerted, but on the contrary, every one of them counted for a host in himself in the organization and definite establishment of the nation. *96*

President Eliot[5] said of the attendance at Harvard in the early days: "The original Harvard College was wonderfully small—a little group of tutors and students. If you look over the Quinquennial Catalogue in which the successive graduates of Harvard are recorded, you will find that no class numbered 10 until 1659 [that is, for more than twenty years], that no class reached 20 until 1690 and 1695 [that is, for more than fifty years], each of which numbered 22, and that the college was over eighty years old before it graduated in 1720 a class numbering 40 or more, and that even this happened only twice down to 1762. The class that contained Samuel Adams and Samuel Langdon numbered only 22 at graduation."

This handful of educated men, trained in the old Scholastic way, taught principles rather than facts, disciplined by old-fashioned methods, drilled in thinking rather than in memorization, impressed themselves very deeply on their generation. We had not come as yet to the time when men felt that one man's opinion was as good as another's or that because a man knew a great deal about one thing, his opinion must be worthwhile with regard to other things. There was respect for education, especially when its results were exhibited as forcefully as in that pre-Revolutionary period.

97 The names of many of these graduates of Harvard have become household words ever since, and they eminently deserve the distinction that came to them. Jefferson, at William and Mary, as we shall see, was so deeply impressed by his professor of ethics that he was quite willing to declare that his destiny had been changed through the influence exerted on him by the president of the college. And Jefferson was one of the great men of that time.

This same thing must have been true in a good many cases in the other colleges. Harvard is a striking example of that. The old-fashioned curriculum, taken for the greater part straight out of

---

5. Charlies William Eliot, *Harvard Memories* (Cambridge, MA, Harvard University Press, 1928).

the heart of the medieval universities, set men to thinking deeply over the truths of Christianity as applied to conduct and supplied them with the definite principles that made for personal ethical development and cultivated that civic virtue which led men to consider their brother citizens and their advantages quite as well as their own. Christ's well-known expression, often supposed to be impossible of literal application, "Thou shalt love thy neighbor as thyself," was exemplified quite literally in the lives of the group of men who together made the sacrifices that were necessary to secure for us in this country the independence from Great Britain and the form of government that we possess. These men had been trained in accord with Scriptural and Scholastic principles, and they had the reasons for the faith that was in them, and their lives were fashioned to exemplify them.

3

The College of
William and Mary

At the College of William and Mary, founded in Williamsburg,   *98*
Virginia, (1693) under the patronage of King William and Queen
Mary of England, who donated out of the royal privy purse a substantial sum for its foundation, the organizers faced the larger problem of establishing higher education in continuous sequence from
the preparatory school to what we would call the graduate (divinity) school. The Virginia college authorities did not, like Harvard
founded more than half a century before, have the advantage of
drawing their college students from well-established Latin schools
in which an intensive preliminary training in Latin was given, so
that the boys came up to college ready even to talk Latin in their
classes. Except in the case of those who had private tutors, and
fortunately in the aristocratic social conditions of the South there
were a number of these, the educational authorities had to provide
for this preparatory school work in connection with the college. As
organized, their grammar school corresponded rather closely to the
Latin schools in New England, and the schoolmaster was "one of
Six Masters of whom with the present scholars the college consists."

99 According to the statutes of the combined institution, "In this grammar school let the Latin and Greek tongues be well taught. We assign four years to the Latin and two to the Greek." The school founders were manifestly dominated by the idea that their teaching should accord with that of the English schools of the time, hence the direction of the statutes: "As for rudiments and grammars and the classic authors of each tongue, let them teach the same books which by law or custom are used in the schools of England."

They were particularly careful about orthodoxy in matters of religion at William and Mary, where the college was under the aegis of the Episcopal Church of England. They were even more solicitous for the suppression of any influences that might incline youth at an impressionable age to immorality, so the statutes decreed, "Let the master take special care that if the Author is never so well approved on other Accounts, he teach no such Part of him to his Scholars as insinuates anything against Religion or good Morals." They were persuaded that there were many passages, even in the best of classic authors, that it would be just as well for pubescent youth not to be tantalized with. They would have been quite ready to reject the idea that innocence is ignorance and yet felt that what youth did not know did them no harm.

While William and Mary received its charter directly from the Privy Council in England at the hands of the king in 1693, its first commencement did not take place until 1700. It never had large numbers of students, but it graduated, as we shall see, some *100* of the most prominent men of the later colonial and Revolutionary periods. Washington in later years was chancellor of the college. He received his surveyor's license from it in 1749. William and Mary greatly benefited by the legacy received from Robert Boyle, the Irish physicist (the father of chemistry and the brother of the great Earl of Cork, as he is described in Irish fashion). The fund left by his will was partly invested in the Brafferton estate in Yorkshire. The income from it was to be used for the education of Indians at Harvard and William and Mary. This continued to be a principal source of revenue for the college. It was lost by the Revolution, but in those days, men were willing to risk property and lose money for the sake of principle.

Most of the students of William and Mary came from old Virginia families and had a social training above the average at that time in the colonies. There was none of the roughness that might be looked for in frontier people, though doubtless there was some of the characteristic fieriness of temper of the Southerners that had to be curbed, so that, from the beginning, special care was taken to secure good conduct among the students. The statute of prohibitions to prevent abuses of various kinds comes under the division of statutes drawn up for the grammar school and runs as follows:

> Special care likewise must be taken of their Morals, that none of the Scholars presume to tell a Lie, or Curse or Swear, or to take or do any Thing Obscene, or Quarrel and Fight, or play at Cards or Dice, or set in to Drinking, or do any Thing else that is contrary to good Manners. And that all such Faults may be so much the more easily detected, the Master shall chuse some of the most trusty Scholars both for Publick and Clandestine Observators, to give an Account of all such Transgressions, and according to the degrees of heinousness of the Crime, let the Discipline be used without Respect of Persons.

101

The custom of having monitors among the students was in accord with the customs of the English public schools, as was also the clandestine observation, though that came to be deprecated during the reform of the schools in the early nineteenth century.

It was a very definite requirement that students should be made familiar with conversational and colloquial Latin while in the grammar school, and the sort of books to be used for that purpose were named. The directions in this matter and the methods of teaching insisted on here enable us to understand just how these colonial Latin schools were able to succeed in having their pupils talk Latin at the age of fourteen or fifteen after four or five years of schooling:

And because nothing contributes so much to the Learning of Languages, as dayly Dialogues, and familiar Speaking together, in the Languages they are learning; let the Master therefore take Care that out of the Colloquies of Corderius and Erasmus, and Others, who have employed their Labours this Way, the Scholars may learn aptly to express their Meaning to each other. And if there are any sort of Plays or Diversions in Use among them, which are not to be found extant in any printed Books, let the Master compose and dictate to his Scholars Colloquies fit for such sorts of Plays, that they may learn at all Times to speak Latin in apt and proper Terms.

102

The same requirements were enforced in the preparatory schools generally, so that the surprise at the speaking knowledge of Latin is lessened. The extent to which they proposed to make the pupils at the end of the grammar school course familiar with Latin as a preliminary to their college studies is probably the most interesting phase of their high school work. They did not treat it, as came to be the custom later, as a dead language but planned to make it of practical daily use in the classes. It was a required mode of expression in the various philosophic subjects during the college years. This would seem almost impossible to headmasters in the modern time, but the school statutes relating to this subject make it very clear that this was their purpose and that it was lived up to. The pupils were supposed not only to have their class work in Latin but to use Latin exclusively for responsions in class and for disputation purposes in their training in mental philosophy. How far this purpose was realized, and was not merely an ideal to be aimed at but not reached, may be judged from the fact that they studied logic, grammar, rhetoric—the *trivium*—and then the *quadrivium* of mental, moral, and natural philosophies, that is, metaphysics, ethics, and physics, as well as even mathematics, in Latin, for all these are presented in that language on the theses sheets which were distributed on commencement day and represented the attainments which the students were supposed to have reached before graduation.

103

82

The statutes of 1736, some forty years later, leave it to the responsible teachers to determine how the education in logic, metaphysics, and natural and moral philosophy and mathematics shall be carried on. The first paragraph of regulations for the philosophy school emphasizes two modes of instruction considered of supreme importance. They are (1) disputations for the training in logical and mental philosophy and (2) declamations for the training in oratory. The students were expected to be ready in thought and speech, capable of responding to objections that might be urged against their opinions but also thoroughly able to persuade hearers. Always the two ideas prominent in the minds of the college authorities of the colonial period were education for the ministry and the magistracy of the colonies. The beginning of the statutes for the philosophy school at William and Mary ran, "Forasmuch as we see now dayly a further Progress in Philosophy, than could be made by Aristotle's Logick and Physicks, which reigned so long alone in the Schools, and shut out all other; therefore we leave it to the President and Masters, by the Advice of the Chancellor, to teach what Systems of Logick, Physicks, Ethicks, and Mathematicks, they think fit in their Schools. Further we judge it requisite, that besides *Disputations*, the studious Youth *104* be exercised in Declamations and Themes on various Subjects, but not any taken out of the Bible. Those we leave to the Divinity School" (emphasis added). Aristotle's physics particularly was behind the age, and the authorities at William and Mary were desirous to be up-to-date.

The charter of the College of William and Mary demonstrates that there was the same purpose in the foundation of the institute of higher learning in Virginia in 1693 as had been exemplified some fifty years before at the foundation of Harvard in Massachusetts. The Virginians were as solicitous for the proper education of ministers of the Gospel as well as the pious education of youth and the conversion of the Indians as their brother colonists of Massachusetts were. The charter of the college begins:

> Forasmuch as our well-beloved and faithful subjects, constituting the General Assembly of our Colony of Virginia, have had it in their minds, and have proposed to themselves, to the end that the Church of Virginia may be furnished with a seminary of ministers of the gospel, and that the youth may be piously educated in good letters and manners, and that the Christian faith may be propagated amongst the Western Indians, to the glory of Almighty God; to make, found and establish a certian place of universal study, or perpetual College of Divinity, Philosophy, Languages, and other good Arts and Sciences, consisting of one President, six Masters or Professors, and an hundred scholars more or less, according to the ability of the said college, and the statutes of the same.

105

The subsequent statutes of the college enlarged somewhat on this statement of the charter. Those of 1758[1] proclaim in their preamble that the purpose of the college is "First, That the Youth of Virginia should be well educated in Learning and good Morals; Second, That the Churches of America, especially in Virginia, should be supplied with good Ministers after the Doctrinal and Government of the Church of England." The order of the purposes has been reversed, but the emphasis on either of them has not been lessened. The third purpose is set down, "That the Indians of America should be instructed in the Christian religion and that some of the Indian youth that are well behaved and well inclined being first well prepared in the Divinity School may be sent out to preach the gospel to their countrymen in their own tongue after they have been duly put in Orders of Deacons and Priests." This had also been the fond hope of Harvard, but the Indians did not prove amenable to such education as would make this beneficent

---

1. *William and Mary Quarlerly*, xvi, first series.

purpose a practical success. In neither of these early colleges did the education of the Indians succeed to any extent.[2]

---

2. Benjamin Franklin, in the chapter "Remarks concerning the Savages of North America" in his *Autobiography*, tells the story of the attitude toward college life assumed by the Indians, which may account for the failure of the proposal to furnish college instruction to the Indians North and South. One would be *106* prone to wonder where Franklin secured the word-for-word speech he reports with all the forthrightness of Thucydides. He says that, after the signing of the treaty of Lancaster (1744), "the commissioners from Virginia acquainted the Indians by a speech that there was at Williamsburg a college with a fund for educating Indian youth; and that if the chiefs of the Six Nations would send down half a dozen of their sons to that college, the government would take care that they should be well provided for and instructed in all the learning of the white people. It is one of the Indian rules of politeness not to answer a public proposition the same day that it is made; they think it would be treating it as a light matter, and that they show it respect by taking time to consider it as of a matter important. They therefore deferred their answer until the day following when their speaker began by expressing their deep sense of the kindness of the Virginia government in making them that offer: 'For we know,' says he, 'that you highly esteem the kind of learning taught in those colleges, and that the maintenance of our young men while with you would be very expensive to you. We are convinced, therefore, that you mean to do us good by your proposal, and we thank you heartily. But you, who are wise, must know that different nations have different conceptions of things; and you will therefore not take it amiss if our ideas of this kind of education happen not to be the same with yours. We have had some experience of it. Several of our young people were formerly brought up at the colleges of the northern provinces; they were instructed in all your sciences; but when they came back to us they were bad runners, ignorant of every means of living in the woods, unable to bear either cold or hunger, knew neither how to build a cabin, take a deer, nor kill an enemy, spoke our language imperfectly; were therefore neither fit for hunters, warriors, nor counselors—they were therefore actually good for nothing. We are, however, not the less obliged by your kind offer, though we decline accepting it; and to show our grateful sense of it, if the gentlemen of Virginia will send us a dozen of their sons we will take great care of their education, instruct them in all we know, and make men of them.'"

At William and Mary, four schools were founded: first, the grammar school, "in this let the Latin and Greek tongues be well taught"; second, the school of philosophy, the candidates for which were to pass an examination before the president and masters and ministers who cared to attend, showing that they were skillful in the learned tongues before admission to the philosophy school; thirdly, there was the divinity school; and fourthly, as a separate institution, the Indian school.

The statutes emphasize the teaching of philosophy by means of disputations. One of the clauses runs, "Further we judge it requisite that besides Disputations the studious youth be exercised in Declamations and themes on various subjects."

Under the duties specially emphasized for the president was this clause: "Let him take care that the other Two Professors diligently attend their Lectures and Disputations."

Manifestly the disputations were considered of cardinal importance, and the old medieval method of teaching philosophy was being carefully preserved. In the philosophy school, one master was assigned to teach rhetoric, logic, and ethics and the other physics, mathematics, and metaphysics. The course was four years for Bachelor of Arts and seven years for Master of Arts. The last three years were taken in the divinity school.

Since they came up to the philosophy school thus prepared to use Latin in conversational form—indeed, here at William and Mary as well as at the other colonial colleges, fines were inflicted and collected for talking in anything but Latin except during recreation periods—it becomes easier to understand how their philosophical disputations were successfully carried out in that tongue.

Emphasis was laid in various parts of the statutes on the necessity for diligently conducting the disputations. One of the special duties of the president, "a man of Gravity, that is in Holy Orders, of an unblemished Life and Good Reputation, not under thirty years of age," was to see that the other masters and professors

"were not absent from their employments," and above all he was   *108*
admonished by the regulations to visit the schools and "see that the
disputations were carried on properly."

Students were expected to devote themselves to their studies
very faithfully for more than ten months every year. This was the
custom at all the colonial colleges. The statutes divided the year
into three terms: Hilary from the first Monday after Epiphany
(January 6) to the Saturday before Palm Sunday; the Easter term
beginning the Monday after the first Sunday after Easter and ending on the eve of the Sunday before Whitsunday (that is Pente-
cost); Trinity term, beginning the Monday after Trinity Sunday
(a week later than Whitsunday) and ending the 16th of December.
For vacations, then, they had the three weeks from mid-December
until the beginning of the second week in January, the two weeks at
Easter, and one week before Whitsunday. This made slightly more
than six weeks in the year. Our almost four months in the summer with two weeks at Christmas and a week at Easter as well as
other shorter leaves would have seemed a maimed scholastic year
to them. According to the statutes of William and Mary, at the
beginning of every term—hence the word *commencement*—"the
scholars of all the schools are given examinations in public as to
what progress they have made in the knowledge of those languages
and arts in which they have been studying or [as the statutes naively
say] should have studied."

As they filled up the year, so they filled up the day with lit-   *109*
tle time for recreation and not much time spent over their meals,
because these were meager at best. Apparently their daily schedule
of classes and studies was about the same as that of Harvard and
the colleges of the English universities, and the same as the Jesuit
boarding schools of my generation. We arose at 5:30 a.m., and the
day was filled with duties.

Thomas Jefferson, in his *Autobiography* which may be found
in *The Writings of Thomas Jefferson* edited by Paul Leicester Ford,
tells the story of his fortunate experience at William and Mary. His

recollections of the old college were very happy mainly because of his intimate association with one of the professors there who proved to be an inspiration:

> It was my great good fortune and *what probably fixed the destinies of my life* that Dr. William Small of Scotland was then professor of mathematics, a man profound in most of the useful branches of science with the happy talent of communication, correct and gentlemanlike manners, and an enlarged and liberal mind. He most happily for me became soon attached to me and made me a daily companion when not engaged in the school; and from his conversations I got my first views of the expansion of science and of the system of things in which we are placed. (emphasis added)

110 Jefferson's principal reason for thankfulness was not because of what he learned from Professor Small but from the way of looking at the meaning of life and the universe around him that he received through intercourse with him. Professor Small was no narrow mathematician and no mere specialist,[3] but on the contrary was a man of broad education and developed intelligence. This brought him into a broader teaching field. As Jefferson says, "Fortunately the philosophical chair became vacant soon after my arrival at college and Small was appointed to fill it, *per interim,* and he was the first who ever gave in that college regular lectures in philosophy, ethics, rhetoric and *belles lettres.*" (For what was included under the

---

3. What we know of Small apart from his relationship to Jefferson and the College of William and Mary indicates that he was a man of parts, intimately in touch with the current of thought in his time. There is a tradition that he was a close friend of Watt, who invented the steam engine and who consulted Small at times with regard to the application of principles of physics to the details of his invention. He is also said to have been a rather close friend of the elder Darwin, Charles Darwin's grandfather, the poet naturalist to whom we owe the first hint but rather thoroughly elaborated of the theory of evolution.

88

term *philosophy* in the colonial colleges, see Provost Smith's definition in the chapter on the University of Pennsylvania.)

At the time of his graduation from William and Mary, Jefferson was eighteen.[4] During the two preceding impressionable years, he had been under the tutelage of Professor Small and had been well grounded in the ethics commonly taught at the colleges in those days. We have no theses from William and Mary, because of the fire, but the ethical theses that are available from the four colleges, Harvard, Yale, Princeton, and Brown, are all sufficiently alike *111* to make it clear that they represent the moral philosophy teaching of the time. Under ethics or politics at most of the colleges, they defended the proposition that authority for government devolved originally on the people and was by them transferred to the ruler. If he did not rule for the benefit of his people, they had a right to remove him and substitute another. This is the teaching that was in many minds at that time as the result of their college theses, and it was this that was incorporated in the Declaration of Independence, the source of whose theory of government must be found in this ethical philosophy that was the common teaching of all the colonial colleges and had for centuries been the teaching of the universities generally, unless they were under royal influence.

The deep influence exercised upon Jefferson by Small in his teaching of ethics seems also to have extended to the question of

---

4. According to tradition, Jefferson began his schoolwork in one of the Virginia Latin schools at the age of nine. He succeeded so well that when he entered William and Mary at the age of fifteen, he was given a class standing that allowed him to graduate at the age of eighteen. His knowledge of Latin stood him in good stead in the latter part of his life, because a great many of the scholarly books of that day were written in Latin, and of course all the books almost without exception of the preceding generations had been published in Latin. This was true not only for books on philosophy but also mathematics and science, because Latin was the language of scholars, and they were saved the necessity of knowing a series of modern languages, since all the scholars of the different countries wrote in Latin.

the injustice of Negro slavery. It has always been more than a little difficult to understand how the man who wrote so confidently, "All men are created free and equal," should have himself kept slaves, though that produces no greater surprise than to find that the men

112 around him who were readiest to accept that declaration were themselves slave owners. Many of the theses condemn slavery, and this was particularly true in New England, but that must have been the ethical teaching also at William and Mary. Jefferson tells us in his *Autobiography* that when he was elected to the House of Burgesses in Virginia, he made a formal motion to the House to secure permission for the freeing of slaves. At this time, according to an act of King George II, no slave was to be set free upon any pretense whatever except for some meritorious service to be adjudged and allowed by the governor and council. Jefferson's motion was rejected. Indeed, no trace of it is to be found in the journal of the House of Burgesses. It was either expunged from the minutes or deliberately omitted as if to be considered only the hasty expression of a very young man. What is interesting is that, thus early, Jefferson was applying these ethical principles derived from Professor Small at William and Mary in practical life.

During the twenty years immediately preceding the Revolution, there were over three hundred graduates of William and Mary, less than a score of whom came from outside of Virginia. Harvard during this period had an annual average of somewhat more than forty graduates, Yale about thirty-three, Princeton about twenty, and William and Mary about sixteen. The College of Philadelphia (University of Pennsylvania) with two vacant years (without commencements), 1758 and 1764, averaged in the twenty pre-

113 Revolutionary years a little over seven, and Columbia with its first Commencement in 1758 somewhat less than six. These colleges drew their students from their immediate surroundings. Harvard and Yale drew their matriculants from the New England colonies with some from New York. Princeton's student body came mainly from New Jersey with a few from Pennsylvania and New York, mainly those for whom Presbyterianism was the source of attraction, and the Presbyterian element in Philadelphia contributed largely to the college roster. The College of Philadelphia drew from the lower counties of Pennsylvania, but some were attracted also to William and Mary in Virginia, where they might be expected to go because that institution was under the discipline of the established Anglican Church. In spite of the smallness of the numbers in attendance and the fewness of the graduates, the little college in Virginia proved the foster mother of a group of men who could think deeply and sanely with regard to human problems and who stamped their personalities profoundly upon the life of a great nation destined to be a leader in human affairs.

The graduates helped, perhaps more than any other set of men of the colonial period, to secure for us the great experiment in liberty that was afforded humanity by the creation of our American republic. The alumni of William and Mary were substantially a unit in that spirit of patriotism that was expressed in the Declaration of Independence, and they were cardinal factors in organizing the colonies for the Revolution. When independence had been won and the failure of government under the Articles of Confederation seemed for a time to demonstrate that a democracy could not succeed in the colonies, the Virginians, led by William and Mary graduates, helped more than any others in the drawing up of the Constitution of the United States, and their example inspired the creation of the constitutions of the various States under which our government has been carried on successfully—in spite of many prophesies to the contrary—for more than one hundred and fifty years and seems to be destined for a lengthy future.

114

Among its graduates just before and during the Revolution were such men as Thomas Jefferson and James Monroe. James Madison, whose cousin Bishop Madison was appointed professor of natural philosophy at William and Mary in 1773 and elected president of the college in 1777, graduated from Princeton but must have been deeply influenced by the spirit and tradition of the institution with which his family was so intimately associated, for Bishop Madison continued in the presidency of William and Mary until his death on March 6, 1812.

Among the signers of the Declaration of Independence, William and Mary gave Jefferson, Benjamin Harrison, George Wythe, and Carter Braxton. Half a dozen at least of the governors of Virginia, representing some of the most powerful influences on the life of the American republic in its early development, and a number of senators of the United States and governors of other states, owed their education to these combined classical and philosophical courses at William and Mary.

115

Virginia soon came to be known as the "mother of presidents," because out of the first five of our presidents, no less than four were natives of that state. Each of them served two terms in the presidency, showing that their first administration had been so satisfactory to the people that they were continued in the office for as long as the tradition established by Washington in the matter permitted.

Fifty years later, Jefferson wrote from Monticello to Henry Lee, who had suggested that the Declaration of Independence was not Jefferson's but had been copied from other writers, that the ideas incorporated in the Declaration of Independence were not in any sense of the word *new*, though he did not copy them directly from "any particular or previous writings." On the contrary, he suggested in this letter that they were the ideas very commonly accepted at that time and without any claim to originality. He insisted that the principles behind the Declaration were to be found in the elementary books on public rights, as Aristotle, Cicero, Locke, Sidney, etc. He felt that they represented just the teaching of the time, as everybody was influenced by it who received the higher education. He said,

> When forced therefore to resort to arms for redress, an appeal to the tribunal of the world was deemed proper for our justification. This was the object of the Declara-

tion of Independence. Not to find out new principles or new arguments never before thought of, not merely to say things which had never been said before, but to place before mankind the common sense of the subject in terms so plain and firm as to command their assent and to justify ourselves in the independent stand we are compelled to take. Neither aiming at originality of principles or sentiments nor yet copied from any particular or previous writings, it was intended to be an expression of the American mind and to give to that expression the proper tone and spirit called for by the occasion. *116*

Jefferson is often said to have been influenced in his conclusions with regard to government by the French philosophers and especially by Rousseau, but here is his own testimony as to what had influenced him most deeply. The old-fashioned philosophy of the schools, which had come down through many centuries since Aristotle's time and which had continued to constitute the curriculum of the European colleges and had been carried across the sea to Virginia, was what exerted the deepest influence over his impressionable adolescent years. Jefferson is a striking example of the fact that it is the teacher above all who counts, and his gratitude for what was done for him in this regard is very striking.

Undoubtedly Jefferson's underlying philosophic principle as to the seat of authority under government was expressed in the Declaration of Independence, which, it must not be forgotten, was written when Jefferson was about thirty-three, that is, when men are still accustomed to be under the influence of their education more than they will be later in life. Jefferson declared, "Governments are instituted among men deriving the just powers from the consent of *117* the governed." In explaining this afterward, he said, "After all it is my principle that the will of the majority should prevail." Unfortunately, we have not the exact theses which they demonstrated and defended at William and Mary, but the theses at the other colleges are so much alike that there does not seem to be any room for doubt left that Jefferson, in drinking in the great principles of ethics from

93

his favorite teacher, Small, must have had implanted in his mind this doctrine rather early in life. Many of the theses at other colleges contain this idea, and they also express in various ways the famous formula of Patrick Henry: "Give me liberty or give me death." Men had inherent rights, and if they could not exercise these, they had the right, and much more, the duty, to fight for them even though at the peril of their lives. Jefferson's formulas with regard to the equality of men, the seat of authority in the people, the right to be consulted in the levying of taxes, are all definite propositions in medieval philosophy taught at all the colonial colleges.

The disputations with regard to these and the answering of objections must have impressed these political principles deeply on the minds of students. This is the principal way in which the Scholastic education of the time made for the training of the minds of the Founding Fathers. This can be illustrated rather readily by propositions chosen from among the commencement theses defended at the other colonial colleges.

118   For instance, at Princeton in 1750, that is, some twelve years before the publication of Rousseau's *Contrat social*, which is sometimes said to have influenced the colonists deeply, two of the theses with regard to government were,

> In the state of nature with the exception of certain individual qualities men are equal so far as government is concerned; therefore
> The right of kings had its original foundation from popular compact.

In 1771 among the ethical theses at Brown we find "Government when it is not by the voice of the people verges toward tyranny."

In 1765 at Harvard, there was the thesis under ethics: "Absolute monarchy tends to the destruction of the happiness of the human race."

In 1778 at Harvard, they had among the ethical theses: "No civil law is just unless it agrees with the principles of the natural law." There was no paltering with the idea that an unjust law had to be obeyed, and they evidently reserved the right to determine whether a law was just or unjust to the individual conscience.

At Harvard also that same year (1778), there was the ethical thesis "The will of God accords perfectly with the happiness of society."

At Brown in 1772, they had the thesis "The best form of democracy is that which comes from their own delegates chosen by popular suffrage."

119

At Harvard in 1770, they had these rather striking theses connected conclusionally:

> The closest bond of civil society is the oath; therefore
> The persuasion of the existence of God is necessary for
> the preservation of civil society.

There is a definite similarity among the theses at all the colonial colleges. The propositions were almost identical, and as a rule, there are only word differences. This is true not only as regards colleges so distant from each other, as distance was in those days, as Harvard and Princeton and the University of Pennsylvania, but also as regards difference in time. Harvard one hundred and fifty years after its first commencement, and Yale nearly a hundred years after its initial disputation, was still setting up practically the same theses for "manful defense" as they did at the beginning. They all evidently drew from the same sources. Though we have no theses from William and Mary or King's College (now Columbia), we have the tradition of their having been in existence, and there seems no doubt that if we had the originals, they would be practically identical with those that are extant from the other five colonial colleges.

120

4

YALE COLLEGE

It is typical of the intense interest of the colonists in education that   *121*
when the Reverend John Davenport came down from Boston in
1638 to found a colony at New Haven, he had already worked out
a complete scheme of education which he hoped to develop. In
Boston they were just in the midst of their foundation of Harvard
College in New Town across the river from Boston, afterwards to
be called Cambridge, after the English university town, because
it housed the college. It is not surprising, then, to find the idea of
an institution for the higher learning fermenting in Davenport's
mind. His scheme included "schools for all where the rudiments of
knowledge might be gained; schools where the learned languages
should be taught; a public library; and to crown all a college in
which youth might be fitted for public service in church and state."

Always in these colonial college foundations, emphasis is
placed on the provision of education for the sake of church and state.
Only rarely is there any mention of education for the personal benefit of the student. Provided with an education, it was supposed that
he would use it to the best of his ability for the benefit of his fellow
citizens. That was why the men of the time were so ready to make
sacrifices in order to secure the establishment of these early colleges.   *122*

They felt that they were doing a service that would accrue to the benefit of the community for as long as the commonwealth endured.

It is easy to understand that Davenport's scheme was utopian under the circumstances. The struggle to survive was too hard in the young colony during the first generation to think seriously of taking up in any practical way such a reduplication of educational facilities. The project was not abandoned, however, only put off for a more favorable time. A generation later, at the beginning of the last quarter of the seventeenth century, the project came up for consideration again, and the faculty at Harvard quite properly protested that there were scarcely students enough available for a single college in New England. As a matter of fact, until the end of the seventeenth century, Harvard's graduating classes averaged less than ten per year, and there were altogether scarcely more than fifty students in attendance at the college at this time.

Shortly after the beginning of the eighteenth century, definite efforts were made to bring about the organization of a college at New Haven, but too much friction developed in the course of the enterprise. There was a strong feeling at this time that New England should have another college besides Harvard. This was largely due to the wish to inculcate a more orthodox Congregationalism than that exemplified in the teachings of the older institutions. During the early part of the eighteenth century, schools claiming collegiate rank were founded at Wethersfield and Saybrook (Connecticut).

123

New Haven forged ahead in population and influence, and after a time, the college at New Haven came to be looked upon as the representative collegiate school of Connecticut. Because of Elihu Yale's substantial gift of books to the institution in 1718, it was called after him. The books at Saybrook were reclaimed by the sheriff that same year, and the school at Wethersfield adjourned to New Haven in June 1719.

The man to whose scholarship and unremitting efforts in the cause of education Yale owes more than to any other was Reverend Thomas Clap, who gave up the pastorate at Wyndham,

Connecticut, where he had been located for some fifteen years, to become rector of the collegiate school at New Haven during the preliminary unsettled period for some six years and then for twenty-one years as president of Yale College. He was considered by those whose own scholarship gave them a right to an opinion in the matter the most learned man in the colony. He specialized in mathematics and astronomy, but so far from limiting his scholarly interests to these subjects, he was looked up to as intimately acquainted with all the other subjects of the college curriculum of those days and perfectly capable of turning his hand to the teaching of any of them.

During his administration, one of his unfailing duties was to *124* preside at college exercises two days in the week when the juniors and seniors held disputations with regard to various subjects in philosophy. Those familiar with disputations as college exercises in argumentation will know that their success depends to a very great extent on the presiding official. The principal subject of these disputations was, as in the other colleges of the time, mental and moral philosophy, or metaphysics and ethics as they were called on the commencement broadside theses sheets distributed to those who cared to take an active part in the proceedings. Almost needless to say, President Clap must have considered these college exercises, which under the name of disputations or sometimes *disputes* are so often sadly misunderstood in the modern time, to be of supreme importance. Otherwise, as a college executive, he would not have given so faithfully the hours demanded every week all during the college course to make this feature of college work the success it should be. As a matter of fact, presidents were not left free to consult their own judgment in this matter as a rule, and we have a number of passages from the statutes of the various colleges which commend the disputations to the care of the president and make it incumbent on him to attend them regularly in person.

Unfortunately, President Clap's personal tendency to dictate his opinions and his refusal to listen to others on disputed points

125 eventually impaired his usefulness to the college, and after more than thirty years as its presiding officer, he was forced to resign. It has been very well said of him that "for untiring zeal and disinterestedness in laboring for the best advantage of what he thought the best interests of the college, there is no one in the whole line of presidents more worthy of the grateful remembrance of the alumni than President Clap."

What we are interested in particularly here is President Clap's relation to the disputations and his intimate connection with the syllogistic training of mind which went with them. This same feature of college education is to be found, as we have seen and shall see further, in all the colonial colleges. The departure from it represents that wandering off into the many-featured course with a multitude and variety of all sorts of studies which gradually developed in the nineteenth century. This development brought with it many definite reasons to complain that instruction has taken the place of education, that is, that the cultivation of memory—the mere accumulation of facts—is replacing that study and pondering of principles, so valuable for the bringing out of powers of the mind, which is represented by the etymology of the word *education*.

At Yale the curriculum, as can be readily seen from the number of annual theses sheets which have been preserved for us— there are more than fifty of them—demonstrates very clearly that at least as much emphasis was placed on the *trivium* and *quadriv-* 126 *ium* here as at Harvard. *The Annals of Yale College (1700–1766)*, printed in New Haven in 1766, give a resume of the curriculum. The author of this work was Reverend Thomas Clap, president of Yale at the time when he wrote. He was himself very much interested in mathematics, so it is not surprising to find that he calls particular attention to the amount of mathematics that might be learned at the new college. He said, "In the first year the students learn Hebrew and principally pursue the study of the languages (Latin and Greek) and make a beginning in logick and some parts of mathematicks. In the second year they study the languages but principally recite on the subjects of logick, rhetorick, oratory, geography and natural history."

It is to be noted that while the students principally *pursue* the languages in the first year, they principally *recite* in philosophic subjects the second year. Clap continues, "Some acquire a good proficiency in trigonometry. In the third year they learn natural philosophy, mathematicks and algebra and some of them proceed to conic sections and fluxions. In the fourth year they devote themselves to metaphysicks, ethicks and divinity."

The study of divinity, or theology, as exemplified by these theses was not meant solely for those studying to be ministers but represented, as we have seen at Harvard, what used to be, and in philosophy classes is still, called natural theology, that is, such a knowledge of God and man's relation to him and to the universe as may be secured by the human mind through its own light of reason apart from revelation. It is perfectly clear what great significance they attributed to metaphysics and ethics, since practically the whole fourth year at college, just when the student was attaining his maturity and when he was receiving the deepest impressions to be obtained from his college course, was devoted to these subjects. *127*

President Clap adds the very pertinent remark that "on Monday they [the students] gave themselves to disputing in the syllogistic fashion." Everywhere in the history of the colonial colleges, there is this emphasis on the disputation or exercise of argumentation that was a heritage from the old medieval universities and was considered of so much importance that nearly everywhere there is special legislation on the part of college faculties and boards of trustees with regard to it. As we have seen and shall see in subsequent accounts of particular colleges, practically all of the American college statutes of the eighteenth century carry special injunctions on this subject of the disputation, which was manifestly considered a cardinal factor in college education.

Yale, like Harvard, was deeply intent on having a broad education in the arts and sciences but also, like its rival on the banks of the Charles, was intent on cultivating religion in the minds and hearts of its students. In the prospectus of Yale written in order to attract students, there is the declaration that the faculty intended to make of it a place "wherein youth may be instructed in the arts and sciences who through the blessing of Almighty God may be fitted for public employments both in Church and civil service." At all of the colonial colleges, these sentiments were expressed in almost the same terms. Their thoroughgoing conviction was that the all-important function of the college was to make men better and above all better citizens. They were not educating people for personal success in life but for the benefit which they would confer on the community.

128

Oviatt, in his volume *The Beginnings of Yale: 1701–1726*,[1] says that the first-year men "studied logick and elementary Greek and Hebrew and the Sophomores the same, the Juniors principally physicks and the Seniors metaphysicks and mathematicks." All the classes had to prepare disputations, and at Yale, as everywhere else, these disputations were emphasized and manifestly rated of very great importance for thoroughness of philosophic study.[2]

---

1. Edwin Oviatt, *The Beginning of Yale: 1701–1726* (New Haven, CT: Yale University Press, 1916).

2. Oviatt is very much inclined to think that while the entrants into college were supposed to know Latin well enough to speak it, this was much more of a supposition than a reality. He mentions that Danekaerts and Sluyter visited Harvard at the end of the seventeenth century and were scandalized by the bad manners and the illiteracy they found there. They went into Harvard Hall, for instance, and found ten scholars smoking tobacco in a room that smelled like a tavern. They tried Latin on these youths and were astonished at the sad response. Oviatt is inclined to think that they would not have found the Yale students at the end of the first quarter of the eighteenth century any better. It is very probable, however, that the specimens out of the student body who would be sitting around in Harvard Hall smoking until the place "stank like a tavern" would not prove anything like a fair test of the scholarship of the student body. Smoking students were much rarer than in our day.

How supremely important the religious element was consid-   *129*
ered to be at Yale is very well demonstrated from an expression that
was used by President Clap in 1754: "The original end and design
of colleges was to instruct and train up persons for the work of the
ministry. ... The great design of founding this school was to educate ministers in our own way." Yale was strictly Congregational in
those early days and had no sympathy with the tendency toward a
more liberal theology, with already a hint of Unitarianism, which
even at that early time was making itself felt at Harvard.

Oviatt quotes from the statutes with regard to the personal
cultivation of religion by the students: "Every student shall exercise
himself in reading the Holy Scriptures by himself every day and
hold private prayers 'for wisdom for himself' in his room of nights."

The students were rigidly kept at work except for a half hour
after breakfast, an hour and a half at noon after dinner, and "after
ye evening prayer till nine of ye clock."

Yale very soon became a serious competitor of Harvard so far
as the number of students in attendance was concerned. Ruggles
in a note to his Semicentennial Address (1864) proudly calls atten-   *130*
tion to the fact that in the one hundred sixty-two years from its
first commencement down to that time, Yale promoted altogether
7,116 academic students to the degree of AB. Harvard during this
same period graduated with the same degree only 6,973, or very
nearly one hundred fifty less than its younger rival at New Haven.
Curiously enough, in the year 1862, both colleges graduated the
same number of students with the degree of AB—ninety-six. The

---

There are always hangers-on among students in all colleges and times who
just barely succeeded in maintaining their places in college. They should have
been plucked out early in their course but for some reason or another were
not. Committees of investigation would find very much the same thing true
at the present time, and if the loafers around college rooms were taken as the
average of scholastic attainments, a very serious injustice would be worked to
the student body.

younger college had caught up with her older rival, but within the decade, there was to be a new president at Harvard who was to change completely the status of education there and, by means of an extension of courses and the introduction of the elective system, was to attract a great many more students.

The curriculum of the two colleges during the colonial period was almost exactly the same. This may be seen from the theses presented by both on commencement day. Both colleges confined themselves to the granting of degrees of Bachelor of Arts and Master of Arts, though Harvard had vindicated for itself the right to give further degrees by conferring the doctorate of theology on President Increase (Crescentus) Mather (of Harvard) during his presidency. This made it clear that the college felt it had the right to confer the doctor's degree, though this is the only example that we have of the exercise of it. Yale once conferred the honorary degree of MD in the same way.

131 Only Harvard has more of her commencement theses preserved than Yale. It would be comparatively easy to illustrate most of the phases and all of the familiar phrases of Scholastic philosophy from the Yale theses that are extant. Over and over again, freedom of the will is formulated in different modes of expression. The principle of causality is appealed to confidently. The natural law and the divine law are emphasized as well as the place of conscience in life. Universals are discussed, matter and form as an explanation of the constitution of matter is proclaimed, happiness is declared dependent on submission to God's will, the distinction between essence and existence is emphasized. In general, if one wanted a rather thoroughgoing introduction to Scholastic philosophy, it would be quite easy to obtain it from a study of these theses which were the examination papers of the Yale students for their degrees of Bachelor of Arts. While President Clap was more deeply interested in physics and mathematics than in ethics and metaphysics, he was careful to see that his students received a similar training in mental and moral philosophy to that which was being given at the other colonial colleges as well as in the European universities.

In the lists of theses at Yale, the investigator finds on occasion that there is no subdivision for ethics or for metaphysics. It might seem as though Yale, which was one of the most progressive of the colonial colleges, was getting away from the medieval Scholasticism, which still formed the basis of its teaching during the last two years of college work, and becoming more modern. It takes only a little research, however, in the lists of theses to show that under other rubrics, many ethical and metaphysical theses are to be found. For instance, at Yale in 1768, they had no rubric *ethics*, but under the heading *theses physicae*, there are some propositions that would seem to have very little place in this galley and which serve to indicate that the Yale students were required to defend propositions that came under metaphysics and ethics in other colleges. The twenty-fourth proposition, for instance, for that year under physics, printed in italics and with an index which showed that students must be prepared to defend this proposition particularly, was the familiar formula with regard to the freedom of the will: *Voluntas coactioni non subjicitur*, "The will is not subject to coercion." This proposition in other colleges is usually placed under ethics or under ontology.

132

Yale, even before the middle of the eighteenth century, was deeply interested in physical science and continued to be conspicuous for this interest until our own time. Hence, it is not surprising to find that in 1751 at Yale, no less than thirty-eight (nearly one third) of the more-or-less one hundred and twenty-five theses presented for the public act on commencement day—all in Latin of course—were under the rubric *theses physicae*. They began with the definition:

> Physics is the investigation of the laws of nature and the explanation of phenomena from them.

105

133   1. [with an index and in italics] The laws of nature are only the general rules according to which natural phenomena are immediately produced by God.

Then follow a dozen of propositions in mechanics followed by a series of propositions properly physical and then a dozen of propositions in astronomy. Among the physical propositions—some of which have been superseded by the progress of science—are

9. Water when frozen in a vacuum does not expand.

10. Every definite quantity of air can be expanded to fill up any portion of space.

11. Air (gas) is generated by dead animals but is consumed by living ones.

12. Although inflammable bodies are set on fire by the electric spark, no heat can be perceived in it.

13. The electric spark does not liquefy bodies by calefaction.

14. The electric spark is especially attracted by water.

15. The electric spark is a real element permeating all bodies.

16. The phenomena of lightning and the aurora borealis are most readily explained by electricity.

17. Every homogeneous light according to the degree of its refrangibility has its own color.

18. The proper objects of vision are only colors.

19. Objects seen at different distances are not the same.

134   20. We always see the same number of visible points.

21. The periodical times in ellipses are the same as in circles whose diameters are equal to the major axis of the ellipse.

Metaphysics is represented in proposition 23 just below: *Anima rationalis potest agere inorganice.* This is the familiar declaration universally defended in the Middle Ages that the soul can function without the body: "The rational soul can act inorganically" (without the bodily organs). The demonstration of this proposition disposed of the objection that the soul was absolutely dependent on matter for its intellectual functions and that, therefore, there could be no conscious life after the death of the body.

Under logic that same year, there are to be found certain metaphysical theses which indicate very clearly that though there was no special list of metaphysical theses presented for the public act on commencement day, that fact furnished no evidence that metaphysics was neglected. For instance, there is the proposition, *Genus non existit a parte rei*, "Genus does not exist in things" (but only intellectually). Following that thesis is the proposition *Differentia specifica non oritur a forma substantiali*, "The specific difference between things does not arise from the substantial form." Then there is the thoroughly Scholastic proposition with which they had been very much occupied in the Middle Ages, *Forma oritur ex dispositione materiae*, "Form arises from the disposition of matter." They were evidently very much occupied with matter and form as the explanation of the composition of matter.

135

How little the theses had changed, so far as their Scholastic character is concerned, is very well illustrated by the theses from Yale for 1797. If there had been any even slightest disrepute for metaphysics, it had ceased. For instance, under the rubric *theses metaphysicae*, there is the definition "Metaphysics treats of the knowledge of spiritual beings and their essences and properties as well as of the reasons for things moral." Then come the following propositions:

1. As to what is the substratum of matter or spirit is altogether and entirely hidden from the human race.

2. The properties of spirit as well as matter are very well known to many.

3. That matter thinks can neither be demonstrated nor even shown to be at all probable.

4. The existence of spirit is much more probable than the existence of matter.

THESES TECHNOLOGICÆ

Technologia est generalis Artium et Scientiarum tractatus.

1. CUJUSVIS populi felicitas politica è religione pendet.
2. Ejusdem speciei sunt animalia quorum progenies procreare possunt.
3. Quivis diligentiâ et assiduitate potius quam ingenio naturali celebris et illustris fiet.
4. Generi humano linguâ divinitùs data fuit.
5. Quo minus ad imitandum scriptores veteres quisque fide dederit eo plùs iis similis fiet.
6. Dei existentia quibusdam nationibus vel hodiè prorsùs ignota est.
7. Humani generis coloris et formæ varietas è æquali physicâ omnino probetur.
8. Algebra seu ratio analytica ratiocinandi exemplar perfectissimum præbet.
9. Matheseos philosophiam naturalem terminare debet, non procreare aut generare.
10. Scientiæ veræ janua est Mathesis.

THESES GRAMMATICÆ

Grammatica est Ars cujusvis Linguæ ejus instituens.

1. LINGUÆ fundamen est Grammatices.
2. Verba et pronomina Hebraica personæ primæ vel secundæ terminationibus variis genus ostendunt.
3. Characteres tres tantum vocales, 182 autem consonantes linguæ Arabicæ designant.
4. Adjectiva quæ in linguâ Anglicanâ etiam in aliis abnormè comparantur.
5. In pronunciatione vocalium E, I, A, O, U, vocis accentus gradatim remittitur.

THESES LOGICÆ

Logica est ars investigandi et communicandi veritatem.

1. IDÆA simplex definiri nequit.
2. Idæa abstracta generalis non datur.
3. Ut in Geometria triangulus quivis particularis triangulos omnes similares repræsentat, ita etiam, in cæteris rebus, idæa particularis omnes idæas ejusdem generis exhibet.
4. Idæa generalis abstracta quasi fui ipsius contradictio à dialecticis ...
5. Rhetorum et Poetarum genius à facultate idæarum componendarum omnino pendet.
6. In comparatione idæarum et propositionum generalium formatione, quæ vulgo abstractio nominatur, mathematicorum, dialecticorum, et metaphysicorum ingenium omnino versatur.

THESES RHETORICÆ

Rhetorica literas politiores edocet artemque dicendi.

1. EX affectatione literarum venustatis naturalis perceptio oritur.
2. In vultu, accentu, et gestu oratoris, plus licet eloquentiæ quam verborum delectû.
3. Raro fit ut cuivis curritissimè et perspicaissimè pollicam.
4. Exhibito spectaculo vel naturales quidem, non autem obviæ vel communes sunt et compositæ.
5. Oratoris vitia facilius et citius quam venustates ad decora cernuntur.

THESES MATHEMATICÆ

Mathesis numerabilia, et mensurabilia tractat.

1. ANGULUS ad interfectionem circuli cujusvis arcûs tangentem ...
2. Frusti seu zonæ sphæræ cujusvis superficies curva, frusti seu zonæ altitudinis et sphæræ peripheriæ rectangulo æqualis est.
3. Arciâ cujusvis sinus, inter feminalium et duplicis arcûs sinum versum medium et proportionale: Ergo,
4. Cujusvis arcûs sinus versus logarithmicâ differentiæ inter sinum ... æqualis est.
5. Secundi ... cujusvis quadratus rectangulo lateris recti et abscissæ in sectione parabolica æqualis, in sectione autem hyperbolica major est. — Unde sectionum trium conicarum nomina ducuntur.
6. Verticis seu loci cujusvis in ellipsium solarium projectione orthographica semita nunquam ellipsis vera est.
7. Duorum quantitatum ferè æqualium, medium arithmeticum medio geometrico æqualis est.

THESES PHYSICÆ

Physica est legum naturæ investigatio, et Phænomenorum ex illis solutio.

1. CREPUSCULUM vespertinum crepusculo matutino subducitur dius est.
2. Æquatio seu motus, mercurii in thermometro subductionem non efficit.
3. Aquæ congelatione atmosphæræ calor augetur.
4. Siglaciei temperatura—20° Farenheiti æqualis erit, electricus fiet.
5. Et frigore et calore externâ, levitas redditur aqua.
6. Luna, agenti 2321, milliaribus, 349 terræ propius accessit.
7. Fluidorum calor fiu conservatur, rarcani proportionalis est.
8. Plumborum in ævo subsole est.
9. Sulphuris consimili vapor sulphur ipso ponderosior est.
10. Alcohol in carbonem convertatur.
11. Quercus humilis fruticosus florifici et anni spatio interspam fructum edit.
12. Sit in eodem vase oleum et aqua infundantur, aquæ superficies volenter agitari jussa, aqua innotescit manente.
13. Frigore extremo et placitis et nivis minus ponderosè redduntur.
14. In aëre calido plus aëris quam in frigido continetur.
15. Aquæ per tubum fluentis velocitas media est, inter velocitatem apud axem et latus tubi medium arithmeticum.
16. Quadratus radicis quadratæ velocitatis superficialis aquæ per tubum quodvis effluentis —1, velocitati apud partem maxam æqualis est: cujus dimidium et velocitas media.
17. Aëris inflammabilis et puri combustione aqua ponderis æqualis fiet.
18. Terra, temperaturæ hyemali, Soli propius quam in æstivâ 2,750,000 milliaria accedit.
19. In novilunio celerior et vegetatio quam in plenilunio.
20. Vegetatio fine luce effici non possit.
21. Et frigus communi et electricitas ex magneticam corrumpunt.
22. Si duorum planetarum distantiæ fint ratione 1:2, prioris gravitas quadruplex erit posterioris: si duarum chordarum musicarum longitudines fint in eadem ratione 1:2, et posterior quadruplici pondere prioris tendatur, tonos similes edent: Ergo,
23. Si à Sole usque ad planetas singulos, chordæ musicæ extensæ fuerint, et ponderibus ratione distantiarum quadratarum tensæ symphonicè erint chordæ.
24. Inde principium dicit doctrina illa Pythagoræ de harmonia sphærarum excelsâm.
25. Sit cujusvis perpendicularitur projectum velocitate quasi milliarium 420 temporis minuto à terra semper decedere, nunquam reversurum si obliqua fuerit projectio, veri parabolica erit femita: si autem impetu eo velocitate paulo minore projiciatur in ellipsi admodum eccentrica revolvetur.
26. Sol atmosphærá induetur.
27. Analogia tantum, et non phænomenis, gravitatem ad stellas usque fixas extendam vel porrectam esse, probatur.
28. Ex gravitatione mutua planetarum Jovis et Saturni irregularitates quædam minore oriuntur: Ergo,
29. Dato tempore, in angulo ætatis ... æquales temporibus æqualibus describere haud absolutè vera est.
30. Si satellitis in conjunctione gravitas Solem versus fit major quam versus primarium, femita ejus Soli concava erit: si minor, con-
vexa: si æqualis, ad conjunctionem ipsam recta erit femita, atque utnique, solem versus, concava.
31. Sit aeris fanus varios ... 390 dict ... 390 percurrit, facilè diameter apparens non augeretur.
32. Cujusvis corporis ad extremiarem ordinari axzern per focum ductâ revolventis velocitas angularis est velocitati apud verticem ratione 1:2 si sectio fit parabolica : majore autem ratione erit velocitas si fit elliptica, et minore si in hyperbolica sectione revolutio efficiatur.
33. Observationes astronomicæ accuratissimæ systema solare Herculis constellationem versùs moveri verisimile reddunt.
34. Sunt circuli duo, quorum prioris centrum distat à centro posterioris inter revolutiones periodice primariæ revolutioni syndicalis satellitis i sum, si posterioris .... longitudine in .... ratione distantiæ facilis a planetá sua, epicycloidem describeret; facilitis super planam immobile femitæ similem.
35. Gypsum, regionum maritimarum fertilitatem non auget.
36. Aëris temperatura in patriâ aliis in quovis climate, inter temperaturam æstivam et hyemalem climatis illius est medium arithmeticum.

THESES ETHICÆ

Ethica est bene beatèque vivendi.

1. OMNE mendacium est culpabile.
2. Æquitas, Ethicæ folùm fundamen in scripturis facrofanctis reperitur.
3. Æqualitas, vera non est scientiæ, honoris, aut divitiarum, sed jurium æqualitas.
4. Leges, populi ingenio et moribus adaptari oportet.
5. Experientia folùm artem gubernandi perfectam reddere potest.
6. Ex commercium et scientiâ politicâ finili gradu adhuc progrediuntur.
7. De ratione et vi obligationis naturalis philosophi semper et ubique gentium dubitârunt: Ergo,
8. Obligationis moralis fundamen in nullum stabile et certum philosophia præbere potest.
9. Sine virtute et literaturâ nulla respublica felix et libera existere potest.
10. Ut Civis virtute et intelligentiâ fint præditi, literis et moribus probos reddere institutæ necesse est; Ergo,
11. Influentibus talibus neglectâ, respublica felix et libera haud existere potest.

THESES METAPHYSICÆ

Metaphysica Entium spiritualium æternaque essentias et proprietates, rerumque moralium rationes tractat.

1. VEL materiæ vel spiritûs substratum quid sit, generi humano profus et omnino latet.
2. Spiritûs æquè ac materiæ proprietates hominibus perrorae sunt.
3. Materiam cogitare nec demonstrari nec etiam probabile reddi potest.
4. Spiritûs quam materiæ existentiâ multo probabilior est.

THESES THEOLOGICÆ

Theologia est scientia quæ DEUM et perfectiones ejus contemplatur.

1. DEI cognitio divinitùs generi humano data fuit. ... Scripturæ facrofanctâ cognitionem Dei inter homines conservaverunt.
2. Dei unitas ratione humanâ probari non potest.
3. Dei peccata remissurum esse ratione humanâ probare non potest: Ergo,
4. Deum peccata remissurum ratio humana probare non potest.
5. Ratio humana, felicitatem futuram adspicientem modum nullum hominibus ut quam præbuit, aut præbere possit.
6. Polytheismi et acretalistæ, sceptici vel athei, philosophorum plerique semper fer ... :
7. Et Religioni naturali et revelatæ, et virtuti, et felicitati humanæ, philosophi maxima ex parte obfuerit et perniciei fuit.

H : antecedit Oratio Salutatoria.

Habita in COMITIIS ACADEMICIS NOVO PORTU Connecticutensium, M,DCC,XCVII.

YALE THESES, 1797

108   (136)

Among this last set of theses that we have from Yale (1797) under *theses ethicae* are these propositions following the definition:

Ethics is the art of living well and happily.

1. Every lie is culpable.

2. The sole foundation of ethics is found in the most holy Scripture.

3. The true equality of man is not a matter of science or honor or riches but an equality of rights.

4. Laws ought to be adapted to the genius and customs of the people.

5. Experience alone can render the art of governing perfect.

6. Both commerce and political science have so far progressed to the same extent.

7. As far as reason and the force of moral obligation is concerned, the philosophers of the various nations have always and everywhere hesitated; therefore

8. Philosophy can provide no stable and sure foundation of moral obligation.

9. Without virtue and literature, no republic can exist happy and free.

10. In order that citizens may be gifted with virtue and intelligence, it is necessary that they should be instructed in letters and good morals; therefore

11. Such institutions being neglected, a free and happy republic cannot exist.

The *theses physicae* at Yale in 1797 illustrate very well how deeply interested they were in physical science at the same time that they were devoting themselves so strenuously to metaphysics and ethics. In spite of the fact that their summation of their knowledge of physical science was in Latin and evidently studied to a great extent in that language, their interests were not conventional but were broad and liberal and represented the most important up-to-date subjects of scientific discussion. While they entitled this series of

137

theses *physics*, under it were discussed astronomy, chemistry, and often also what we call biology, though the term was invented later, and some agricultural chemistry. In the Yale thesis sheet for 1797, there are no less than thirty-six different propositions under physics, and these comprise all the scientific interests of that time. Here is a selection from them that shows the breadth of their scientific interests and the number of various subjects that were treated. Those who would like to read them all will find a copy of this thesis sheet among the illustrations.

138

Sometimes the formulas no longer represent the truth in our modern science, but on the other hand, it is surprising how many propositions from that old time represent advances in science supposed to have been made much later than the end of the eighteenth century:

6. The moon in 2,221 years has come nearer to the earth by 349 miles.

18. The earth in the winter time is 2,750,000 miles nearer to the sun than in the summer time.

19. At the new moon vegetation grows more quickly than at the full moon.

20. Vegetation will not grow without light.

21. Ordinary fire and electricity diminish magnetic force.

26. The sun is provided with an atmosphere.

27. By analogy alone, but not from actual observation, it is proved that gravity extends to the fixed stars.

28. In the mutual attraction of the planets Jupiter and Saturn, certain minute irregularities arise; therefore

139

29. The teaching of Kepler that the planets describe equal areas in equal times is not absolutely true.

Among the *theses physicae* at Yale in 1797, there are some chemical theses which indicate that the study of chemistry was gradually attracting attention. For instance,

8. Lead is soluble in water [as many a drinker of water through new lead pipes has found to his cost in the modern time].

9. The vapor of burnt sulphur is heavier than sulphur itself.

10. Alcohol is converted into carbon.

They were becoming more interested also in various agricultural problems; those descriptive of the influence of light have already been quoted:

35. Gypsum does not increase the fertility of maritime regions.

Theses 23 and 24 are with regard to the music of the spheres:

23. If from the sun to each of the planets musical chords were stretched by weights in ratio to their quadrate distances, the symphonic chords would be sounded; and

24. Thence comes the basis of that doctrine of Pythagoras on the harmony of the spheres.

While they were devoting so much time to physics, they were not neglecting theology at Yale at the end of the eighteenth century, and the *theses theologicae* for 1797 illustrate this very well. After the definition of theology as "the science which treats of God," the theses run,

1. The knowledge of God was divinely revealed to the human race; and

140

2. Holy Scripture preserved the knowledge of God among men.

3. The unity of God cannot be proved by human reason.

4. Human reason cannot prove that God will remit sins; therefore

5. Human reason has never provided and never will provide any means for man to secure future happiness. [Even the wise Greeks made a mess of religion, and in

their Olympic mythology, they made their gods like themselves but with more emphasis on the evil than the good of human nature.]

6. Polytheists, materialists, skeptics and atheists were for the most part philosophers; therefore

7. Philosophy has for the most part proved an obstacle and a pernicious influence for religion natural and revealed, and for human virtue and happiness. [This is a rather striking variation of the old maxim that a little philosophy leads men away from God, but deeper knowledge of it leads them back again. By philosophers they doubtless meant at Yale very much what the old Greeks expressed by the word *sophist*— they had a word for this as for everything else—which originally had no innuendo of what we have come to call sophistry.]

As a matter of fact, then, the students at Yale were being brought in rather intimate touch with all the subjects of special academic interest in their time. Yale's particular devotion to physical sciences might seem to indicate an evolution of college interests away from Scholasticism and especially from metaphysics, but the commencement theses do not reflect any such diminution of interest. The old Scholastic philosophers were always intent on the cultivation of all the knowledge that they could secure. Their main purpose was to apply Scholastic principles to knowledge of every description so as to bring it under their system of thought. Neo-Scholasticism, the Scholastic system of thought in our day, sets great emphasis on that point. Yale was only following up the efforts of the older Scholastics and anticipating the new Scholasticism in this special attention to the physical sciences which we find exemplified in the theses. They were not eliminating Scholastic influences, but they were adding to their curriculum whatever called for thoughtful consideration and rounded out the store of knowledge.

141

I submitted a number of these commencement theses from Yale to Professor Chenu, who is the director of the Institute for Medieval Studies at the University of Ottawa. His reply was, as I have quoted elsewhere, these are all "pure Scholastic formulas." Almost needless to say, such an expression from a man who is steeped in Scholastic lore and has occupied most of his life with it is very definite evidence that Scholasticism lived on in our American colleges until well on in the nineteenth century. The old tradition of the schools in education, which existed for some fifteen hundred years, was maintained. Scholastic education, like so many   *142* medieval achievements, is now coming back into its proper meed of appreciation once more. Like the art and architecture of the Middle Ages, as well as the literature and the arts and crafts, the educational system founded on medieval Scholasticism is renewing the influence that made it such a precious factor in the life as well as the education of the older time.

5

The College of New Jersey
(Princeton)

The institution now known as Princeton University—it had been   *143*
Princeton College until almost the end of the nineteenth century—
came into existence shortly before the middle of the eighteenth
century. Its title at the beginning was The College of New Jersey,
and that continued to be the name for over a hundred years. The
first courses were given at Elizabethtown (now Elizabeth) in 1747
and were continued at Newark for the next ten years and finally at
Princeton in 1756, where the college has been ever since.

The account of the first commencement, as given in the
*History of the College of New Jersey from Its Commencement Anno
Domini 1746 to 1783 Prepared Originally for the Princeton Whig by
a Graduate*,[1] demonstrates the Scholastic character of the teaching
of the college, which in this followed the examples set by Harvard
and Yale as well as William and Mary:

> On Wednesday, November 9, 1748, the trustees met
> according to appointment at Newark. They agreed that the

---

1. William A. Dod, *History of the College of New Jersey, from Its Commencement,
    A.D., 1746, to 1783* (J. T. Robinson: Princeton, NJ, 1844).

144

> Commencement for graduating candidates who had been examined and approved for that purpose go on this day.
>
> In the afternoon the president delivered a handsome Latin Oration and after the customary Scholastic disputations, the following gentlemen were given the degree of Bachelor of Arts.

Then follows the list of the graduates at the first commencement. It is worthy of note that the author of this history, writing near the middle of the nineteenth century, speaks of the exercise in which the graduating students took part on commencement day as a "Scholastic disputation." This expression, taken together with the sets of theses, makes it very clear that at Princeton the faculty from the very beginning were following closely the medieval traditions in education which harked back in their origin to the times when the philosophy of the Schools, or Scholasticism, was in vogue.

The theses broadsides which were issued at Princeton, as at the other colonial colleges, give lists of propositions in the seven liberal arts: rhetoric, grammar, logic, and then the three philosophies—natural, mental, and moral, that is, physics, metaphysics, and ethics—as well as in mathematics, which were to be demonstrated by members of the class called upon for this purpose and then defended against all objections that might be urged by other members of the class or by the faculty or by any of those present who wanted to take part in the disputation. The contents of the theses are almost invariably those that were familiar in the medieval universities.

145

We have from President Finley, the fourth president of Princeton, a manuscript descriptive of the public exercises of commencement as conducted under him in September 1764. This would seem to be the preliminary sketch made out to guide him in the order of the exercises and preserved in the college archives for future reference. The proceedings began with the *orator salutatorius*. Distribution of the theses broadsides to those of the audience who cared to take part in the disputation followed. Then came the first disputation syllogistically treated. The first thesis was, *Mentiri ut vel Natio conservetur, haud fas est*, "To lie even though to preserve the nation is not justifiable." Then there was an English forensic dispute on the subject of dreams, the title of which, however, was announced in Latin: *Somnia non sunt universaliter inania et nihil significantia*, "Dreams are not universally inane and without significance." The other theses followed: *Lex Rationis sola incitamenta ad virtutem satis efficacia non praebet*, "The law of reason alone does not furnish incitements to virtue that are thoroughly efficacious" (There is need of revelation to help man in life). Then there was a final disputation on the very interesting proposition *Nullam veram Virtutem habet qui omnes non habet*, "He possesses no real virtue who has not all the virtues."

President Finley includes in his sketch of the commencement of 1764 an amplified account of the disputation so that we are able to secure an excellent idea of just how the defense and objection to the theses were carried on. The student selected as defender of a particular thesis first gave his proof for it in syllogistic form, and then the objectors also in syllogistic form presented the difficulties they found in accepting the defender's thesis and his proofs for it. For instance, with regard to the first thesis, which condemned lying even though the salvation of the country might depend on it, President Finley presents in Latin the determination, or initial proof, given by the defender:

146

DETERMINATIO

Mentiri quacunque de causa, ignobile et sua Natura pravum esse, res ipsa clamat, et ferme ab omnibus praecipue Virtutem colentibus conceditur. Quod si omnino fas esse possit, Deus comprobat; et si ille possit probare, non est necessario verax; sed impossibile est eum mentiri, ergo et mendacium probare. Nec ratio Veritatis ab hominum Felicitate sed Dei Rectitudine pendit; et quoniam sibi semper constare necesse est non potest non esse rectum. Ergo falsum necessario improbat ut

ejus naturae oppositum; et vetat malum facere ut quidvis
Bonum inde sequatur etiam ut Natio conservetur.[2]

147   President Finley gives more at length the determination, or proof, for the forensic dispute on the subject of dreams. As this is in English, it will furnish an excellent example of the mode of argumentation which was followed. Almost needless to say, the Scriptures were taken as representing quite literally Gospel (God's word) truth, and arguments founded on it were considered to be absolutely unanswerable. It is not so much the matter, however, as the manner of the dispute, or disputation, that we are occupied with here:

DETERMINATION

Although I see no necessity of accounting for all dreams from the agency of other Spirits, anymore than to interest them in the Reveries of the Mind when lost in mere imaginary Scenes while we are awake without reflecting that they are not realities; Yet that foreign Spirits have access to ours as well when we are asleep as when awake is inconsistent with no Principle of Reason. And if some dreams cannot otherwise be accounted for than by having recourse to foreign spirits we must then admit their agency; since there can be no effect without cause. And though it must be granted that our own Spirits at the same time think, yet there is no Inconsistency in supposing that other Spirits gave Occasion to their thinking of Some

---

2. This may be translated, "To lie for any reason whatever is ignoble and vicious by its very nature. The thing itself cries out and is conceded by practically all who cultivate virtue. But if it could be right [to tell a lie] God approves of it, and if He could possibly approve He is not necessarily truthful; but it is impossible for Him to lie, therefore also to approve a lie. And the basis of truth does not depend on the happiness of man but the righteousness of God, and since He must be consistent with Himself He cannot but be righteous. Therefore He condemns necessarily what is false as opposed to His very nature and He forbids that evil be done that any good whatever should follow from it even though the country should be saved thereby."

Subjects rather than others as is the case of conversing together when we are awake.

What has been matter of fact is certainly still possible and we know that in some Cases infinite Wisdom chose to employ Angels to communicate divine Instructions in Dreams; which establishes the general Doctrine. And Experience assures us that Impressions made on these Occasions are very deep and lively; and as has been observed those very Dreams that came from fullness of business or other Causes mentioned show us the Temper of our Minds and in that view are useful and significant.

148

Four sets of the theses printed for the Scholastic disputations on various commencement days at the College of New Jersey are extant: those for 1750, 1752, 1760, 1762.[3] When compared with the theses from Harvard, Yale, the University of Pennsylvania, and Brown, it is perfectly clear that in New Jersey they were using the same Scholastic method as well as Scholastic principles in the series of propositions chosen for defense by their students. All the colleges were manifestly following as closely as possible the models set for them by the European colleges, above all by the English and Scotch universities. The metaphysical and ethical courses were considered the most important in the latter two years of college life and were usually taught by the president. Many hours of classwork were spent in presenting them to the students and many more in disputing about them, so that they would not in any sense be mere memory exercises but represented seriously thought-out propositions, the proof of which could be given and the objections against which could be solved, by those who took the course successfully.

149

---

3. Professor Collins tells me that while they have only four printed copies, they have the texts of all programs from 1760 to date, besides those of 1748, 1749, 1754 and 1756, giving the subjects disputed and the various forms of the disputation.

We have some notes from students at Princeton which help us to understand the curriculum and how it was taught. Blair's *Account* of Princeton issued in 1764, only four years before the coming to Princeton of Witherspoon as president and less than twenty years after the foundation of the College of New Jersey, gives an excellent idea of the curriculum followed at the college, which was carried on by the new president from Scotland. This curriculum enables us to know exactly the education afforded the generation that planned the Revolution and made the colonies independent but also organized the basic structure of our republican government through the federal Constitution and the constitutions of the states which were written at this time. In both the Revolution and the Constitutional Convention, Princeton representatives—such men as James Madison and Witherspoon—were leaders and more deeply influenced than any others, except possibly the graduates of William and Mary, the discussions among the delegates which led up to these achievements.

The daytime hours of study and recitation during the first scholastic year were, according to Blair, devoted to the classics. The authors studied were Horace and Cicero in Latin, Lucian and Xenophon in Greek. An interesting specialization during this first college year was that the students had public declamations five nights of the week after supper. This must have proved often an interesting diversion at the end of the day, and diversions were rare enough in college life at that time. Above all this practice must have brought home to the minds of the college men the definite realization, even from the very beginning of their college course, of the two confessed purposes of higher education at that time: the training of men for the ministry and the magistracy, the two professions that demanded facility and forcefulness in public speaking.

In the sophomore year, less attention was paid to the classics, and indeed the Latin classics were entirely omitted from the curriculum with the understanding that whatever knowledge of them

150

120

was considered necessary was looked upon as completed. Homer was still studied faithfully, doubtless because of the knowledge of men and their ways and the motives of their actions which he presented so picturesquely; Longinus was taken up, especially his essay "On the Sublime," for that quality was supposed to be exemplified in religious and secular eloquence. In this sophomore year, moreover, the students received their introduction to mental philosophy through logic in combination with rhetoric, thus demonstrating once more the value placed upon public speaking as an important factor in the curriculum. For the scientific side of their training, they had mathematics and geography.

In the junior year, neither the Latin nor Greek classics had *151* a place in the curriculum, and the students devoted themselves entirely to the three philosophies, mental, moral, and natural. Under natural philosophy, they had physics and astronomy and in connection with that devoted special attention to mathematics. In mental philosophy, they devoted themselves to metaphysics, beginning with ontology as the study of being in general, but they also took up such special subjects as pneumatology, by which term they understood the study of human and animal psychology but also of spirits—immaterial beings—their existence and qualities.

In the junior year, they held weekly public disputations in philosophy as well as weekly declamations. The disputations were very formal in character were conducted in Latin, usually presided over by the president himself or the professor of philosophy and were looked upon as an extremely important exercise for the sharpening of wits and the provision of the arguments which supported the knowledge they possessed with regard to the basic principles of human existence and its relations. The students were expected to learn the reasons for the faith that was in them with regard to religion, and young men learned not to accept propositions of various kinds just because they were asserted but to demand reasons for them and be able to solve objections that might be made with regard to them.

152 In the senior year, they reviewed the contents of the curriculum of the preceding years, not a little time being devoted to the rereading of the classics, and they took up very seriously the study of the sciences, philosophy, and mathematics. The greatest attention was given to moral philosophy, the teacher of which was the president of the college. Seniors also reviewed logic and metaphysics as well as other phases of philosophy in order to secure, as far as that might be possible, a thorough comprehension of these subjects. The examinations at the end of the senior year included the whole subject matter that had been studied during the four college years, with the exception of the classics. This almost universal examination on all the college work is a consummation devoutly to be wished in our day. Its practice can be clearly seen from the theses presented on commencement day, which included propositions from all of the developed seven liberal arts, the *trivium* and *quadrivium* of the older time. The rubrics were logic, grammar, rhetoric— the old *trivium*—and mental, moral, and natural philosophy and mathematics—the developed *quadrivium*—which completed the seven liberal arts as they had been modified in the course of the evolution of knowledge, especially through physics and the related natural sciences.

Besides these philosophic and mathematical studies, certain hours on Saturdays were devoted during the earlier college years to the study of catechism, that is, a brief survey of religious truths and principles. Catechism was studied at Princeton in two forms, Presbyterian and Episcopalian, the *Westminster Shorter Catechism*

153 and the *Episcopal Catechism* with the Thirty-Nine Articles, according to the wish of the students and their parents. Princeton was predominantly Presbyterian, securing its greater presidents by direct invitation from Presbyterian pulpits and colleges in Scotland, and continued to be Presbyterian until toward the end of the nineteenth century.

This liberalism in the matter of the form of faith to be taught is interesting and shows that the bigotry which had characterized colonial life earlier was beginning to give way through the enlightenment which came with the foundation and organization of the colleges. None of the colleges founded about the middle of the eighteenth century in this country, Princeton in 1746, King's College (after the Revolution, Columbia) in 1754, the University of Pennsylvania in 1755, Brown in 1764, Rutgers in 1766, Dartmouth in 1769, imposed religious tests. Such tests were still in existence in the English universities, and it was difficult for a non-Conformist to secure an education and almost impossible for Catholics. Here in America, there was a growing spirit of tolerance which eventually led to that enactment of freedom of worship, which was such a surprise and has proved such a blessing.

Fortunately, a number of notes with regard to college life at Princeton made by other students have been preserved for us. Besides Blair's *Account* just quoted from at length, we have a letter of Joseph Shippen of Philadelphia as well as some notes with regard to his course that give us some very definite information *154* about the curriculum and the daily order of studies. Shippen was the son of Judge Edward Shippen, a trustee of the college, and in a letter to his father, written in French for practice's sake, he has left us a vivid picture of the life of the students of Princeton at this time, which above all brings out the place of the disputation in the college curriculum.

He was a sophomore, and this was the order of his day: "At seven in the morning we recite to the president lessons in the works of Xenophon in Greek and Watt's Ontology. The rest of the morning until dinner time (11 a.m.) we have a recitation on Cicero's *De Oratore* and Hebrew grammar. The remaining part of the day we spend in the study of Xenophon and ontology in preparation for the recitation the next morning, and besides these things we dispute once a week after the syllogistic method and now and then we study geography."

Seven o'clock, I fear, would seem, in modern college parlance, "entirely too soon after midnight" to college students of our day to meet even the president for several hours in Greek and ontology, but in those days, the practice of turning night into day, such a notable feature of our modern mode of living, had not come in. They used the daylight hours to the best advantage.

According to Shippen's notes with regard to his course, he says that in his freshman year, besides the classics, logic was taken up in the second term. He adds that, for training in this, there were "disputations once a week after the syllogistic method." In the sophomore year, they studied rhetoric, ontology, and elementary mathematics. In the junior year, they studied moral philosophy (ethics), astronomy, and navigation. Senior year was devoted largely to a review of all these subjects of the preceding years, including the classics, which were studied more intensively.

We are interested here mainly in the curriculum in so far as it concerns philosophic studies. It is surprising to note the amount of time beginning with the freshman year that was devoted to mental philosophy. In the second term, logic was taken up, and even at this time, there were disputations once a week. In the sophomore year, they took up what was called ontology, as can be seen from the theses, and this of course represented metaphysics. The emphasis on ethics was evident from the number of ethical theses on the commencement broadside as well as from the fact that, as a rule, this branch was in all the colleges taught by the president of the college. Men must have gone out of college deeply impressed with the principles of right and wrong which had been not only expounded to them but which they themselves had to defend against objections urged very strenuously and often with telling ingenuity. After all, in these disputations there always entered an element of competition, and a man who could not defend his thesis against strenuous objection was considered to have failed in the contest of wits, something

155

156

that I need scarcely say youth is particularly likely to resent and react against to the uttermost of its ability.

Another Princeton student who left some notes of his college experiences, Samuel Livermore, records that on graduation an examination was held in Hebrew, the Greek testament, Homer, Cicero, Horace, logic, geography, astronomy, natural philosophy, ontology, ethics, and rhetoric. There is confirmation of what we find in Blair's and Shippen's notes with regard to the curriculum of Princeton among these papers. In 1770, as a freshman, he studied the classics, Horace, Longinus, Lucian. In 1771, as a sophomore, he continued the classics and had a rather broad course in logic. In 1772, as a junior, he began ethics and also metaphysics, studied Euclid, also trigonometry and Martin's philosophy. In the senior year, there was a review of these courses and then an examination for the degree. They believed in a terminal examination that included most of the subjects of the course in order that students might not have the feeling that they could dismiss subjects from their minds as having been completed.

There are some very interesting students' notes on President Witherspoon's lectures. The president took to himself the whole field of philosophy except natural philosophy. He lectured on psychology, mental and moral philosophy, ontology, and natural theology. The president's lectures were looked upon as the culminating course not only of the senior year but of the whole college curriculum. In the time he was able to devote to these large and profound subjects, he could not have treated seriously more than the important points, but his lectures reviewed during the senior year the philosophy courses of the preceding years. These students' notes taken in connection with the theses sheets show that the old Scholastic philosophy, and especially its ethics, was looked upon as the most important feature of the curriculum for training in thoughtfulness and in the principles of philosophy. Graduates who were ere long to have the formation of the federal government of the new republic as well as the drawing up of the federal Constitution on their

157

125

hands, and who succeeded in bringing their efforts to a successful issue, were given their ultimate mental molding in this way.

For its first twenty years, the College of New Jersey had a rather difficult task to maintain itself. It owed its eventual success very largely to the Reverend Dr. John Witherspoon, Scotch Presbyterian minister, a graduate of Edinburgh University, who was invited to become president of Princeton in 1768. He devoted himself wholeheartedly and successfully to the task of making of the struggling institution a college deserving of the name. Some of the accounts of the Princeton commencements that we have after Witherspoon became president are interesting because they show how many intellectual interests were being cultivated.

158   The commencement of 1770 as reported in the *Pennsylvania Chronicle*, October 15, 1770, was one of the very busy commencements of the time. The reporter says,

> The exercises began with an English oration on "The Utility of the Study of History" to which succeeded a Latin syllogistic dispute on the following thesis: *Tenentur et obligantur subditi, ex Lege Naturae, ut Regi suo, immani Saevitia grassanti, vel Civitatis Jura evertenti, resistant, et Libertatem suam defendant,* "Subjects are bound and obliged by the law of nature to resist their king whenever he inflicts intolerable cruelties on them or overthrows the rights of the state; and they must defend their liberties." This was followed by an English forensic debate, "The Non-Importation Agreement Reflects a Glory on the American Merchant and was a Noble Exertion of Self-Denial and Public Spirit." An English dissertation on this subject, "Every Religious Profession which Does not by its Principles disturb the Public Peace ought to be Tolerated by a Wise State." A disputation ... "That National Characters depend not upon Physical but Moral Causes" ... an English oration on "The Utility of American Manufacturers" ... an English oration on "The Advantages of Trade and Commerce." ... Next followed a Latin syllogistic

debate on this thesis: *Omnes Homines, Jure Naturae, liberi sunt,* "All men by the law of nature are free." ... An English dispute on the following ... "The Different Religious Professions in any State if Maintained in their Liberty Serve it by Supplying the Place of a Censor Morum." ... This proposition was then controverted: "The Study of the Dead Languages is for the Emolument of Science even in a State where every useful and ornamental branch of learning is copiously treated in the Language proper to that state." ... A Valedictory Oration on the Subject of "Public Spirit." *159*

Some of the items mentioned in these reports of commencements are interesting from the standpoint of what was happening at this time in the colonies. For instance, in the report of the commencement of 1774, the *Pennsylvania Journal* for October 12, 1774, notes that the Latin salutatory oration that year at Princeton had for subject, *Bellum servituti anteponendum,* "War must be preferred to slavery." This was almost simultaneous with the expression of Patrick Henry, not a college man, "Give me liberty or give me death." The English forensic dispute that same year took up for consideration the subject that is occupying a good deal of attention at the present time: "Whether a state which derives all the necessary conveniences of life from its own territories is preferable to a state which by means of foreign commerce is supplied with all the elegancies of different climates." There was but one Latin thesis argued that year, and that under the rubric *ethics*: *Benevolentia erga proximum et Amor proprius nunquam inter se re vera pugnant,* "Benevolence toward one's neighbor and love of self never really conflict." The valedictory that year was on "The Horrors of War," and the colonies were just arming for the Revolution.

In the midst of his busy educational work, Witherspoon *160* somehow found the time to become an American of the Americans. Above all he became deeply interested in the question of securing independence for his adopted country as well as liberty and stability for the new nation that came into existence as the result of the Revolution. He succeeded particularly in arousing such a spirit of readiness to make sacrifices for national freedom in the minds not only of his students but also of others around him with whom he was brought in intimate contact that he has been deservedly hailed as one of the fathers of the country. He was a signer of the Declaration of Independence and a delegate from New Jersey to the Continental Congress. He was a member of the New Jersey Provincial Congress in 1776 and also of the New Jersey Constitutional Convention. While acting as president of the college, he gave instruction in divinity, philosophy mental and moral, Hebrew, rhetoric, and occasionally other subjects when teaching emergencies arose.

In this story of the early days of Princeton, emphasis is laid on the strictness of examinations, which gave the college a special reputation in the educational world of that day. Princeton's educational standards have been maintained at a high level ever since. Nassau Hall at Princeton had been founded by the Scotch Presbyterians, and the College of New Jersey was influenced deeply by their strictness and rigor. This gave it a special prestige among the colonial colleges. The discipline at Princeton, as became a faithful Scotch Presbyterian institution, was rather stern and rigid. This is best illustrated by the statute with regard to absence from school during term time. The sanction was not a punishment, but the deprivation of a right, and perhaps carried a hint of student participation in discipline, which became so noteworthy at Princeton later on.

161

Absence from the campus without license was considered a rather serious offense and was punished accordingly. For absence of a week during the two longer terms, any right that a student had to his room was forfeited, and it might be taken by anyone else. The Princeton statutes were strict in that matter and declared that "any student so absenting himself shall forfeit all his right and title to the same." This same statute applied also for a single day's absence "without license" during the shorter summer and winter terms.

In the sketch of the early history of Princeton which was written by a graduate shortly before the middle of the nineteenth century and which is a valuable source with regard to the early days of Princeton, high compliment is paid to Dr. Witherspoon for the influence which his character had over the students. The writer says, "The piety, erudition and knowledge of the world and deep insight into human nature possessed by Dr. Witherspoon qualified him in an eminent degree for the presidency of the college."

And yet with all this, which might hint at a life devoted very largely to study and devotion to books, Witherspoon proved a very practical college president. He succeeded in collecting what must *162* have been very large sums of money in those days, and he was quite as successful as any modern university president—one of whose main duties is usually considered to be financial—in securing funds that would enable him to maintain the high scholastic standards that he had set up.

During the more than twenty-five years (1768–1794) just before and after the Revolution while Witherspoon was president of Princeton, he came to be an extremely important factor in the thought of this country. While teaching metaphysics and ethics, it is easy to understand that he was the most important molding influence of his day on the minds of the students. His influence was diffused very widely all over the country, because of the very interesting fact that no less than thirteen of the graduates of Princeton during his presidency became college presidents themselves in various parts of the country. They carried on diligently the tradition of old-fashioned Scholastic education in which Witherspoon had been drilled himself in Edinburgh and with which he made it his definite purpose to form the minds of his students in Princeton.

When the list of the colleges over which Witherspoon's graduates came to be presidents is brought together, it is easy to understand how wide must have been the educational influence which he exerted over the United States after the Revolution. Among them were such institutions as Hampden-Sydney College

163 and Washington in Virginia; Washington and Jefferson in Pennsylvania; the University of North Carolina and Queens College in the same state; Mt. Zion in South Carolina; Washington, Tusculum, Greenville, and the University of Nashville in Tennessee; Transylvania in Kentucky; and Union College in New York. They were all followers of the Witherspoon traditions, which mainly concerned mental and moral philosophy, metaphysics, and ethics.

 Princeton's educational influence quite literally dominated much of the thinking in educational circles all over the country. Witherspoon himself was a born teacher—and teachers are born, not made—thoroughly capable of arousing the interest of his students and producing in them a spirit of emulation. If there was one thing these Scotch Presbyterians could do, it was think, and they were not afraid to tackle the deeper problems of life and above all the questions of the rights and duties of mankind and their relations to their Creator, as well as their obligations as citizens not only to the State but also to their fellow men. Princeton continued to be, down to our own day, one of the great foci of conservative thinking. Just a century after Witherspoon, another Presbyterian clergyman, Dr. James McCosh, brought over from Ireland, was to renew Princeton's influence in this regard very happily.

 Princeton, in the early days particularly, provides an excellent illustration of the place that graduates of colonial colleges came to occupy in the political life of the country during the latter half of the

164 eighteenth century. A whole series of holders of important offices in the generation just after the Revolution had been students in the College of New Jersey and had there received the stimulus which made them worthy representatives of their alma mater in constructive statesmanship. Among them there were a president and vice president of the United States, twenty-one United States senators, thirty-nine members of the House of Representatives, nine members of presidential cabinets, three Supreme Court justices, twelve governors of states, thirty-three judges, as well as more than twenty commissioned officers in the Revolutionary army. Princeton had six very important members of the Continental Congress and had

130

no less than nine delegates to the Constitutional Convention. It was mainly through the influence of Princeton graduates that one of the two plans presented to the Constitutional Convention for the determination of representation in the Congress was the New Jersey plan. The other was known as the Virginia plan. These two colonies exerted a paramount influence in the organization of the colonies before and after the Revolution and had much to do with the construction of the American republic as we have it.

I submitted the theses that were printed in 1750 and 1752 at Princeton under the rubric *metaphysics* to the Reverend Father Pyne, SJ, professor of Scholastic philosophy at Fordham University, to have him indicate just which theses represent propositions concordant with Scholastic philosophy and which do not. The definition of metaphysics as given at the head of the theses is in perfect accord with old-time philosophical ideas: "Metaphysics treats of beings considered abstractly in themselves and of their causes, kinds and relationships." Altogether, there are seven propositions under metaphysics, and Reverend Father Pyne marks four of them as thoroughly Scholastic; one as probably so, there being a question of terminology to disturb the comparison; and two that are questionable for the same reason. These seven propositions are:

165

1. A series of causes cannot proceed to infinity. [That is definitely Scholastic.]

2. Metaphysical truth in perfection [certitude] does not admit degree. [This is Scholastic.]

3. The moral perfections of God are not exercised from natural necessity [which Father Pyne marks as probably Scholastically right].

4. Physical possibility can exist apart from moral possibility. [This is definitely Scholastic, so is number 7, which is preceded by an index finger indicating its special importance.]

7. A conscious succession of thought is not necessary to constitute personal identity.

PRÆSTANTISSIMO

Optima Eruditione, Dignitate ac Pietate ſublimi, omnique fœliciſſime gubernandi Ratione VIRO perilluſtri,

JONATHAN BELCHER, Armigero,

Provinciæ *Novæ-Cæſariæ* GUBERNATORI, Mariſque contermini Vice-Admirallo,.

Conſummatiſſimo;—Neo non hujus Academiæ Patrono colendiſſimo;

Reverendo pariter ac honorando D. AARONI BURR, *Collegii Neo-Cæſarienſi*, PRÆSIDI, Fideliſſimis etiam

Ejuſdem Curatoribus, Literatura ac Pietate conſpicuis;

Vigilantiſſimis etiam, Eccleſiarum CHRISTI paſſim Paſtoribus, Doctrina et Pietate aromatis;—Omnibus denique, Rei literariæ Cultoribus, de noſtra Accademia bene merentibus, ſumma Gratitudine ſemper proſequendis; Hæc Philoſophemata quæ (DEO Opt. Max. favente) ſub Præſidis Moderamine ſunt agitanda, Juvenis Artibus initiati.

Hugo Bay,
Jacobus Beard,

Alexander Clinton,
Daniel Farrand,

Jacobus Frielinghuyſen,
Simeon Mitchel.

Devotiſſima cum Obſervantia ac Humilitate,—D. D. D. C. Q.

THESES TECHNOLOGICÆ.

TECHNOLOGIA de omnium Artium ac Scientiarum generaim, regulis ac Terminis verſatur.

1 Omnis Res Rhetoricæ eſt propria, quæ ornate dici, graviterque debeat.

2 Mentis Operationes & Termini quibus exprimuntur, adequatum Logicæ Objectum, conſtituunt.

3 Algebra, Quantitatem Quæſitam, five Numerum, five Lineam, ut datum aſſumit.

4 Inter Trigonometriam planam & Sphæricam, quædam datur certa Relatio ac Harmonia.

5 Ergo accurata hujus Obſervatio, ad illam perdiſcendam, multum conduceret.

6 Excellentia omnium Artium ac Scientiarum, a Tendentia ad Gloriam Dei & Hominum Fœlicitatem promovendum, pendet.

THESES GRAMMATICÆ.

GRAMMATICA, in quavis Lingua, Ideas Verbis apte & dilucide communicandi, Artem docet.

1 Sine Verbo expreſſo vel ſuppreſſo, Sententia eſſe nequir.

2 Grammatica per quam Lingua ignota docetur, Linguâ vernaculâ ſcribi debet.

3 Quo paucioribus Verbis quævis Lingua conſtat, eo-facilius intelligi poteſt.

5 Inter poſitivas & primitivas Quantitates nulla datur Ratio.

6 In Hyperbola, Quadratum Axis conjugati, tranſverſi Quadrato, ac Parameter Axi tranſverſo, eandem habent Proportionem.

7 Sphæra Pyramidi eſt æqualis, cujus Baſis Superficei, et Altitudo Sphæræ Radio ejus, ſunt æqualia.

8 Pyramidum æqualium Baſis & Altitudines, reciprocam habent Proportionem.

9 Sinus Arcuum ſimilium, Radiis eorum, eandem habent Rationem.

10 Sphæræ Superficies, Circuli Arcæ, ab ejus Radio deſcripti, eſt quadrupla.

THESES PHYSICÆ.

PHYSICA, Phænomenorum in Mundo Naturali ſecundum Leges Stabilitas Orientium, Solutionem indicat.

1 Altitudo Atmoſphæræ, ob inæqualem Denſitatem, accurate determinari nequit.

2 Inæqualis Atmoſphæræ Denſitas, partim ab ejus Elaſticitate, oritur.

3 Vi Solis ac Lunæ attractivâ, Fluxus ac Refluxus in Atmoſphera, æque ac in Mari, efficitur.

4 Soni Velocitas Aeris Elaſticitati eſt proportionalis.   Ergo,

5 Ceteris paribus Æſtate quam Hyeme eſt major.

6 Velocitas Lucis eſt 10210 major quam Terræ in ejus annua Orbita.   Ergo,

7 Parrallaxis Syderum fixarum apparebit contrarie quam aliter effet.

8 Reflectio Radiorum Lucis, ab Atmoſphera elaſtica, quamvis Particulam Lucis,

4 Cognitio Vocafium Mutationis, ad Linguam Hebraicam intelligendum, non est absolute necessaria.
5 Inter Hebræos Adverbium negandi sæpe intelligitur.
6 Hebræi, Gradum superlativum per Adverbium, exprimunt.
7 Omnium Linguarum Hebraica est antiquissima.

THESES RHETORICÆ.

RHETORICA est Ars Veritatem copiose et eleganter illustrandi.
1 Perfectio optimorum Authorum præsertim veterum Poetarum, ad Oratorem formandum, multum conducit.
2 Sine multum scribendo, Orator perfectus existere non potest.
3 Tamen Oratio sine Scriptis pronunciari debet.
4 Ortio, non minus Oratori quam Audientibus prodest.
5 Penitus Rei Cognitio, Memoriæ Lumen maxime adfert.
6 Vocis, Vultus, & Gestus, Moderatio cum Venustate, Orationem reddit jucundam.
7 Vox ultra Vires urgenda non est.

THESES LOGICÆ.

LOGICA est Ars, in Veritatem investigando ac aliis communicando, Ratione bene utendi.
1 Extensio & Comprehensio Idearum mutuo sese excendunt aut contrahunt.
2 Affirmatio Ideæ, Comprehensionem ejus, semper includit.
3 Differentia inter Species nominales, Differentiam inter reales, non arguit.
4 E Premissis particularibus, ad Conclusionem generalem, Consequentia non valet.
5 In Premissis, unus Terminus universalis, magis quam in Conclusione semper esse debet.
6 Veræ Conclusiones a veris Principiis Oriuntur.
7 Ideæ simplices explicari non possunt.
8 Nomina, ad Ideas communicandas, non sunt absolute necessaria.
9 Ex diversis Ideis, eidem Nomini affixis, mutarum Controversiarum oritur Causa.
10 Nomina particularia, cuivis Ideæ simplici annexa, Causam Erroris in Ideis communicandis suffulerent.
11 Sed hoc, quamvis Linguam, redderet nimis obscuram.

THESES MATHEMATICÆ.

MATHEMATICA, de, Quantitate & ejus Relationum, Natura & Analogia tractat.
1 Circulus Triangulo est æqualis cujus Basis Peripheræ et Altitudo Radio sunt æquales.
2 In omni Parrallelogramite, duorum Diagonalium Quadrata, quatuor Laterum Quadrato sunt æqualia.
3 Privitivæ Quantitates, etsi realium sunt Defectus, tamen minores vel majores esse possunt.
4 Primitivæ positivis Quantitatibus, sunt heterogeneæ et vice versa. Ergo,

circumambiente efficitur.
9 Corpusculum, in quavis Parte Sphæræ concavæ que attractivæ, erit quietum.
10 In Divisione Sphæræ, solida Materia ut Cubi, Superficies autem ut Quadrata Diametrorum minuuntur. Ergo,
11 Corpora parva in Fluido, in Proportione solidæ Materiæ, magis quam magis resistuntur.
12 Retrocessio Poli Equatoris circa Eclipticum, solis ac Lunæ Vi attractivâ, efficitur.
13 Unde apparet Terram esse Figuræ Sphæroidalis.
14 Dies Solares, nec fideriis Diebus nec sibi ipsis, sunt æquales.
15 Hujus Inæqualitatis, Revolutio Terræ circa Solem et eccliptica Orbitæ Figura sunt Causa.
16 ☞ *Omnia Phænomena, in Mundo naturali, immediatâ Dei Energiâ, efficiuntur.*

THESES METAPHYSICÆ.

METAPHYSICA est, de Entibus in se abstracte consideratis, et eorum Caufis, Generibus, ac Relationibus, Tractatus.
1 Subordinatio Caufarum ad Infinitum procedere non potest.
2 Metaphysica Veritas & Perfectio Gradus not admittunt.
3 Perfectiones Dei morales, e Necessitate naturali, non exercentur.
4 Possibiles naturalis absque Possibilitate morali existere potest.
5 Omnia, Necessitate Consequentiæ, sunt necessaria.
6 Sed hæc Necessitas, in Voluntatem Agentium moralium, nullam Influentiam habet.
7 ☞ *Consilia Successio cogitandi, ad personalem Identitatem constituendam, non est necessaria...*

THESES ETHICÆ.

ETHICA, summam Fælicitatem per Praxin Virtutis, Rationem obtinendi docet.
1 Summum Bonum, in Fruitione Entis perfectissimi, constat.
2 Sine Respectu ad Deum, ut ultimum Finem, Actiones formaliter bonæ esse non possunt.
3 Judicium privatæ Discretionis, cuivis Agenti morali, est essentiale.
4 Sine Voluntatis Consensu Peccatum existere nequit. Ergo,
5 Libertatis Abusus Mali moralis fuit Origo.
6 Sine Virtute non potest esse alicujus Boni vera Fruitio.
7 Dictamina Rationis sunt iis Sensuum anteponenda.
8 In Statu Naturæ, (quibusdam Cognatis excepti) quoad Imperium, Homines sunt æquales. Ergo,
9 Jus Regum, e Compacto Populi, originale Fundamen habuit. Ergo,
10 Competitor Gæorgii Secundi (optimo Jure) nostri Regis, Imperium *Magnæ-Britanniæ,* non minus injuste quam inaniter sibi vindicat.

His præcedit Oratio Salutatoria:

Habita in Comitiis academicis Novarcæ. in Nova-Cæsarea, Sexto Calendas Octobris, MDCCL.

PRINCETON THESES, 1750. COMMENCEMENT HELD AT NEWARK

(167)   133

The other two propositions which are connected:

5. All things by the necessity of consequences are necessary,

6. But this necessity has no influence over the will of moral agents,

168 are questioned as regards their relationship to Scholastic philosophy, because it is not quite sure what the terminology employed might connote, but they seem to be Scholastic, for they emphasize the fact that there is freedom of the will, since necessity has no influence over the will of a moral agent.

In 1752 at Princeton, the definition of metaphysics is "the science which treats of the abstract relations and causes of things." Under it there are nine propositions, practically all of them, when submitted to professors of Scholastic philosophy in our time, proving to be thoroughly Scholastic in character. They run,

1. The essences of mathematical entities [abstract ideas] are immutable.

2. Whatever consists of parts cannot be infinite.

3. A simple being insofar as it is such is prior to and more perfect than one that is a compound.

4. All the essences of things existed in the mind of God from eternity. [Father Pyne's commentary on this is "Platonism preserved through Scholasticism."]

5. The possibility of a thing is deduced from the non-repugnance of the [notes constituting the] idea.

6. Cyclogenesis [the genesis of living beings in a cycle, that is, each from the other without any beginning] is impossible; therefore

7. The existence of God can be demonstrated from effect to cause. [Here is the principle of causality invoked as a proof of God's existence.]

8. All the divine ideas are wanting in archetypes. [Father Pyne notes this as Platonic.]

9. [With an index] Moral evil does not take away the *169*
perfection of this world. [Here is the problem of evil
obtruding itself once more and yet without at all disturbing the faith of the men of that time in the existence of a beneficent Creator and the perfection of the
world from the standpoint of reason.]

At Princeton as early as 1750, a full twenty-five years before
the Declaration of Independence, there was a series of propositions
among the *theses ethicae* which show that the philosophers of New
Jersey, under the influence of the Scotch at Edinburgh, were insisting on certain principles of government and its origin that harked
back to the sixteenth century and the later Middle Ages. This series
of propositions runs, "In the state of nature (with certain exceptions)
so far as government is concerned men are equal; therefore, the right
of kings has its original foundation from a compact of the people;
therefore, the rival of George II, our king (by the highest right) vin-
dicates for himself the right to rule in Great Britain not less unjustly
than vainly." The reference of course is to the Pretender, Charles
Edward Stuart, the grandson of Charles I, who shortly before this
time had been defeated at the battle of Culloden and had escaped
and was still from France proclaiming his right to the rulership of
Great Britain, though without justice on his side and therefore in
vain, for his claim was not supported by the majority of the people.

At Princeton in 1760, the class in which Benjamin Rush
and Samuel Blair graduated, the theses demonstrate that eth- *170*
ics was looked upon as by far the most prominent feature of the
curriculum, for there were no less than twenty-nine propositions
advanced. The proposition which is marked with an index and is
printed in italics and was, therefore, a proposition to be demonstrated and argued in the commencement disputation ran as follows: "A perfect system of ethics in the present condition of men
cannot be constructed without the help of divine revelation."

Some of the other propositions in ethics in 1760 at Princeton
serve to show very clearly how much they were occupied with the

personal sense of right and wrong and with the effort to maintain individual righteousness. For instance, proposition 3 runs, "The propensity of nature toward moral evil even when vehement does not do away with responsibility." Number 4 runs, "Mere speculation in matters of prudence without experience and observation is not sufficient to direct men well." Number 5 runs, "Actions which are materially good can be at the same time formally bad." The Latin expressions are *secundum materiam* and *secundum formam*, definitely Scholastic terminology. Number 6 is "A rational being acting according to reason cannot do evil."

Succeeding propositions run,

7. The obligation of an intelligent being is increased or diminished according to the strength of nature and the opportunity of action.

8. The evil of a sin is to be estimated from the quality of the delinquent and the dignity of the personality who is affected by the injury.

9. In the state of nature, a man is the owner of all that he secured possession of before others.

10. The number of each sex is throughout all the centuries nearly equal; therefore

11. Polygamy is not in accordance with reason, nor does it belong to the institution of God as Creator and Providence.

15. Human society cannot exist without the observance of truth.

16. The faculty of distinguishing good from evil is essential to a moral agent.

17. The liberty of a creature may crave the faculty of performing an action but does not require it.

22. Moral obligation supposes reason and the congruence of things, but

23. God is the cause of things and therefore also of the relations of the same; hence

24. God is the cause and the exemplar of reason and of the congruence of things.

25. The moral sense is only indeed a mode of perceiving moral obligation.

26. In all men there is present a moral sense of eternal obligation as is plainly to be seen from the judgments which men make with regard to the actions of others.

27. Parents in accordance with their condition in life are bound to imbue the minds of their children with doctrine [education].

28. A clement, mild government conduces very much to the increase of the number of subjects and of rendering them obedient to the laws.

172

29. To be affected by a sense of the Deity and of His Providence is the greatest incitement that we have to the practice of virtue.

In 1762 at Princeton, there were twenty-one propositions under the rubric *ethica*. The first one ran, "The highest perfection of men depends on their liberation from all sin." The second ran, "Truths that are known of themselves (intuitively) exist in ethics," from which the conclusion is drawn in a proposition printed in italics and with an index finger: "Therefore, Moral truths can be demonstrated equally with mathematical truths." The next two propositions are connected in the same way and complete the idea: (4) "Ethical ideas are for the most part more complex than numbers; therefore (5) Ethics is more difficult to prove than mathematics."' Number 6 is a political thesis: "Absolute liberty belongs to no form of government." Number 11, printed in italics with an index finger, is a key proposition: "The moral sense in so far as it is a simple perception and the foundation of moral obligation does not exist." At Princeton they were quite sure that ethics was not easy, and they must have felt the need of casuistry, that is, the discussion of particular cases in order to be able to point out the bounds of moral obligation. Proposition 12 ran, "The present life is to be estimated not as an end but in so far as it provides an opportunity for the securing of eternal happiness." Proposition 20: "The idea of virtue is definite and also immutable." The last proposition, printed in italics and with an index, runs, "A ruler endowed with civil virtue though without military glory is much preferable to a prince who though without civil virtue is very illustrious for his courage in war."[4]

173

---

4. Almost exactly a century after Witherspoon, Reverend James McCosh of Belfast was invited to become president of the rising College of New Jersey. Princeton owes as much to this nineteenth-century Irishman as to its eighteenth-century Scotch president. McCosh probably influenced the academic world of America as deeply in the second half of the nineteenth century as Witherspoon did in the eighteenth. During his presidency, the number of students increased from two hundred to six hundred. The tradition among the professors of Scholastic philosophy in the Catholic colleges of the country in his time was that Dr. McCosh was distinctly Scholastic in his philosophic teaching. I recall our own professor of philosophy at Fordham dwelling on this. He was particularly struck with the attitude of Reverend Dr. McCosh toward error and sin and quoted from McCosh, "Our academic moralists are commonly averse to look at or consider these two topics, but if there be truth in our world there is also error; if there be good there is also evil. ... Malice and deceit and adultery are as much realities as good will, integrity and purity." I have recently consulted Father Pyne, professor of Scholastic philosophy at Fordham University, with regard to the Scholastic quality of Dr. McCosh's teachings. He wrote me that, in a general way, Dr. McCosh follows "the line of thought of the Scholastics holding the same fundamental positions that God is the Creator of all things outside Himself, that the soul in immortal, that God has established a moral law and that there will be judgment after death pronounced by God upon the individual man in accordance with his observance or violation of the moral law."

6

King's College
(Columbia)

Just after the middle of the eighteenth century, a number of men   *174*
in the colony of New York took up the discussion of a project to
establish an academy and college in Manhattan. Harvard, William
and Mary, Yale, and Princeton had succeeded in this purpose in
spite of many difficulties, and prominent inhabitants of New York
felt that their city should have an institution of this kind. Mr. William Smith, after finishing his divinity studies at Aberdeen, but not
yet ordained to the ministry, came over to New York as tutor in the
family of Colonel Morton. The agitation for the foundation of an
institution for higher studies caught his attention, and Mr. Smith
wrote a pamphlet with the title *Some Thoughts on Education with
Reasons for Erecting a College in This Province and Fixing the Same in
the City of New York*. The following year, he wrote at much greater
length under the title *A General Idea of the College of Mirania*, in
which he expressed his ideas as to a liberal education. These publications were sent to Benjamin Franklin in Philadelphia, because
there was agitation at this same time for the establishment of an
institute of higher learning over there. Franklin, who was deeply

175 interested in the provision of opportunities for higher education, expressed himself as well satisfied with the scheme of education outlined by Mr. Smith.

Mr. Smith's volume *The College of Mirania* bears the subtitular dedication "Addressed more immediately to the consideration of the trustees nominated by the legislature to receive proposals relating to the establishment of a college in the province of New York." It bears also the imprint "New York, printed and Sold by J. Parker and W. Weyman, at the New Printing Office in Beaver Street, 1753." In spite of this dedication and definitely expressed purpose, the pamphlet was destined to provide its author with an opportunity to put his theories of education into practice not in New York but in Philadelphia. A discussion of his book finds a more appropriate place in the chapter on the College of Philadelphia, of which Smith was the provost for some twenty years. His outline of a scheme of education emphasizes the place of Scholastic philosophy, that is, the *trivium* and *quadrivium*, in the education of that day, and the commencement theses of the College of Philadelphia make it very clear that the principles laid down by Smith and which attracted the attention of Franklin were carried out in the college of which he became the first executive.

The first president of King's College, New York, was Reverend Samuel Johnson, pastor of the Episcopal Church at Stratford, Connecticut, who was our first American writer on philosophical subjects. His writings, as we shall see, confirm very strikingly the
176 idea that Scholasticism constituted the heart of the curriculum in the colonial colleges. Johnson had been deeply influenced by Dean, afterwards Bishop, Berkeley, the Irish philosopher with whom, as a young man, he was brought intimately in contact during Berkeley's visit to the colonies in 1729. He had lifted himself above that influence, however, and his philosophic writings were very conservative. He was undoubtedly the most distinguished writer and thinker on philosophic subjects in this country. Benjamin Franklin tried to

secure Johnson as the head of the college that they were founding in Philadelphia, but Johnson preferred to stay in New York not too far away from his congregation at Stratford, Connecticut. Besides, he had many personal friends among the founders of King's College.

In spite of his preoccupation with philosophic subjects, Dr. Johnson proved to be an excellent organizer, and King's College, as is evident particularly from the roll of its graduates and the extremely important influence which they exerted upon their generation, became a distinct asset to the city during the years before the Revolution.

Dr. Johnson was the son of a deacon of the Congregational Church in Guilford, Connecticut. What little schooling he received came from his grandfather and certain of the ministers in the neighboring towns, several of whom volunteered their services as teachers. Even at the age of ten, however, he set them down as "such wretched poor scholars that they could teach him little or nothing." When he was about eighteen, he was afforded the opportunity to read the works of some of the best English poets, philosophers, and divines, and their effect on Johnson was, as he says himself, "truly revolutionary." During the next six years, he discovered not only the New Learning but also the Anglican Church. The English ecclesiastical writers not only made him conscious of the doubtful validity of his Congregational orders but also introduced him to a rich, scholarly tradition of which he had been quite ignorant. After some years of hesitation and deliberation, he and a few friends in 1722 finally resolved to take orders in the Anglican Church. He came to be considered the most scholarly representative of that Church in the country, and his selection to the post of president of King's College demonstrates that the organizers were intent on securing the best talent there was for the new institution.

He had already been some thirty-two years a minister of the Anglican Church when he was chosen the president of King's College. The charter granted by the English king, George II, for the

177

141

foundation of a college in the province of New York to be called King's College dwells particularly on the primacy of influence which the Church of England, by law established, was to exert in the colony. In this charter, Reverend Samuel Johnson was nominated specifically as the first president with the proviso for his successor that "the president of the said college for the time being shall forever hereafter be a member of and in communion with the Church of England as by law established." That charter called for representation on the board of trustees of King's College of the ministers of the other principal churches of the city. Among them were the senior minister of the Reformed Dutch Protestant Church, the minister of the Ancient Lutheran Church, the minister of the French (Huguenot) Church, and the minister of the Presbyterian Church.

178

After the terms of this charter became known generally to the people of the city, the Church of England in New York fell under suspicion of trying to create a monopoly in education that would accrue to the advantage of the Church rather than the citizens and the province itself. When the Dutch surrendered New York into the hands of the English, they were solemnly promised that they should enjoy "the liberty of their conscience in divine worship and church discipline." On the foundation of King's College, the ministers of the Dutch Reformed Church set forth that they needed education for their ministers, and this being represented to the king, he declared, "We being willing and desirous that all our loving subjects, the members of the Reformed Protestant Dutch Churches, should have the opportunity for the training of their ministers, granted this privilege to King's College of educating for the ministry."

The education afforded these ministers of the Dutch Reformed Church according to the subsidiary charter was to be such as would "conform to the doctrine, discipline and worship established in the united provinces by the national synod of Dort."

179

This same religious curriculum was to be open to "any other students that may be desirous to attend its lectures."

The professor of theology in this department of the college was to be nominated by the "ministers, elders and deacons of the Reformed Protestant Dutch Church in New York." Provision was thus made for the education in the theology of the Dutch Reformed Church not only for ministers but also for such of the laity as cared to devote special attention to this form of belief.

The royal charter was quite frank in the added declaration that the crown did this all the more readily because the privilege thus conceded promised "to promote the prosperity of the said college and an increase in the number of students." Almost needless to say, the number of students at the beginning was quite small, and the registration at King's College did not increase rapidly until long after the Revolution.

For some time before the granting of these charters, there had been considerable discussion as to the advisability of having a college in New York City, and a pamphleteer created quite a sensation by suggesting that New York, being a city of considerable size, though it was then much smaller than Philadelphia, was not a suitable place for the gathering of young men into a college, because they would be subjected to all sorts of temptations. In answer to *180* this, another pamphleteer said that opponents of the erection of a college in New York "admit that the Conversation of polished Citizens would be of great Advantage to their Sons, but say they, in such a large place there never fails to be worthless, rakish Individuals to debauch unwary Youth and lead them into what (to oblige delicate ears) is called the polite Vices." He adds that "to preserve the Morals sound ought to be the chief aim of education" but emphatically declares that that can be accomplished as well in New York as in any other town.

Perhaps this discussion before the opening of the college led the authorities to emphasize the place that religion was expected to

143

hold in the new foundation. There is an advertisement published June 1754 from the pen of the first president, which was evidently intended to neutralize any bad impression that might have been produced by the preceding discussion and to attract parents' attention to the new institution by proclaiming the religious aims of the founders and their purpose to make better citizens of the students by making them better Christians. Doubtless it was hoped also to attract the attention of benefactors, since the avowed aim of the new institution was to benefit the community by the training afforded future citizens: "The chief thing that is aimed at in this college is to teach and engage the children [*sic*] to know God and Jesus Christ and to love and serve Him in all Sobriety, Godliness and Righteousness of Life with a perfect Heart and willing Mind."

181

Always in the colonial colleges the necessity of teaching religious principles was emphasized, and the knowledge and worship of God was presented as the culmination of intellectual development. A striking example of this is to be found in the charter of King's College, which provides for the instruction and education of youth in the learned languages and in the liberal arts but emphasizes also the value of religious education. The announcement of the opening of the school reads as follows:

> A serious, virtuous and industrious Course of Life being first provided for, it is further the Design of this College, to instruct and perfect the Youth in the Learned Languages, and in the Arts of Reasoning exactly, of Writing correctly and Speaking eloquently; And in the Arts of Numbering and Measuring, of Surveying and Navigation, of Geography and History, of Husbandry, Commerce, and Government; and in the Knowledge of all Nature in the Heavens above us, and in the Air, Water, and Earth around us, and the various Kinds of Meteors, Stones, Mines, and Minerals, Plants and Animals, and of every Thing useful for the Comfort, the Convenience, the Elegance of Life, in the chief Manufactures relating to any of these things;

> And finally, to lead them from the Study of Nature, to
> the Knowledge of themselves, and of the God of Nature,
> and their Duty to Him, themselves and one another; and
> every Thing that can contribute to their true Happiness,
> both here and hereafter.

182

After the granting of the charter, a considerable sum of money was raised by a collection in England and by a public lottery. Ground being donated by Trinity Church, a suitable building was erected. The first president, after some eight years, returned to his pastorate at Stratford, Connecticut, which he had not resigned, probably because he felt that the pastorate was more important for him than the presidency of this new small college, whose future it was rather difficult to foresee at the beginning. The second president was Reverend Miles Cooper, an ardent Royalist, who on the breaking out of the Revolution returned to England. A great many of the old New York families continued to be royalist in sympathy, but in the course of the Revolution, a change of attitude, particularly among those associated with King's College, took place. During the Revolution itself and the occupation of New York by the British, college work was suspended, but this was true to a great extent also of all the other colonial colleges.

After the Revolution, it was reopened as King's College in 1784, but a change of name necessitated under the circumstances was made in 1787, and the title Columbia College was adopted. This continued to be the formal title of the institution until 1896, when the name was changed to Columbia University with the removal to its present site on Morningside Heights. In spite of the fact that New York early in the nineteenth century became the metropolis of the country, growing more rapidly than any other city, Columbia College was slow in growth. By the middle of the nineteenth century, it had scarcely more than a hundred and fifty students. By the end of the century, there were only some two thousand students, including large law and medical schools. Its growth

183

to the huge institution which registers nearly forty thousand students was a matter of the twentieth century and especially the time since the Great War.

The curriculum of King's College was similar to that of the other colonial colleges. They had the *trivium* and the modified *quadrivium*. The secretary of the university tells me that there are no theses broadsides extant for Columbia, but they have the receipted bills for the printing of some of them to prove their use. The account of the first commencement which has come down to us shows that there were disputations both for the bachelors' and masters' degrees. We are told that a metaphysical thesis was learnedly defended against two objectors, so there is no doubt of the Scholastic character of the exercises. They had their public act on commencement day as had the other colleges.

This description of the first commencement held at King's College shows that the disputations constituted an extremely important part of the exercises and make it very clear that King's College was not different from the others in this regard. In the *New York Mercury* for June 26, 1758 (n. 306), there is a communication manifestly from someone deeply interested in the college, probably a member of the faculty, describing the exercises, in which we find the following passage:

184

> Dr. Johnson, president, from the pulpit opened the solemnity with a learned and elegant *Oratio Inauguralis*. The exercises of the Bachelors were introduced by a polite salutary [*sic*] Oration delivered by Provost [one of the graduates] with such Propriety of Pronunciation and so engaging an Air as greatly gained for him the Admiration and Applause of all present. This was followed by a metaphysical Thesis learnedly defended by Ritzema [another of the graduates] against Verplanck and Costello with another held by Reed and opposed by the two Ogdens. The Bachelors' exercises were closed by a well composed genteel English Oration. Mr. Treadwell in a clear and concise

manner demonstrated the Revolution of the Earth around the Sun both from astronomical Observation and the Theory of Gravity and defended the Thesis against Mr. Cutting and Mr. Whitmore, a candidate for the degree of Master of Arts. This dispute being ended, the president conferred the degrees.

The most direct and authentic evidence of the content of what was called philosophy, that is, mental philosophy, or metaphysics, and moral philosophy, or ethics, as taught not only in King's College but in all the colonial colleges is to be found in the writings of President Johnson. In Ueberweg's well-known German *History* *185* *of Philosophy*,[1] in the chapter on "Philosophy in North America," Samuel Johnson is given the title "Father of American philosophy." Fortunately, the material for analysis of his philosophy is readily available in the biography of the first president of King's College prepared by the Schneiders: *Samuel Johnson, President of King's College, His Career and Writings*, edited by Herbert and Carol Schneider, in four volumes.[2]

In the second volume are reprinted Johnson's *Encyclopedia of Philosophy* and his *Elementa Philosophica*. The first volume consists of some 1,271 theses or propositions which Johnson wrote out when he was about eighteen years of age and which he considered to be a systematic summary of "all learning" and was ready to defend. Of this Schneider says, "The terminology is highly technical, and almost impossible to translate into intelligible English; but a glance

---

1. Friedrich Ueberweg, *Grundriss der geschichte der philosophie* (Berlin: Mittler 1928), VI.
2. Herbert Schneider and Carol Schneider, eds., *Samuel Johnson, President of King's College, His Career and Writings* (New York: Columbia University Press, 1919). Volume 1 bears the title *Autobiography and Letter*; vol. 2, *The Philosopher*; vol. 3, *The Churchman*; and vol. 4, *Founding King's College*. All quotations are from vol. 2.

at this treatise is sufficient to reveal its Scholastic methods and categories as well as the preoccupation with purely formal distinctions."

Not long after Johnson completed this, he very fortunately came into the possession of Lord Bacon's *Advancement of Learning*, and this took the conceit out of him that he knew nearly all that

186 was worthwhile knowing. The select collection of books brought over from England by Dummer, a colonial agent, completed his disillusionment as to his intellectual attainments. Johnson secured the opportunity to read not only the works of the best English poets and philosophers, Shakespeare, Milton, and others, but also Boyle and Newton of the physicists and mathematicians, as well as the writings of a great many prominent English divines, including Harrow, Tillotson, South, Sherlock, and others. As he himself said in his *Autobiography* (written in the third person), "All this was like a flood of day to his low state of mind."

Some years later, after he had had the opportunity to digest some of this serious reading, Johnson wrote what he called *An Outline of Philosophy*, in which he defined philosophy as "the love and study of truth and wisdom, that is of the objects and rules conducive to true happiness, for to be happy being our great aim and chief good this is the chief end of philosophy." In 1731 he published an *Introduction to Philosophy*, the second edition of which was published in London in 1746. An enlarged edition of this was printed by Franklin in Philadelphia under the title *Elementa Philosophica*. Franklin had been very much taken with Johnson's work and secured Johnson's own annotated copy for his enlarged Philadelphia edition. Franklin was so much impressed by it that he invited Johnson to become the head of the college which they were about to found over in Philadelphia, but Johnson had already been

187 engaged by King's College, New York, and so it came about that William Smith, who had written his booklet *The College of Mirania* in order to stir up interest for the establishment of a college in New York of which he hoped he might become the head, was invited to become the provost of the College of Philadelphia.

148

Johnson's *Elementa Philosophica* published by Franklin came to be rather well-known throughout the academic world of the colonies, so that it is not surprising that Johnson is hailed as the "Father of American philosophy." Even a little study of this volume makes it very clear that Scholastic philosophy had influenced Johnson not only in his younger years but continued to influence him all during his career. It is perfectly possible to illustrate most of the phases of Scholasticism out of Johnson's book, and after reading it, it becomes clear that the old medieval mode of thinking and teaching was still very much alive and was influencing deeply the minds of the teachers in the colonial colleges.

Johnson believed firmly in the principle of causality and trusted his own mind and his logic enough to follow it to an ultimate deduction. He said,

> Whatever being began to be must have had a cause and depend on some other being for its existence. By the word cause we mean that being by whose design and activity, force or exertion, another being exists; and that being which exists by the design, force, action or exertion of another, is called an effect; what is called an effect, therefore, must be supposed not to have existed and consequently to have had a beginning of existence or at least a dependent existence and must therefore have had a cause by the force or activity of which it came into existence and without which it would not have been. And this must be the case of everything that is till you come to a first cause, that is to a being that never had a beginning or dependent existence but exists by the absolute necessity of its own nature having an original perfect fullness of being in and of itself without depending on any other being and deals out being and perfection to all other things in various measures and degrees as pleaseth him. And such a being there must be, otherwise nothing could ever have been unless you suppose a thing to be its own cause, that is to act before it is which is impossible; or unless you suppose an infinite succession of causes and effects which in effect

188

would be an infinite effect without any cause at all. But an effect without a cause is a contradiction in terms.

Johnson discusses many of the problems that were favorite subjects of the Scholastic philosophers and asks and answers many of the questions that were the subjects of argumentation in the schools of philosophy of the Middle Ages. He has long paragraphs on such subjects as "Of Real and Apparent Causes," "Of Necessary and Voluntary Causes," "Of Final Causes." He has nearly a page of discussion of matter and form and a similar discussion of the distinction between the essence of things and their existence. He says,

189

> By their essence, we mean those constituent principles, properties and powers in them, which are necessary to nature, as being what they are, whether considered only as conceived in the mind of an intelligent being or existing in *rerum natura*. ... We have as clear an idea of a rose in winter, as in June, when it is before our eyes and under our noses. ... Whereas by existence we generally mean things being actually in fact and nature as well as in idea or conception. ... Hence existence always implies essence though essence does not necessarily imply existence except in that of a necessarily existent being and in whom necessity of existence is implied in His very essence and accordingly His original name, Jehovah, given by Himself does literally signify The Essence existing.

In chapter 4 of the *Elementa Philosophica*, under the title "Of the Mind Reasoning and Methodizing Its Thoughts," there is a discussion of the syllogism, its nature, and various figures and of the place that it has in the acquisition of truth. He discusses the enthymemes, or condensed syllogisms, and the irregular forms of the syllogism, the dilemma and the sorites. In a dilemma, the major proposition is a conditional whose consequent contains all the several suppositions upon which the antecedent can take place, which being removed in the minor, it is apparent the antecedent must also be taken away. He gives as an example of this form of reasoning: "If God did not create the world it must either have

150

been self-existent or have derived from mere chance; but it could *190* neither be self-existent nor derived from chance; therefore it must have been created by God."

Dr. Johnson defines the sorites as a method of arguing in a series of propositions so connected together that the predicate of the first becomes the subject of the second, and so on until we come to a conclusion in which the predicate of the last proposition appears from those intermediate propositions to be connected with the subject of the first. He gives as an example of the sorites the following way of reasoning to prove the natural immortality of the soul:

1. The soul is a conscious, intelligent, active, self-existing being.

2. A conscious, intelligent, active, self-existing being as such is entirely of an opposite and different nature and kind from that of bodies and therefore can have nothing in common with them but their existence.

3. A being which as such is entirely of a different nature from bodies and hath nothing besides existence common with them, can have no corporeal properties and affections such as solid extension, continuation of parts and divisibility or discerpibility.

4. A being that having no corporeal properties and so does not consist of solid extended parts divisible or discerpible cannot be naturally liable to dissolution.

5. What is not in the nature of it liable to dissolution *191* must be naturally immortal. Ergo.

6. The soul is naturally immortal. And here these intermediate propositions may be reduced to so many categoric syllogisms beginning with the last and ending with the first.

Almost needless to say, this argumentation is characteristically Scholastic in method and content.

Dr. Johnson emphasizes that the rules for the syllogism as he has given them, if duly attended to, would effectually prevent all sophistical reasoning but considers that some attention should be devoted to the sophisms, or false reasoning. He numbers four of these:

1. *Ignoratio elenchi*, when the dispute proceeds upon a mistake, occasioned by not attending to the state of the question.

2. *Petitio principii*, when the thing is taken for granted which has to be proved. This, as Dr. Johnson says, is called in English "begging the question."

3. *Fallacia quatuor terminorum*, which occurs when the intermediate term bears a different sense in the minor from the sense in which it was used in the major.

4. *Non causa pro causa*, a mistaking for a cause what was not a cause, as when a person perceives his health consequent to the using of a medicine and ascribes it to that, when perhaps it might really be due to a medicine which he had used before;

And fifthly, there is the *association of ideas*, in which, because such ideas are connected merely by custom, we are apt to conceive they are connected in nature as terrors with darkness. Dr. Johnson follows this with the very practical advice, "On account of this it is of great importance in education to take care that no ideas become associated by habit or custom with those that are connected in nature: and on the other hand that those ideas that are really connected in nature be associated by habit or custom, that a sense of their connection may operate with a greater force on the conduct of life."

Reverend Dr. Johnson's treatment of the passions, their end and use, and the due government of them is so different from the corresponding treatment of this subject in the secular colleges at the present day and yet so closely resembles the corresponding

192

treatment in the Catholic colleges of the present time, and indeed for the past seven hundred years and more, that it seems worthwhile to quote what he has to say:

> These passions are natural to us, and, as such, must be considered as part of the frame of our natures, and consequently as being implanted in us by the Author of our nature, for answering very wise and good ends, relating to our happiness; and therefore are so far from being evil in themselves, that they have the nature of good, as well as all our other faculties, and so, like the rest, become morally good or evil, according to the good or ill use we make of them. Now as God hath so framed us, that our happiness should depend on a vigorous activity in the use of the powers and faculties he hath given us, his design in planting these passions in us, was, that they might be, as it were, spurs and incentives in us, to put us upon such a vigorous activity, in avoiding those things that are mischievous either to ourselves or others, and pursuing those things in which our happiness or that of others consists. For the passions are, as it were, the wings of the soul, by which it is carried on with vehemence and impetuosity in its several pursuits; and, as it were, its springs, by which it is animated and invigorated in all its exertions. Thus love, desire and hope, vigorously animate and spur us on to the pursuit of those things that we love, desire and hope for, as being connected with our well-being and happiness; and hatred, abhorrence and fear, engage us with the utmost vehemence to fly from, and guard against, those things that we abhor and dread, as tending to our misery. And as benevolence, compassion and gratitude, inspire us with a delight in all those good offices in which both our personal and social happiness consists; so malevolence, aversion and anger, are useful to inspire us with indignation and zeal, in opposing all those impious and injurious practices that tend to the mischief and misery of society in general, as well as each particular person.

193

As regards the due government of the passions, Reverend Dr. Johnson would be much more in accord with Huxley's expression in his address on *A Liberal Education and Where to Find It* than with any of the present-day teachers in secular universities that I know of. Johnson, like Huxley, insists that the passions must be brought to heel under the guidance of a tender conscience and the power of a strong will:

194

> So that the passions are designed to be, and are, in their nature, capable of being subservient to a multitude of excellent purposes; and all that is necessary to render them so, is, that there be a right judgment made, what objects we ought to affect or disaffect, as being really connected with our happiness or misery, either personal or social; and that they be duly balanced one with another, and rightly governed and moderated in proportion to the real value and importance of their respective objects. And for this purpose were we furnished with the powers of reason and conscience, that they might preside over our passions, and make a right judgment of their several objects, and thence prescribe laws to them, and restrain them from all exorbitancies and irregularities; that we might know what we ought to love or hate, to hope for or fear, to be pleased or displeased with, and in what proportion, and not to suffer them to exceed the real value and importance of things with regard to our true happiness. Since, therefore, the great Author of our nature aims at our happiness, and hath given us our passions to be subservient to it, and furnished us with reason, to govern and regulate them in such a manner as to render them useful to that end, it must be his will and law, and the law of our nature, that we should duly exercise our reason in the right government of them, so as not to suffer them to hurry us into such actions as our reason and conscience disallow, as being contrary to the eternal laws of justice and benevolence: and one of the chief concerns in culture and education is, to discipline

195

and moderate the passions, and to inure them to a ready submission to the dictates of reason and conscience.

Johnson held ethics in the highest esteem and considered it the keystone of the arch of education. He said, in his *Introduction to the Study of Philosophy*, a brief essay which he suggested as exhibiting a general view of all the parts of learning, "Our Blessed Savior hath exalted ethics to the sublimest pitch and His admirable Sermon on the Mount is the noblest and exactest model of perfection," and then he added,

> Ethics explain the laws of our duty as we are men in general and which indeed are the eternal and immutable laws of right that equally bind all intelligent creatures. ... But as we cannot well subsist without being combined into particular societies; and as societies are of two kinds: the one founded in nature, viz., families, the other in compact, viz., civil governments; hence spring two other branches of moral philosophy, viz., economics which relate to the regulation of the family [the word has had a much wider signification given to it in the years since] and politics which treat of the constitution and good government of cities, kingdoms and republics. And as good policy provides for everything that may contribute to the public good and happiness of mankind it does in effect comprehend and sum up the whole of philosophy. And lastly as it provides for the happiness of men both temporal and spiritual, both with regard to this life and that which is to come, it must consist of two great branches, viz., civil and ecclesiastical politics. And the facts in the moral world are related in biography and in civil and ecclesiastical history.

196

A favorite proposition among the theses of the colonial colleges was the formula which suggested that the ground principles of ethics are as firmly fixed as those of mathematics. Dr. Johnson was evidently of this same persuasion, and in the introduction (advertisement) to his treatise with the title *A Short System of Morals*, which forms a part of the *Elementa Philosophica*, he says,

> We know there are a great number of truths in mathematics and natural philosophy, which not one in ten thousand of the bulk of mankind would ever have thought of, if it had not been for such great men as Euclid, Apollonius, Archimedes and Sir Isaac Newton, etc., which yet may, safely, and with great advantage, be received upon their authority, and be accordingly practised upon by those who have not leisure or ability to attend to the reasons of them. And now they have led the way it is not difficult for those who are capable of thinking closely to enter into the demonstrations of them. The case is much the same as to moral truths and duties with regard to the authority of prophets and lawgivers. It is the part of the prophet or lawgiver, as such, to discover truths and enjoin laws as rules of behavior to the people who are to receive them upon their authority as having but little leisure or capacity to exercise their reason about them, and therefore if they found no weighty reason against them they act rationally in so doing. And it is the part of the philosopher as such, as far as it is practicable, to enter into the reasons and demonstrations on which those truths and duties are originally founded.

197

The concluding sentence of the advertisement to his *Short System of Morals* in the *Elementa Philosophica*, which is called "The Religion of Nature," runs, "As we are reasonable creatures and obliged as such to yield unto God, the author of our beings, a reasonable service, it may be of very good use for us as far as it will go, with an implicit submission to Him for the rest, to exercise our reason upon these great and important subjects." This sentence was added to the second edition, as was also the following sentence: "As our reason in these things is, at best, but very dark and weak it is of the greatest importance to us that we diligently study the holy oracles in which we have the sublimest and most advantageous instructions and incentives to practice with regard to these matters which are of the utmost importance to our true and everlasting happiness." These are the fruits of his more serious thought and lengthier consideration of the moral truths which he considered of such paramount importance in education and life.

Undoubtedly the most interesting part of Dr. Johnson's *Elementa Philosophica* are the chapters on ethics: part 1, "The Speculative Part of Moral Philosophy," part 2, "The Practical Part of Moral Philosophy." In the colonial colleges, as is very clear from a number of passages in this book, they emphasized duties much more than rights. Dr. Johnson began by suggesting, "Let everyone seriously ask himself this question: what am I?" In the second edition, he adds the comment, "A question that I doubt few seriously think of, or much concern themselves about and so live and die great strangers to themselves however near and dear that self of ours is to us." He then emphasizes the distinction between the animals and man, emphasizes the place of intelligence in human life, and above all the role of the will: *198*

> I can excite imaginations and conceptions of things past or absent and recollect them in my mind at leisure and reject or keep them under consideration as I please, at least in a good measure, and am at liberty to suspend judgment till I have carefully examined them and to act or not to act in consequence of my deliberations as I think fit. In the impressions of sense, indeed, and the perceptions of evidence I am passive but in all these I am evidently active and can choose or refuse will or nil, act or forbear, from a principle of self-exertion; which are all truly great and noble powers.

In beginning "The Practical Part of Moral Philosophy," Dr. Johnson says, "Having thus considered the nature of my being and of that glorious cause from Whom I derive and on Whom I depend and observed in the structure of my nature and His attributes what I must suppose to have been the great end of that being *199* and nature which He hath given me; I proceed now from the truths I have found in the first or speculative part of this essay to deduce the duties that result from them which constitute the second or practical part of it." He emphasizes above all the obligations of intelligent creatures to God: "And since I am accountable to Him for all the powers and talents He hath bestowed upon me and must expect He will call me to account for them and see what regard I have had to His end in the bestowment of them; it is necessary that I be above all things concerned to act and conduct myself in such a manner as to be able to give a good account of myself to Him."

Dr. Johnson sets forth the purpose of life in thoroughly Scholastic form, quite as ever so many teachers had done in the Middle Ages:

> The great end of my being is that my rational and immor-
> tal nature may be completely and endlessly happy. The
> happiness of my rational nature consists in that pleasure
> and satisfaction that naturally attends its being conscious
> to itself of its union with its proper objects. The proper
> object of the intellect is truth and that of the will and
> affections is good, so that the highest happiness of our
> nature must consist in that pleasure which attends our
> knowledge of truth and our choosing and delighting in
> good; and consequently pursuit of these must in general
> be the great duty of my life.

200

The future president of King's College emphasized very properly the coordination between duty and happiness and the dependence of the human being on his Creator:

> My duty and happiness must in general consist in the
> union of my will with His: in sincerely choosing what He
> chooseth and delighting in whatsoever He delights in; in
> submitting to whatever instructions He shall think fit to
> give or whatever laws He shall think fit to enjoin either
> by nature or revelation; and in resigning to the whole
> system of constitution which He hath established both
> natural and moral; and consequently in patiently bearing

whatever He is pleased to allot and in conducting toward every person and thing as being what it really is and what He hath made it as He Himself doth and in governing myself and my whole temper and behavior by all those rules which promote the general weal of the whole system as God doth Himself; always avoiding what is wrong or hurtful as being contrary thereunto; and doing what is right or beneficial as being agreeable to it on all occasions as they offer.

The subject of free will the president of King's College taught almost exactly in the old Scholastic fashion, and what he has to say is farthest possible from the modern ideas that are included under the term *determinism*. Reverend Dr. Johnson is sure that the exercise of the will strengthens it, and he would have agreed thoroughly *201* with the Comte de Maistre, who, in his *Soirées de St. Petersbourg*, insisted that the practice of doing something hard every day was the best possible method of strengthening willpower so as to be able to accomplish whatever one wanted to do no matter how difficult it might be. Reverend Dr. Johnson said,

> And lastly, in consequence of any object's appearing agreeable or disagreeable to our minds, as tending to our pleasure or uneasiness, and being accordingly affected or disaffected, the last things I mentioned, of which we are conscious in ourselves, and which I shall here briefly take together, are the powers of choosing the one, and refusing the other, and our wills to act, or not to act, with a power of free activity, whereby we are able spontaneously to exert ourselves for obtaining the one, and avoiding the other. Now, as our true happiness consists in being secure from all pain or uneasiness, which is called natural evil, and in being possessed of such pleasures and satisfactions as are suitable to our nature in the whole of it, which are called natural good; so our highest natural perfection consists in being capable of rightly judging and choosing for ourselves, and of a free and vigorous activity, conformable to our best judgment and choice, for avoiding the one, and

202

attaining the other. And as our reason was plainly given us, to enable us to make a right judgment what we ought to choose and avoid, and to do and forbear, in order to our true happiness, in the whole of our nature and duration; and our will consists in freely resolving and determining ourselves to the one or the other, as they shall appear to our judgment; so our highest moral perfection consists in actually making a right judgment, what we ought to affect or disaffect, and to do and forbear; and in freely and habitually exerting ourselves in choosing and doing the one, and rejecting and forbearing the other, comformable thereunto. I say, freely; for freedom or liberty consisteth in having the power to act, or not to act, as we please, and consequently to suspend judging or acting, till we have taken opportunity to make as deliberate and exact a judgment as ever we can, what is best for us in the whole, to do or forbear; as necessity, on the other hand, considered as opposed to liberty, implieth, that it is out of our power to suspend acting, or to do otherwise than we do, in which there can be neither praise nor blame.

In this "Practical Part of Moral Philosophy," there are chapters with the titles "Of the Duties in General Resulting from the Foregoing Truths," "Of the Duties Which We Owe to Ourselves," "Of the Duties We Owe to God," "Of the Duties Which We Owe to Our Fellow Creatures or to Those of Our Own Species in Society in General and to Our Relatives in Particular," and then "Of the Subordinate Duties or Means for the More Ready and Faithful Discharge of the Duties above Explained." The sixth chapter has the title "Of the Connection between the Law of Religion, of Nature and Christianity."

203

The last paragraph of the ethics, or moral philosophy, in the *Elementa Philosophica*, which is also the last paragraph of the whole work, is a fervent confession of faith and hope in Christianity and in the rewards that will come to a man who has fulfilled his duties and accomplished his proper purposes in life:

Now therefore, all those who do firmly believe all the great truths of this holy religion, whether natural or revealed, i.e., whether founded in nature, or merely depending on revelation; and who under the influence of them, do by faith look for assistance and acceptance, only through His mediation, and in the method which He hath prescribed; and who, conformable to this holy discipline of Christianity, do heartily repent and forsake their sins, and return to their duty, and faithfully live and act in all their behavior, both towards God and man, from a sense of duty and gratitude to God, their great creator and benefactor, and to Jesus Christ, their great mediator, lawgiver and judge, and persevere in their obedience, faithful to the death, all these are said to be true Christians; and, even while they continue here, they belong to that heavenly community which is called His Kingdom, whereof He is the head, lord and king, the great vice-regent of God the Father, and shall, through His merits and mediation, be accepted in Him, and be inconceivably happy with Him, in his glorious kingdom in the life to come.

All of this is thoroughly familiar to those who have studied *204*
Scholastic philosophy, and they will recognize at once that with certain modifications of no great importance, Johnson's *Elementa Philosophica* represents the precious inheritance of philosophic thinking that has come down from the Middle Ages, not alone from the university period but most of it from the very early days of the medieval period, where a direct connection between Scholasticism such as this and the philosophy current among the Greeks and Latins may be traced. President Johnson's work undoubtedly influenced very deeply the philosophic thinking and teaching of that period here in America, and it represents an extremely important contribution to the education of that time. Undoubtedly, all of the colleges of the period just before the Revolution were deeply affected by it. Johnson's work represents the best textbook out of which to secure a very definite idea of just what was the teaching in

the last two years of the college course, which is represented fragmentarily but unmistakably in the commencement theses, which have been so little understood, though they constitute the most important element in the history of early American education.

In the brief twenty-two years of its existence before its closure as the result of the disturbance incident to the Revolution, King's College had graduated only a few more than one hundred Bachelors of Arts, but it was destined to contribute through them in a remarkable way to the welfare of the country. Among King's College students were such men as Alexander Hamilton, deservedly looked upon as one of the founders of the nation; John Jay, whose service as diplomat and afterwards as chief justice of the Supreme Court of the United States was to mean so much for the country; Chancellor Livingston, one of the most distinguished of the jurists in the country, who shaped law as it was to rule New York in the after time; Gouverneur Morris, distinguished for legal ability; John Stevens, after whom the Stevens Institute was named, well-known engineer who made great improvements in steamboats and who pointed out later on how much railroads would mean for the development of this country; Right Reverend Samuel Provoost and Right Reverend Benjamin Moore, the first and second Episcopal bishops of New York; as well as many others noted for their influence in this country in constructive statesmanship and the formation of public opinion for the task of self-government.

Dr. William Samuel Johnson, the third president of King's College, and the first president after it had adopted the name of Columbia College, was the son of the first president of the institution, the Reverend Samuel Johnson. Almost needless to say, he had been deeply influenced by his father's philosophic writings. His place in the country may be best appreciated from the fact that he was chosen a member of the committee of five referred to by the Congress in its legislation as a "Grand Committee" which was "appointed to frame a Federal Constitution and to devise such further provisions as were necessary to make the Constitution of the

205

206

162

federal government adequate to the demands of the United States." The makeup of this committee is the best possible demonstration of the influence which the college men of the time wielded as regards the formation of our government and above all the framing of the great legal instrument which was to safeguard the progress of this country in the path of liberty.[3]

---

3. After the resignation of Dr. Johnson on July 16, 1800, there was an interregnum in the presidency of Columbia until the election of Reverend Charles H. Wharton, the rector of St. Mary's Episcopal Church, Burlington, New Jersey, May 25, 1801. Perhaps the duties of the two positions proved incompatible, for his resignation was received in August of the same year. Reverend Mr. Wharton had been a Jesuit, set free from his order but not his priesthood by the suppression of the Society of Jesus by the Pope in 1773. It might be thought that his education as a Jesuit would be very different from that of the colleges in this country at that time, and his selection might seem for this reason inappropriate. As a matter of fact, his training in philosophy among the Jesuits had been exactly that of the colonial colleges and of the European universities of that time. The Jesuit ratio studiorum created for their schools a curriculum combining classical studies with Scholastic philosophy almost exactly identical with that of the colonial colleges.

7

THE COLLEGE OF PHILADELPHIA
(UNIVERSITY OF PENNSYLVANIA)

The Academy and College of Philadelphia was the first of the colo- *207*
nial institutions for higher education in English speaking America
to assume the more ambitious name of *university*. The name was
first suggested in 1771 and first taken in November 1779, although
in the opinion of historians of education, the institution might
fairly have assumed the title in 1769, when it gave the first medical
degrees in addition to those in arts. The college was the culmination
of the earlier academy, which served to provide the students, after
the fashion of the Latin schools of New England, with the necessary preliminary training for college work. The trustees felt that
there was a distinct advantage in having a single directing board,
one faculty, and a continuous curriculum from the beginning of
education to the attainment by the students of their bachelor's or
even their advanced degrees.

The first president of the board of trustees of the Academy
and College of Philadelphia was Franklin, and the members of
the board comprised the pick of the representative men of the old
families of Philadelphia, bearing such names as Logan, Lawrence,

208 Shippen, Willing, Bond, Peters, Taylor, Hopkins, Coleman. The Mifflins, Tilighmans, Chews, Cadwaladers, and Biddles came to be members later. It is easy to appreciate, then, that the institution and its provost had the support of the most cultured in the colony.

For proper understanding of the foundation and early history of the College of Philadelphia, and above all to appreciate its pre-Revolutionary status and the curriculum which formed the minds of its students, it is essential to know its first presiding officer, Reverend William Smith. He wrote out his views with regard to education more fully than any other educator up to that time in the English colonies. It was after thorough acquaintance with these views on the part of the trustees of the Academy and especially Franklin as president, who was very much interested in education, that Mr. Smith was invited to accept the post of head of the institution. A sketch of his career, then, is an important contribution to the history of colonial education, especially because his resume of college work illustrates very clearly the vogue of Scholasticism in the colonial colleges.

As we have told in the chapter on King's College (Columbia), when there was question of the foundation of a college in New York, Mr. Smith wrote a pamphlet with the title *Some Thoughts on Education with Reasons for Erecting a College in This Province and Fixing the Same in the City of New York*. There was manifestly a great awakening in education in the colonies about that time. It is *209* a striking historical coincidence that the colleges in Philadelphia, New York, and New Jersey were all established in the same decade. The following year, Mr. Smith published a longer pamphlet, a small book with the title *A General Idea of the College of Mirania*, in which he set forth his views on ideal college education.

The formal title of the book, following the fashion of the time, is rather long and comprehensive: *A General Idea of the College of Mirania with a Sketch of the Method of Teaching Science and Religion in the Several Classes and Some Accounts of Its Rise, Establishment*

*and Buildings, Addressed More Immediately to the Consideration of
the Trustees Nominated by the Legislature to Receive Proposals relating
to the Establishment of a College in the Province of New York.*[1]

This account of the College of Mirania begins in the conventional way of a number of the ideal commonwealths of the six-   *210*
teenth and seventeenth centuries. There is a chance meeting with
a stranger—quite as in Sir Thomas More's *Utopia*—who tells the
story of his experiences in the solution of educational problems
while at the College of Mirania and, thus, furnishes the background for various opinions: "While I was ruminating upon the
condition of the several colleges I had either personally visited or
read of without being able to fix on anything I durst recommend as
a model worthy our imitation, I chanced to fall into the company
of a valuable young Gentleman named Evander who was a person
of some distinction in the province of Mirania. After some conversation he was led to give me an account of the seminary established
about twelve years ago in that province."

---

1. The title page has quotations from Horace and Seneca. The first is *Quid Leges
sine Moribus vanae proficiunt?* "What do vain laws avail without morals?" A
modification of this Horatian phrase, *Literae sine moribus vanae*, became the
motto of the University of Pennsylvania and is inscribed around a pile of
books on its seal. These words might have been set down as the motto of all
the colonial colleges, for they were all intent on making men better as well as
making them scholarly, and while they had the two aims, they considered the
first by far the more important. The quotation from Seneca runs, *Nullum Animal morosius est; nullum majore Arte Tractandum quam Homo. Natura sequitur
melius quam ducitur*, "No animal is harder to get along with, none must be
treated with greater tact, than man. Nature follows rather than is led." A copy
of the little volume (New York, 1753), which is very rare, may be consulted in
the reserve room of the New York Public Library, where, through the kindness
of the special librarian, Mr. Wilberforce Eames, I have had the opportunity to
study it.

167

He said that "the objective Thing always kept in sight in the seminary in Mirania was the easiest, simplest and most natural method of forming youth to the knowledge and exercise of private and public virtue: and therefore they did not scruple to reject some things commonly taught at colleges nor to add others; and shorten or invert the order of them as best suited the circumstances."

The Miranians often quoted Tillotson's aphorism that "the knowledge of what tends neither directly nor indirectly to make better Men and better Citizens is but a knowledge of Trifles; it is not learning but a specious and ingenious sort of idleness."

211 They felt that they were arranging their education for two classes of students. There were, first, those designed for the learned professions, among which they included not only divinity, law, and physics—that is, the ministry, the bar, and the medical profession—but also agriculture as well as the chief officers of the State, that is, the magistracy. The second class included those designed for the mechanical professions and all the remaining people of the country. Education must not be confined merely to the higher classes but must be provided for all, and educational institutions must be so arranged as to secure this. The education for the great masses of the people, he added, was "best exemplified in the English school at Philadelphia where it had been first sketched out by the very ingenious and worthy Mr. Franklin."

In the College of Mirania, as its curriculum was outlined by Reverend Mr. Smith, no Latin was studied. That language was supposed to be completed in the Latin school or academy, and the young men were expected to use Latin as a living tongue in their study of philosophy but also of mathematics. In his outline of the classes that were to be taken up in college were, first, Greek, second, mathematics, third, philosophy, and fourth, rhetoric, under which term was included poetry, criticism, composition, and the training of taste. In the fifth class, they were to study animal anatomy and agriculture. In the colleges of that time, physics was taken up as a rule, that is, natural philosophy, and undoubtedly this as well as moral philosophy (ethics) was included in what Reverend Mr. Smith called philosophy. The special practical studies of animal anatomy and agriculture were introduced probably because he was already in touch with Franklin, and he knew that Franklin had the feeling that a college must include in its curriculum more of the practical subjects in the sense of training in knowledge that would be useful, especially for those who would take up the life of a farmer. At this time, Philadelphia was ever so much more important as a city than New York, and while Mr. Smith was writing in New York and for New York, his eye was fixed on Philadelphia, and his selection as the provost of the college there showed that his special attention had not been in vain.

In the fifth or highest class at Mirania, the principal, who has taken various classes up through the course from the beginning in the Greek class, instructs this group about to be graduated in agriculture and animal anatomy. The reason for this choice of subjects is stated to be that the students may have the knowledge necessary for the proper care of their health and their bodies. One of the principal purposes of the teacher of this class must be to trace the analogy between plants and animals. One would be inclined to think that there was some question in this of sex teaching for protective purposes some two hundred years ago. History was the third important subject of study in this fifth, or highest, class, but it was not to be studied merely for the knowledge of the events that had taken place, but because it furnished a background for the proper understanding of events in their own time. It was the philosophy of history that was to be studied and not merely the facts.

The students at the college were to be between their fourteenth and nineteenth year. The Miranians were very positive in this matter of the age of the college students. It is clear that Provost Smith disagreed with many of the American college customs. Graduation from most of the colonial colleges took place earlier

212

213

than this, at times even as early as fifteen to sixteen, but Smith thought this too young to complete the study of philosophy and receive the degree of Bachelor of Arts.

Mr. Smith had a very high ideal of education and of the time that should be devoted to securing higher education in the true sense of that word. He said, "Ten years is the best time that can be allowed for finishing the studies laid down for those intended for the learned professions." It is curiously interesting to note that this is about the time that our better-class universities are demanding at the present time for the learned professions or at least for medicine.

Mr. Smith recognized that the college could not be supported properly on fees received from the students. The problem of endowment was difficult to solve, and for the money needed at the beginning, he went over to England and, in connection with Mr. James Jay of New York, secured permission from the Archbishop of Canterbury to make a collection in England, Ireland, and Scotland for the colleges which were then being founded in Philadelphia and New York. Both of the institutions benefited also by lotteries which were held for them until religious consciences in this country woke up to decide that the securing of money for educational purposes by gambling was not setting a good example to the rising generation.

As we have said, Reverend Mr. Smith sent copies of his booklet on education to Benjamin Franklin and the Reverend Richard Peters of Philadelphia, both of whom were very much interested in the foundation of a college in Philadelphia. They felt that the most important factor for the successful foundation of the college would be a suitable director of the institution. Franklin's estimation of the value of a teacher was very high. He felt that the possession of a talent for teaching carried with it a very definite duty to use that talent to the best advantage. He made every effort to secure the services of Dr. Samuel Johnson, so well-known because of his contributions to American philosophy. Dr. Johnson was already committed to New York, so Franklin took up correspondence with

214

Reverend Mr. Smith, to whom he wrote, "I think, moreover, that talents for the education of youth are the gift of God and that he on whom they are bestowed whenever a way is found for the use of them is as strongly Called as if he heard a Voice from Heaven; Nothing more surely Pointing out Duty in a public service than Ability and Opportunity of performing it."

After further correspondence with Franklin, Mr. Smith *215* returned to Scotland to take holy orders and then came back to be the head of the academy and college. The presiding official of the College of Mirania was called the provost (*prefectus*), and that has been the name of the presiding officer of the University of Pennsylvania ever since: "When Dr. Smith arrived in Philadelphia in May, 1754, one of the most important epochs in the history of the province was about to open. In less than two weeks his friends, Franklin and Peters, set out for Albany to meet representatives of the other colonies to consult about their common defense; and it was to that gathering that Franklin presented his famous plan for the union of the colonies."[2]

At the College of Philadelphia, the provost was deeply intent on the study of philosophy—mental, moral, and natural. In his discourse delivered at the first commencement, May 17, 1757, he described what he meant by the term *philosophy*. Even a little careful study of this explanation makes it very clear what was the significance of the series of commencement theses at the colleges of this time:

> A person who knows himself endued with reason and understanding, will not be content to take his knowledge entirely at second hand, on subjects so important as the nature and fitness of things, and the Summum Bonum

---

2. George B. Wood, *Early History of the University of Pennsylvania*, 3rd ed., with supplementary chapters by Frederick D. Stone (Philadelphia: J. B. Lippincott, 1896).

of man; he will not care to rely wholly on a Historical Knowledge, founded on the Experience and Testimony of others; however much his labors may be shortened thereby. He will think it his duty to examine for himself, and to acquire a Moral and Physical knowledge; founded on his own Experience and Observation. This is what we call Philosophy in general; comprehending in it the knowledge of all things Human and Divine, so far as they can be made the objects of our present inquiries. Now the genuine branches of this Philosophy or great system of Practical Wisdom, together with the necessary instrumental parts thereof, may be included under the following general heads; it appearing to me that the nature of things admits of no more:

1. *Languages*, which have been already mentioned rather as an Instrument or Means of Science, than a Branch thereof.

2. *Logic* and Metaphysics, or the Science of the Human Mind; unfolding its powers and directing its operations and reasonings.

3. *Natural* Philosophy, Mathematics, and the rest of her beautiful train of subservient Arts, investigating the Physical properties of Body; explaining the various phenomena of Nature; and teaching us to render her subservient to the ease and ornament of Life.

4. *Moral* Philosophy; applying all the above to the business and bosoms of men; deducing the laws of our conduct from our situation in life and connections with the Beings around us; settling the whole Economy of the Will and Affections; establishing the predominancy of Reason and Conscience, and guiding us to Happiness thro' the practice of Virtue.

5. *Rhetoric*, or the art of masterly Composition; just Elocution, and sound Criticism; teaching us how to elevate our wisdom in the most amiable and inviting

garb; how to give life and spirit to our Ideas, and make our knowledge of the greatest benefit to ourselves and others; and lastly, how to enjoy those pure intellectual pleasures, resulting from a just taste for polite letters, and a true relish for the sprightly Wit, the rich Fancy, the noble Pathos, and the marvelous Sublime, shining forth in the works of the most celebrated Poets, Philosophers, Historians and Orators, with beauties ever pleasing, ever new.

Deeply interested as Provost Smith was in the development of the minds of his students, he would have considered the education provided at a college under his control as sadly lacking unless it made better citizens by making better Christians. This, as at all the colonial colleges, was emphasized very strongly. His own words on the subject are deeply impressive: "Thus I have given a sketch of the Capital Branches of Human Science: and all of them are professed and taught in this Institution. But there is yet one Science behind necessary to compleat all the rest, and without which they will be found at best but very defective and unsatisfactory. 'Tis the Science of Christianity and the Great Mystery of Godliness; that *218* Sublimest Philosophy, into which even the angels themselves desire to be further initiated."[3]

As regards the teaching of religion, Mr. Smith felt that the most important factor for that was not so much class exercises in

---

3. Wherever one turns among the histories of the colonial colleges, one finds the expression of the sentiment that the main purpose of the teaching was to educate men to be better citizens so as to be ready to make sacrifices for the benefit of the community in which they lived. In the charter of the Academy and Charitable School in the Province of Pennsylvania, this is illustrated very well. In that fundamental document, the hope is expressed that "this Academy may prove a nursery of wisdom and virtue and that it will produce men of disposition and capacity beneficial to mankind in the various occupations of life."

it, as the influence exerted by the teacher over individual pupils. He was quite sure that the cultivation of the spirit of religion in the students of institutions of the higher learning particularly depends on the teacher: "He who takes the opportunities with Judgment and Discretion to inculcate Religion will have no reason to join in the vulgar Complaint that Youth will not learn Religion and that Philosophy rather tends to make them free-thinkers."

How Provost Smith introduced these ideas and ideals of his into the curriculum of the new college will be most readily appreciated from the sets of theses which are extant and which demonstrate his endeavor to bring all these various subjects to the attention of the student. The *trivium* and *quadrivium* of the Middle Ages are well exemplified in the theses, and the Scholastic philosophy in content and method is illustrated very thoroughly in spite of the distance in time and space that separated the teaching of the medieval universities and the colonial colleges. It might possibly have been expected that Franklin's influence would have lessened the amount of metaphysics taught in the college with which he was so closely associated, but as a matter of fact, none of the sets of colonial college theses are quite so redolent of Scholasticism as the Philadelphia theses. Provost Smith was emphasizing the Scholastic teaching with which he himself had been so recently and thoroughly imbued in Scotland.

Provost Smith's profound interest in metaphysics and ethics might stamp him for educators in our time as the sort of man who could succeed very well academically and yet prove a failure in practical life and in his contacts outside the university. As a matter of fact, he was an extremely practical man, one index of that being revealed by the fact that he succeeded in obtaining what were for those days large sums of money for the carrying on of the institution of which he was the head. Within a very few years of his election as provost of the university, he came to exert wide and deep influence over the community around him in Philadelphia. It is not too much to say that within ten years of his arrival there, he came to be looked upon as one of the most prominent and revered citizens of his adopted city and province.

Montgomery, in his *History of the University of Pennsylvania 1749–1770*,[4] describes succinctly the position which Smith came to occupy in terms of the admiration which his scholarship and his culture evoked, not only among the students, but all who came in intimate contact with him. He does not hesitate to place Smith just next to Franklin in the educational and political influence he exerted in Philadelphia:

> Could it be a matter of little moment that the founder of their Home of Learning (Franklin) was the foremost man of the day in all public affairs whether of politics or of philanthrophy and was in most of these representing his adopted province at the throne of power pleading for liberty? Could it be a matter of indifference to say that their Provost was taking his share in the controversy whether public or anonymous? Would they not catch at least the echo of these influences and may it not lie in such surroundings that the College and Academy turned into the Arena of the Revolution more men in proportion to their graduates than any other collegiate institute?

We have three sets of commencement theses extant from the University of Pennsylvania, all of them drawn up during Provost Smith's time. They reveal very strikingly the teaching of the college and especially that done by Provost Smith himself in philosophy natural and mental, as well as in rhetoric, grammar, and ethics. The title of these theses proclaims that these propositions in philosophy are *Deo optimo maximo favente*, "God Almighty in His goodness favoring," to be discussed under the guidance or moderatorship of the provost or vice provost. The vice provost of the college, the Reverend Francis Allison, was the rector of the academy and was only

---

4. Thomas Harrison Montgomery, *A History of the University of Pennsylvania from Its Foundation to A.D. 1770* (Philadelphia: George W. Jacobs, 1900).

less favorably known for the place that he had made for himself in education in Philadelphia than the provost under whom he served. In the absence of the provost, he presided at the commencement, and the thesis sheet of 1763 notes *sub vice-praefecti moderamine,* "under the moderatorship of the vice-provost."

These sets of theses began, as at the other colonial colleges, with *theses grammaticae, rhetoricae,* and *logicae,* showing that the *trivium* was cultivated as assiduously in Philadelphia as elsewhere. After these follow *theses metaphysicae* under three heads, *de ente* (*ontologia*), *de mente humana* (*psychologia*), *de Deo* (*theologia naturalis*). Then follow the *theses physicae* and the *theses morales,* the latter with two divisions, *de ethica* and *de jurisprudentia naturali.* The last set of theses on each of the three broadsheets is *theses politicae.* Most of these subjects, with the exception of physics, were taught by the provost himself and represented the culmination of the college course.

Dr. Stone, in his work already quoted, commenting on this first commencement, says, "Franklin had he been at home this spring ought to have listened with delight to such learned debates on his favorite topics, morals, jurisprudence, politics and physics." He says further that we need not be surprised "at the attainments of youth who in addition to the ordinary school classics had read Lucian, Longinus, Plato's laws, and the Greek testament." The reading of the Gospels in Greek was required for entry into the colleges here in America down to the early part of the nineteenth century.

Dr. Stone says further that "the Commencement programs printed in Latin must have been quite unintelligible to the majority of the audience." But to call the broadside lists of theses issued at the various colleges "commencement programs" is, as we have said, to mistake entirely the significance of these documents. The theses were not printed for the general public but for the group of college graduates present, especially ministers of the Gospel, who might be expected to take part in the public act or the commencement disputation and offer objections to the various theses. Almost needless

222

to say, anyone who proposed to take part in the disputation needed to have the exact wording of the propositions before him in order to be sure exactly what the students were prepared to defend. The University of Pennsylvania theses conformed in this regard to the Scholastic quality of the colonial college theses generally, and they constitute further evidence that all the curricula in these institutions were of identical origin and character.[5]

It could very easily be thought that medieval Scholasticism *223* as studied in the colonial colleges would be of scarcely more than passing academic interest and of very little practical significance as a factor in mental development. Those who feel that way will find it very interesting to take the theses that were discussed under Provost Smith and note how many of them comprise principles of thought and conduct which carry with them the solution of many subjects ardently discussed in the modern time. The young men at college were being formally introduced to the great principles underlying politics and government as well as their more personal rights and duties. Most of our collegians of the present day would be utterly at sea so far as regards the knowledge or the application of such principles, unless by chance they had taken certain special studies relating to politics or jurisprudence. These theses were in the curriculum for the training of undergraduates so that they might have clearly before them, once their thinking powers

---

5. Franklin was much more in sympathy with the older methods of education than is usually thought. He tells in his *Autobiography* of finding in an English grammar "two little sketches on the arts of rhetoric and logic, the latter finishing with a dispute in the Socratic method and soon after I procured Xenophon's 'Memorable Things of Socrates' (*Memorabilia*) wherein are a number of examples of the same method." Franklin was charmed with it and, as he says himself, practiced it continually and grew very artful and expert in drawing people of superior knowledge into concessions the consequences of which they did not see. This was not so different in method from the Scholastic disputation, and the passage would serve besides to show Franklin's interest in old-fashioned methods of argumentation.

matured, the fundamental principles of rights and duties as rules of conduct for their relations to other men and the community.

224   Many propositions discussed at the University of Pennsylvania shortly before the Revolution are at the present time the subject of decisions by our courts, and while the principles laid down are old-fashioned Scholastic propositions, most of which come from the Middle Ages, they are far from out-of-date but continue to have interest of a very practical kind down to the present day. It seems worthwhile to call attention to this by adding annotations after certain of the theses. It is all the more interesting to have these propositions from the College of Philadelphia, because ordinarily it would be presumed that Franklin, the president of the board, was entirely too modern minded and practical to encourage what must seem to many very old-fashioned, even medieval, teaching.

Among the political theses at the College of Philadelphia as early as 1761, there were propositions which make it clear that there was more than a hint of the possibility of a struggle for independence, or at least of armed resistance to tyranny on the part of the colonists, so that future citizens were being trained in the application of principles that would give them a consciousness of justification for going to war. Professor Cheyney, the historian of the University of Pennsylvania, suggests, however, that while Dr. Smith protested firmly against English tyranny over the colonies, he never approved of independence or of military rebellion against England.

225   The principles of civil government were set forth straightforwardly. The first thesis runs, "Civil government arises from contracts (*pactis*)." The second says, "The form of government in which the supreme authority is granted to the king, to the nobility, and to the people conjointly is best constituted." In the third proposition, the right of rebellion is stated very straightforwardly: "It is allowed to resist the supreme magistrate if the commonwealth cannot be otherwise preserved." The succeeding proposition may have been selected for the proprietor's eye, for the Penns were in control in Pennsylvania: "Laws by which tributes are imposed that are

necessary for the protection of the State cannot be violated by the citizens without incurring the crime of theft."

In 1761 the theses on the natural law are interesting. They were extremely practical, and one might suspect Poor Richard's influence. The seventh proposition runs, "A good man will not derive any advantage for himself from the unwittingness or the rashness of another." The proposition immediately preceding runs, "The traitor takes away all the social obligations of man from life." The fourth proposition runs, "The substance of law ought to be possible and useful, but the equity which minimizes the rigor of human law does not obtain in divine law." [As was said, perhaps by Franklin himself, "God is good, but a good-natured God is unthinkable."]

The *theses morales* had under the first division, *ethicae*, at the   *228*
Philadelphia College in 1762, the following theses:

1. If a man aspires to true happiness, he must make his actions conform to the laws of God.

2. No one obeys the laws of God who either does deliberately what is proscribed by law or who acts without any contemplation of God and His law.

3. No one knows that his conscience is erroneous until he recognizes his error and then ceases to err; therefore

4. Studiously to inquire whether one's conscience is erroneous or not [to indulge in scrupulosity] is entirely to waste one's time and to be solicitous about an altogether useless matter; therefore

5. The will of God revealed by the light either of nature or of the Sacred Scripture is an adequate rule and norm of conscience.

6. The good or evil of an action arises partly from the object, partly from the end and partly from the remaining circumstances.

7. An action harmful to him for whose benefit it was intended is by no means good because of the intention of the agent unless it is prescribed by the laws of God; AND

VIRIS PRÆCELLENTISSIMIS,
THOMÆ PENN ac RICHARDO PENN, Armigeris,

Provinciæ *Pennsylvaniæ*, nec non Comitatuum *Novi Castelli, Cantii* & *Suffexiæ* ad fluvium *Delaware*, veris atque solis Proprietariis;

VIRO DIGNISSIMO, Literis humanioribus ornatissimo,
JACOBO HAMILTON, Armigero,

Prædictæ Provinciæ & Comitatuum VICE-GUBERNATORI præclarissimo, nec non hujus Collegii & Academiæ *Philadelphiensis* CURATORI;

Cæterisque VIRIS ORNATISSIMIS

Ricardo Peters, Præsidi, *Gulielmo Allen, Josepho Turner, Benjamine Franklin, Gulielmo Shippen, Philippo Syng, Phinea Bond, Thoma Bond, Gulielmo Plumsted, Thoma White, Gulielmo Coleman, Thoma Cadwallader, Alexandro Stedman, Benjamine Chew, Edwardo Shippen, jun. Gulielmo Coxe, Thoma Willing, Jacob Ducké, Lynsford Lardner, Amos Strettell, Andrea Elliot, & Johanni Redman;* ejusdem Collegii & Academiæ CURATORIBUS amplissimis, Artiumque ingenuarum PATRONIS humanissimis;

Toti denique *SENATUI ACADEMICO* dignissimo, nempe Reverendo GULIELMO SMITH, S.T.P. Collegii & Academiæ PRÆFECTO; Reverendo FRANCISCO ALISON, S.T.P. Collegii VICE-PRÆFECTO & Academiæ RECTORI; Reverendo JOHANNI EWING, A.M. Philosophiæ naturalis Professori; Reverendo EBENEZERO KINNERSLEY, A.M. Linguæ Anglicanæ & Oratoriæ Professori; JOHANNI BEVERIDGE, A.M. Linguarum Professori, & HUGONI WILLIAMSON, A.M. Matheseos Professori;

Hæc Philosophemata sub VICE-PRÆFECTI Moderatmine (DEO opt. max. favente) discutienda;

Juvenes in artibus initiati,

ROBERTUS JOHNSON,
JACOBUS LANG,
GULIELMUS PAXTON,

† JACOBUS ANDERSON,
JOHANNES DAVIS,
ISAACUS HUNT.

STEPHANUS PORTER,
JONATHAN SERGEANT, Coll. Nov Cæf. A.B.
JOHANNES STEWART,

THESES *GRAMMATICÆ.*

GRAMMATICA est ars bené & apté loquendi scribendique.
1. In initio & medio vocis ſ vel s ſcribi poteſt, in fine vero s tantum.
2. Verba & cæteræ partes orationis loco nominum poſitæ neutri adhærent.
3. Nomina verbalia, tam ſubſtantiva quàm adjectiva, caſum ſui verbi interdum adſciſcunt.
4. Pleræque nomina adjectiva quæ in us terminantur, item participia & comparativa, longé frequentius e quam i habent in ablativo.
5. Ex vocibus Anglicanis, è duobus ſubſtantivis compoſitis, prima ſemper qualitas et habenda.
6. Verbis imperſonalibus una cum dativo plerumque ſubjungitur infinitivus, qui nominativi à fronte locum ſupplet.
7. Vox Anglicana *Shall* in prima perſona futuri tantum aliquid se futuro parrat, vox autem *will* aliquid vel pollicetur vel minatur.

THESES *METAPHYSICÆ.*

DE ENTE IN GENERE

1. Entia à Deo ſemel accepta, ſemper exiſtunt, niſi ab ipſo Deo in nihilum redigantur.
2. Non ens nec cauſam nec cauſatum eſſe conſtat.
3. Quodcunque moveri efficientem in modum finis, neceſſariò ab eo cognoſcitur.
4. Bonitas metaphyſica nihil eſt præter abſtractam quandam ideam, obſcuram & generalem.
5. Ab animo noſtro ſolo, tempus non menſurari poteſt.

DE DEO

1. Nihil eſt ſui cauſa, ergo datur prima cauſa ab æterno.
2. Deus adeo unicus eſt, ut plures, non tantum ſimul, exiſtere nequeant, verum æque ſucceſſive, alius poſt alium.
3. Deum incſinenter cogitare incubduum eſt.
4. Quod nullum habet initium, à ſe certé non deſtruetur, nec ab alia natura, à quâ exiſtentiam non habet, in nihilum redigetur.

16. Corpus, quod, vi verſus centrum tendente, in ellipſi retinetur, deſcribit areas circa illud centrum temporibus proportionale.
17. Quum quantitas materiæ in corporibus circumrotatis, & diſtantiæ è centro ſunt æquales, vires centripetæ erunt in ratione inverſa quadratorum temporum periodicorum.
18. Detur ſolaris eclipſis, licet lunæ umbra telluris non pertingat.

Summi cum obſervantiâ, M. D. D. C. Q.

THESES *MORALES.*

DE ETHICA.

1. Ad conſtituendam aliquam actionem benam, neceſſe eſt et ex omni parte cum lege congruat, ſed ad conſtituendam malam, ſufficiat in una duntaxat parte deficiat.
2. Omnis actio vacare debet temeritate & negligentia, nec vero ægre quicquam hominem decet, cujus non poteſt cauſam probabilem reddere.
3. Ad ordinem & decorum in genere humano conſtituendum neceſſarium fit, ut normâ certâ actiones hominum continentur.

8. In facunda & terfa perfona vox *will* tantum emarret, vox autem *fuat* femper minatur.

THESES RHETORICÆ.

1. Est oratoris proprium apté, distinEté, ornaté, dicere.
2. In orando, interdio voci, remisfio, flexusque, pertinent ad movendos audientium affectus.
3. Pathetica magis commovent, cum ea videatur non elaborare ipfe orator, fed generare occafio.
4. Ars perfecta est, cum videatur esse natura.
5. Oratoris est femper perfequi perfonam, quam fibi natura impofuit.
6. Inventionis peritia, ordo, difpofitioque rerum, non uno ex verbo, neque duobus, fed tota ex verborum ftructura, appareat.
7. Concifum curtumque nimis dicendi genus, oratoris fublimitati inimicisfimum eft.
8. Vitiofa funt in fcriptis grandia, quæ inania faliaque funt, & ex quibus periculum eft, ne circumagamur in contrarium.
9. Oratori prima fit virtus perfpicuitas, propria verba, rectus ordo, & non in longum dilata conclufio.
10. In omni compofitione tria funt necesfaria, ordo, junctura, numerus.
11. Partim fublimitas efficitur delectu circumftantiarum fummarum, partim autem combinatione electarum.
12. In caufa conjecturali, narratio accuratoris fufpiciones injectas & difperfas habere debet.
13. Spes feré tota vincendi, ratioque perfuadendi, in genere judiciali pofita eft in confirmatione, & confutatione.

THESES LOGICÆ.

1. Omnis, quæ a ratione fufcipitur de aliqua re, inftitutio debet à definitione proficifci, ut intelligatur quid fit id, de quo difputatur.
2. Idea to clarior evadet, quo pluribus fenfibus rem quampiam percipimus.
3. Quo plures ideas mens diftincté concipit fimul, eo capacior eft habenda; *Ergo*
4. In vario literarum genere verfari, & præfertim geometriæ, arithmetices, & algebræ, ad mentem ampliandam permultum valet.
5. Criterion veritatis in plenâ idearum convenientiâ vel difcrepantiâ confiat.
6. Ubi res ad fummam perfpicuitatem devenit, & liberé & necesfariò voluntatis asfenfum præbemus.
7. Propofitiones multæ terminis univerfalibus conceptæ, univerfaliter intelligi non debent.
8. Omne genus ratiocinandi aliquid notum fupponit.
9. Argumentatio per fyllogifmos geometricum includit, & ad veritatem cum aliis communicandam eft utilisfima.

† Juvenum nomina brdine alphabetico difpofita funt.

---

5. Omnes Dei perfectiones ejus naturæ funt esfentiales.
digitur.

DE MENTE HUMANA.

1. Nihil, quod intelligenter e *ctatur*, materiale five extenfum esse potest.
2. Intellectus nunquam operatur fine concurfu voluntatis.
3. Quotics mens noftra rem *hujus* clarè, diftincté aut planè percipit, caufa in mente *habet*, non in re ipfa.
4. Quæ corpus fimul & mentem afficiunt, magis funt hominis perceptioni appropriata, quàm quæ folam mentem.
5. Motus animi permultum à corporis valetudine prudent.
6. Actio libera fufcepta eft ex principio interno, rationis judicio, & denique voluntatis placito.

THESES PHYSICÆ.

Phyfica phænomena naturalia explicat, & illorum caufas trahit.

1. Fermentatio corporum in *se* fe ex inæqualitate attractionis particularum pendet.
2. Lignum penitus arefactum *electricum* fluidum minimè dirigere queat; *sed*
3. Probe frictum, vi mirandi, ex omnibus corporibus vicinis, hoc fibi fluidum attrahet.
4. Metalla omnia fluidum electricum, lacte, fanguine, aut ullo fluido animali, fluidum uni *lacte*, *aqua*, ligno novo feu viridi, ligno novum, *glacie ficca*, melius dirigere queat.
5. Argenum vivum fiat è *calore* & frigore ficum & ductile, & rurfus calore liquefcit.
6. Velocitates penduli, in ipf *verticali* punEto, funt inter fe, ut fubtenfæ arcuum quos *describit* pendulum.
7. Corpus, celeritate data, *distantiam* quamcunque intra maximam amplitudinem, *rejici* potest.
8. Corpus per duas directione *projici potest*, ut in idem punEtum, alicubi intra maximam amplitudinem, cadat.
9. Amplitudines projectionum, *velociate* data, funt ut finus dupicati anguli elevationis.
10. Elevatione data, funt ut *quadrata* celeritatum; *Ergo*
11. Neque elevatione, *neque velociate* data, amplitudines funt ut quadrata celeritatum in finum anguli elevationis duplicati.
12. Tempore, in quibus v*is* *cylindrica* quæcunque evacuantur, funt in ratione *composita* ex ratione bafium directâ, inverfâ foraminum, & *fubduplicatâ* altitudinum.
13. Corporum opacitas *colorum* folis reflectione & refractione pendet.
14. Radii procedentes ab a*tergo* foco ellipfici fpeculi in alterum refractentur.
15. Si corpus moveatur in ell*ipsi* circa ejufdem focum, vis centripeta erit ubique in *duplicata* ratione diftantiæ ab eodem foco reciproce.

---

4. In omni injuftitia permultum interest, utrum perturbatione aliqua animi, an confulto & *cogitata* fiat injuria.
5. Beneficia male locata, mulctæ & fæpè funt.
6. Providendum est, ne fermo odium aliquid indicet inesfe moribus.
7. Omne mendacium etiam jocofum & officiofum est peccaminofum, male honeftum.
8. Multa quæ honefta naturâ videantur esse, temporibus funt non honefta.

DE JURISPRUDENTIA NATURALI.

1. Natura non patitur, ut *uniorum* politii, noftras facultates, copias, opes augeamus.
2. Fundamentum perpetuæ commendationis & famæ est juftitia, fine qua nihil potest esse laudabile.
3. Lex naturalis non vetbis, ast, ratione duce, omnia ex æquo & bono determinat.
4. In pactis femper intelligitur voluntatem adesse fe obligandi, ubi ejus fit fignificatio.
5. Juftitia etiam adverfus inimicos & hoftes est fervanda.
6. *Animalia mactare bruta, & eorum carne vefci, legibus naturæ humano generi conceditur.*
7. Si plures per confpirationem aliquid facinus perpetraverint, omnes pro fingulis, & finguli pro omnibus tenentur.
8. Nulla necesfitas est tanta, ut cuivis mala fibi imminentia in alios immerito conjicere liceat.
9. Parens non potest liberos in perpetuam fervitutem vendere, aut onere quovis prægravare, ultra impenfas, quæ erogandæ funt in eis educandis.
10. ☞ *Bellum fit juftum, quod nec rebus repetitis geratur, nec denunciatum ante fit, & indicitum.*

THESES POLITICÆ.

1. Ea fola potestas civilis est justa, quæ communi infervit utilitati.
2. Divina funt populi, pariter ac imperatorum, jura.
3. ☞ *Eft advocati aut patroni femper in caufis verum fequi.*
4. *☞ nunquam tam falfam etiamfi verifimilem fcienter defendere.*
5. Qui armia politia ad imperatorum fidem confugiunt, si recipiendi funt.
6. Omne officium, quod ad conjunctionem hominum & ad focietatem tuendam valet, anteponendum est illi, quod cognitione & fcientia continetur.
7. Ad virtutem omnem in civitate fovendam, præcipuè conducunt legis ferendæ ad ejufdem explicationem plerumque ducunt temperatorum exempla.
8. Aliquem à morte, vel quovis alio malo, eripuisfe, nullum præbet jus cum in fervitutem redigendi.
9. Communis omnium utilitas, omni, five fingulorum, five cæteorum juri, modum ponere debet.

[Typis HENRICI MILLERI, in vico vulgò dicto *Second-street*.]

8. A man obeying the laws of God does injury to no one.

9. Whatever is honest is useful, nor is there anything useful which is not honest.

In the division of ethics, *de jurisprudentia naturali*, natural jurisprudence, there are the following propositions:

229

1. In every law there are two parts, a precept and the sanction.

2. Law supposes a superior; therefore an equal cannot make a law for an equal.

3. Almost all laws, especially natural laws, refer to the whole human race or to all of a certain class.

4. Wars must be undertaken so that one may live in peace without injury.

5. Inevitable things (*necessaria*) and those which happen to us unknowingly or unwittingly we are not responsible for.

6. All men are by nature equal. [Here is the first proposition of the Declaration of Independence as an ethical thesis fifteen years before the Declaration was signed.]

The next thesis, supposed to follow by an *ergo*, or conclusion from the preceding one, is printed in italics with an index indicating its special significance:

7. A bondsman (in Latin, *verna*) or one born of a slave ought not to be bound to be a slave for his whole lifetime. [The problem of slavery already occupied many minds both North and South at this time.]

8. The right of authority among men does not arise from any superior dignity of nature. [There is no divine right of kings. Authority comes from the people and is conferred on the sovereign by them.]

9. Whatever is opposed to the common good is also opposed to the law of nature.

10. The laws of vice and virtue are eternal and immutable. *230*
    ["The eternal laws that know not change, that are not
    of today or yesterday," were favorite subjects of the
    medieval Scholastics. They were definitely persuaded
    that there was an eternal and unfailing distinction
    between right and wrong.]

11. [Printed in italics with an index] An oath extorted in
    violence and fear by a bandit is not binding.

12. In the state of nature right does not belong to every-
    one in all things. [Some rights must be foregone for
    the sake of others.]

13. [Indexed and in italics] If anyone should come first to
    market with wheat at a dear price knowing, however,
    that others would soon be present with the former
    cheaper price, he is not under the necessity of impart-
    ing his knowledge to the buyers. [This is the familiar
    principle of *caveat emptor*, let the buyer take care of his
    own interests. In our time, it has been suggested that
    the other form of the aphorism *caveat venditor*, let the
    seller take care of the interests of buyers as well as his
    own, should be formulated into law for the protection
    of investors.]

The *theses metaphysicae* at the University of Pennsylvania in
1762 in the category *de ente* begin with paired theses which demonstrate definitely the Scholasticism of the underlying thought,
because they invade that domain of metaphysics in which occurs
the discussion as to the distinction between essence and existence.
The thoroughgoing medieval Scholasticism of the paired theses is *231*
beyond all doubt:

1. Whatever has no existence has no essence; therefore

2. All essences of things cannot have existed in the mind
   of God from eternity.

3. The existence of things outside the mind of man is demonstrated only by causes and effects. [Bishop Berkeley's

subjectivism and philosophic sensationalism attracted attention in this country, because he had spent some time here some years before—hence, doubtless the formulation of this proposition.]

4. The problem of the origin of evil can be solved without impugning the attributes of God. [The existence of evil in the world does not impugn the goodness of the Almighty.]

5. An infinite (endless) series (of effects and causes) plainly implies contradiction.

6. To the actions of finite beings there belong no qualities, virtues or adjuncts that are infinite.

The theses under the category *de mente humana*, "the human mind," or as we prefer to call it, psychology, show that there are many problems in psychology apart from those with which we are most occupied at the present time:

1. There is certainly an analogy between divine and human wisdom. [Such a proposition probably formed the basis of an argument for the spiritual nature of the human mind and its resemblance to that of the Creator, for according to the old Scriptural expression, man was made in the image of God.]

2. The soul cannot but be conscious to itself of its dependence [that is of its created character].

3. A too rapid succession of ideas is often the cause of insanity.

4. It is extremely probable that God granted to the soul the power of moving its own body. [One of the most important problems of the union of the soul and body is how the soul as a spirit can in any way influence the body, which is material. This thesis expresses one solution of the mystery of spirit acting on matter.]

In the category *de Deo*, there are just three propositions. The first of these runs, "By arguing from effect to cause, the existence of

232

God can be demonstrated without difficulty." The following year (1763), the same truth is treated in another way, and the proposition ran, "Nothing is the cause of itself; therefore there must exist a first cause from eternity." This proposition was followed by the thesis: "God is unique to such a degree that several Gods not only cannot exist simultaneously but neither can they successively, one after another."

This was followed by the proposition: "There is no doubt that God thinks ceaselessly," and that in turn by the proposition, "A being that has no beginning shall certainly not be destroyed by itself, nor can it be reduced to nothingness by another nature from which it has no existence." The last of the propositions in 1762 under *de Deo* was, "All the perfections of God are essentials of His nature."

233

Thesis number two under *de Deo* for 1762 concerned the disturbing problem of the foreknowledge of God and the effect that it may produce in impairing or abrogating the liberty of the human will. In Philadelphia under the influence of Provost Smith, there was no hesitancy as to the solution of this problem. Hence the proposition: "God's foreknowledge does not at all take away the liberty of the human will."

Philadelphia during the twenty years before the Revolution was already very much interested in politics. Their *theses politicae* for 1762 are very interesting for this reason. Consciously or unconsciously, they were already training the Fathers of the country in what concerned their relation to government. The first proposition ran, "Society must be cultivated and preserved by every man in as far as he can." This was emphasizing the fulfilment of the duties of citizenship.

The other theses ran,

> 2. The one measure of punishment is not the turpitude of the offense but rather the benefit to the community which would arise from punishment. [This is, I believe, good penology in our time. To most people it will be

a distinct surprise that they were discussing such problems in penology nearly two hundred years ago.]

3. In public wars there are the same just beginnings and the same terminations as in private quarrels. [The conscience of the nation must be as faithful to moral principles as the individual conscience in self-defense.]

4. It is not allowed to give up an innocent citizen to the enemy, even to prevent the imminent ruin of the republic. [This emphasizes the break with some ancient and medieval customs, when men were delivered up as hostages or sometimes were made the scapegoat for revenge. The thesis might have had a very practical meaning for prominent patriots if the Revolution had failed.]

5. Soldiers who doubt whether war is just or not are still bound to take up arms. [This thesis was enunciated well above one hundred fifty years ago, and its enduring significance will perhaps be best judged from the fact that a recent decision of the Supreme Court of the United States has declared that pacifists who would not go to war if the country was engaged in war cannot become citizens.]

6. Arbitrary power over individuals or whole peoples cannot be acquired by conquest.

7. There is no unlimited right of any man over another.

8. Where right ends, there injury begins and the right of resistance asserts itself.

9. All the parts of supreme government may be not improperly reduced to the legislative, federative, and executive. [This thesis was demonstrated and defended nearly thirty years before the drawing up of the Constitution of the United States, which emphasized these divisions of government afterwards to be so important for the republic.]

The *theses politicae*, the propositions in politics, at the College of Philadelphia in 1763 a dozen years or so before the Declaration of Independence, show how deeply interested were the college professors, and through them the students of that time, in the political problems that were to occupy the minds of the people in the course of the next few years. Practically every one of these sets of theses at the colonial colleges contained principles that would justify revolution in case the benefit of the community was not being consulted by the ruling authorities. These theses were just the accustomed propositions formulated by medieval and Renaissance (Jesuit) philosophers and studied very probably without a thought of their current political significance, but producing a definite effect on the minds of students that justified them, a little later in life, to take up arms for the rights which they had been taught were theirs.

The first of the *theses politicae* (1763) was a very definite declaration as to what constitutes just exercise of the civil power: "That civil power is alone just which makes for the common benefit." The second of the propositions declared very simply, "The rights of *236* the people are as divine as those of their rulers." This represented a very significant repudiation of the principle of the divine right of kings. In the fourth proposition, they were urging mercy for captives in a proposition that is very interesting in the light of impending events, though there was probably no deliberate intention of applying it that way. It was just a political proposition to be demonstrated and defended: "Those who throwing down their arms entrust themselves to the faith of their rulers should be received."

The proposition among the political theses which appears in italics and with an index pointing to it, and therefore was to be considered as the most important of the propositions for that year, is a rather striking proclamation of the whole duty of the lawyer. In principle it is still the teaching. In practice it is not always observed. It runs, "It is the duty of the advocate or patron always in legal trials to follow the truth and never to defend falsehood knowingly even though it should seem to be very like the truth."

They had a word also of advice for rulers and emphasized the force of their example: "For the cherishing of every virtue in a city, the most potent influence is the example set by the rulers." They *237* were growing touchy about slavery, hence, the proposition "To have snatched anyone from death or from any other evil does not confer the right of reducing him into slavery." They believed firmly that laws should be reasonable and that the reasons for the making of the laws should be proclaimed: "The reasons for legislation which facilitate the explanation of it conduce to its observance."

They were rather rigorous as to morals at the College of Philadelphia when they were training the future citizens of the country. For instance, the seventh thesis in ethics for the year 1763 runs, "Every lie, even in joke or in the line of official duty, is a sin." And yet they made allowances for the effect of circumstances upon actions. For instance, the fifth thesis ran, "Good deeds under evil circumstances often become evil deeds." The eighth proposition ran, "Many things which naturally seem honest become at times dishonest."

They weighed conditions very carefully in order to determine the real significance of an act. This is illustrated very well by the fourth proposition in ethics that year: "In every injustice it makes a deal of difference whether the injury is done as the result of some perturbation of mind [emotional impulse] or deliberately *238* and intentionally." The first proposition that year ran, "To make an action good, it is necessary that it should agree with the law in every way, but to make it evil, it suffices that it should be defective in a single part."

Under natural jurisprudence that year, there was definite insistence on justice for all: "Justice must be maintained even with regard to people of the lowest degree and toward enemies," and "The foundation of enduring commendation and fame is justice without which nothing can be praiseworthy."

188

All of these theses were not merely memorized but were demonstrated and defended in weekly disputations, usually held under the supervision of the provost. All objections to them had to be solved. This method of testing knowledge by means of argumentation and defense was employed not only in colleges but also in the graduate schools, particularly in the schools of theology in Europe, where of course, because of the connection between theology and philosophy, it might be expected to flourish. Something very similar, however, was practiced in the medical schools, as is illustrated by the account that has been left us by the provost of the University of Pennsylvania of the first commencement of this, the oldest medical school in the country. In 1768 the College of Philadelphia conferred the degree of Bachelor of Physic on a group of candidates, and three years later the degree of Doctor of Physic was conferred. The provost's description shows the method of examination:

> They (the candidates) then presented themselves agreeable to the rules of the college to defend in Latin the dissertations printed for their degrees of Doctor in Physic. Mr. Elmer's piece, *De causis et remediis in febribus* (Causes and Remedies in Fevers) was impugned (objected to) by Dr. Kuhn, professor of botany and *materia medica*. Mr. Pott's *De febribus intermittentibus, potentissimum tertianis* (Intermittent Fevers, above all Tertian) was impugned by Dr. Morgan, professor of the theory and practice of medicine. Mr. Tillton's *De hydrope* (On Dropsy) was impugned by Dr. Shippen, professor of anatomy. Mr. Way's *De variolorum insitione* (Inoculations of Smallpox) was impugned by Dr. Rush, professor of chemistry.

239

The objectors for these dissertations, or theses as they afterwards came to be called, were the leading physicians of this country. Morgan, Shippen, and Rush were all graduates of the University of Edinburgh and were undoubtedly intent on maintaining all the traditions of their alma mater across the water in the establishment of a medical school here in America. Morgan and Shippen collaborated in organizing the medical department of the University of

Pennsylvania. Shippen's devotion to the teaching of medicine was interrupted only by his acceptance of the position of surgeon general of the Revolutionary troops. Rush, who had been elected only that year (1769) as professor of chemistry in the college, was one of the distinguished physicians of the country. His own Latin thesis, or disquisition, in medicine, *De coctione ciborum in ventriculo* (The Digestion of Food in the Stomach), he had had to defend against the objections made by a member of the faculty at Edinburgh, just as he himself was now impugning Mr. Way's Latin dissertation. Shippen's graduation dissertation defended at Edinburgh had for subject *De Placentae cum utero nexa* (On the Connection of the Placenta with the Uterus).

240

The provost's concluding record with regard to the graduation of the first physicians at what deserved the name of the University of Pennsylvania is interesting to us here, particularly from the standpoint of the estimated value of the disputation for bringing out the true significance of thoughts and formulas of various kinds: "Each of these candidates having judiciously answered objections made to some parts of their dissertations, the Provost conferred the degree of doctor in Physic with particular solemnity as the highest mark of literary honor which they could receive in their profession."

The fact that these theses, or disquisitions, in the medical school were written in Latin[6] is the best possible demonstration of

241

---

6. The university statute with regard to the graduation in medicine shows that a high standard of preliminary scholarship was required before entrance to the medical school and emphasizes the necessity for the writing of a thesis on some medical or surgical subject in Latin: "It is requisite for this degree (Doctor of Medicine) that at least three years shall have intervened from the taking the Bachelor's degree and that the Candidate be full Twenty-four Years of Age; who shall also write and defend a thesis publickly in college. ... And his Thesis is to be printed and published at his own expense." This custom of publishing the thesis was a definite requirement in European universities, and the custom still maintains at the University of Paris, though it is no longer required that the thesis shall be in Latin. This thesis in the medical school,

the fact that these educators in colonial times believed very thoroughly in quite definite training of mind in preparation for medical study. When we recall that more than a hundred years later, anyone who wanted to could enter a medical school without any question of his preliminary education, provided he could read and write—and he did not have to write very well—it is extremely interesting to note medical degrees given in the colonial period as the culmination of university work after some six or seven years of study. When President Eliot entered upon his duties at Harvard (1869) and proposed to have the examination in the medical school in writing, the dean, Professor Bigelow, declared that the new young president was surely going to wreck the Harvard Medical School. He said, "He actually proposes to have written examinations for the degree of doctor of medicine. I had to tell him that he knew nothing about the quality of the Harvard medical students; more than half of them can barely write. Of course they cannot pass written examinations."[7]

242

This was the state of affairs at Harvard in the 70s of the nineteenth century. Other medical schools throughout the country were no better as a rule, and most of them were very much worse—if possible.

There is a very prevalent impression that the small colleges of the eighteenth century in this country must have afforded comparatively little education and that surely they were not to be compared with the institutions of learning which developed during the

---

which was a disquisition on a medical topic, has often been confused with the theses sheets, or lists of propositions, which were distributed to those of the audience who might care to take part in the disputations on commencement day. There was a very great difference between the two forms of theses, and yet it must not be forgotten that propositions were sometimes taken out of the medical theses or disquisitions and made the subject of disputations.

7. Charles W. Eliot, *Harvard Memories* (Cambridge, MA: Harvard University Press, 1923).

nineteenth century. Dr. T. G. Morton, in *History of the Pennsylvania Hospital*, is of entirely different opinion. He was himself a graduate of the University of Pennsylvania, deeply interested in the history of his profession and especially the developments in connection with it in Philadelphia, which continued to be looked upon as the medical center of the United States, so far as education was concerned, during most of the nineteenth century.

He does not hesitate to say that the doctors and lawyers of the colonial period were much better educated than most of their successors of the nineteenth century. He was one of the most prominent members of the medical profession in Philadelphia during the second half of the nineteenth century. He was thoroughly disgusted with the lack of premedical education that he saw around him and the failure of young men to secure a background of mental development that would enable them to follow up their professional work more successfully and satisfactorily. Above all he called attention particularly to the number of young men who in the early days crossed the ocean when that was indeed a trying and difficult journey in order to complete their medical education by graduate work and who proved worthy in every way of the time and expense thus devoted to their professional studies. Dr. Morton said,

243

> We find that the professional men of the seventeenth and eighteenth centuries were generally much better educated than most of their successors of the present time. Almost without exception they were classical scholars. Their graduating theses must be written in Latin. Travel was essential, notwithstanding the encumbered modes of motion to which they were subjected. Leyden, Paris, Edinburgh, London, Oxford, Upsal, Bonn, and to some extent Vienna, Berlin and the Italian schools, received and honored them; they, as a rule, by their subsequent career, equally honoring the places which they visited and where they sojourned. They were also men of affairs. It is surprising what a part they took at home in politics (in its strict sense) and government. They were good soldiers,

and freely offered themselves and their services to their country in time of need.

The outstanding commencement of the University of Pennsylvania was that of May 10, 1775, when the guests were General Washington, who was passing through on his way to take command of the troops, and the members of the Continental Congress who were present. The newspaper description of the commencement dwells particularly on the fact that there was a Latin salutatory and a Latin "syllogistic dispute" besides some orations. Several of the orations, especially one on "The Fall of Empires" by the son of the provost, had reference to the existing political troubles and echoed the prevailing tone of patriotism and the love of liberty. One passage brought forth loud applause: "Liberty is our idol!— She is the parent of virtue, the guardian of innocence and the terror of vice. Equal laws, security of property, true religion, wisdom, magnanimity, arts and sciences, are her lovely offspring. She has turned deserts into fruitful fields and villages into populous cities. Without enjoying the blessings which she bestows, the solitary state of nature is preferable to society; and the skins of wild beasts a more honorable covering than all the silken vestments slavery can bestow."

244

It would be easy to think that an institution which occupied the minds of the students to a very great extent during the culminating two years of their course with old-fashioned Scholastic philosophy and the medieval method of teaching it, and which after the middle of the eighteenth century was still largely occupied with training the minds of students by means of the seven liberal arts—the *trivium* and *quadrivium* of the Middle Ages, somewhat developed— would not exert very much influence on its generation. The curriculum would be promptly branded in our time as academic and quite impracticable. No one would ever make a dollar more for having gone through it, and it was calculated even to keep them from making dubious dollars. In spite of any such impression, the College of Philadelphia, which was to become shortly after the

245

193

Revolution the University of Pennsylvania, exerted an immense amount of influence over its students but also on the community in which it was. In his *History of the University of Pennsylvania*,[8] in the series Universities and Their Sons, Edward Potts Cheyney, professor of European history in the university, describes the enviable position attained by the University at the conclusion of what was the first quarter century of its existence: "The Revolution terminated an epoch in the history of the University of Pennsylvania. At no subsequent time until within the last two decades, if then, has the institution played relatively such an important part; at no time has it exerted such an influence on the community in which it has been placed as it did during the greater part of the administration of Dr. Smith, the period from the acquisition of its second charter in 1755 to its closing on account of the Revolution in 1776."

During the score of years immediately before the Revolution, a number of men who were afterwards to be very well-known for their attainments and accomplishments were students at the college. Not a few of them reflected high honor on their alma mater. Francis Hopkinson, a pioneer American literary man, a signer of the Declaration of Independence, who held legislative, judicial, and administrative offices subsequently in New Jersey and Pennsylvania as well as holding office under the federal government, is a striking example of these University of Pennsylvania men. Among those who were in the college at this time, though they did not stay long enough to take their degrees, were Benjamin West, the well-known American artist, who afterwards became the president of the Royal Academy in England, as well as Lindley Murray, the grammarian, whose English grammar was probably the most used in the history of education. In the class of 1759 was William Paca,

246

---

8. Edward Potts Cheyney, Joshua Lawrence Chamberlain, and Ellis Paxson Oberholtzer, *University of Pennsylvania: Its History, Influence, Equipment and Characteristics* (Boston: R. Herndon, 1901).

a signer of the Declaration from Maryland and a holder successively of almost every legislative, judicial, and executive position under that colony and state as well as many under the United States government. Also in attendance was Philomen Dickinson, who held positions in New Jersey similar to those of Paca in Maryland. In the class of 1760 were Thomas Lipton, afterwards general in the Revolution, governor of his state, and president of Congress; also John Cadwalader, member of Congress and judge in many courts. His brother Lambert as well as Whitmel Hill, active in the Revolution in the subsequent history of North Carolina, were also members.

In the class of 1761 were Richard Peters, who held many *247* offices under the government during the Revolution and was subsequently a member of Congress and a Pennsylvania judge. In the same class were Tench Tilghman of Maryland, military secretary to Washington during the whole war, and John Nielson of New Jersey, who had an active Revolutionary career and served in Congress afterwards.

Among the graduates in 1762 was Samuel Jones who helped in the foundation of the College of Rhode Island, afterwards to be known as Brown University. He became its president on the death of its first presiding officer. A number of others might be mentioned, but these demonstrate that during the twenty years under Provost Smith, the College of Philadelphia was amply fulfilling its purpose and that of all the colonial colleges of providing educated, conscientious men for the ministry and the magistracy in the difficult circumstances of the time.

During this period, thirty-four matriculates are known to have become clergymen, sixteen physicians, and forty lawyers. The greater number of its students and graduates were from Philadelphia and its immediate neighborhood, but quite a number were from the adjoining provinces, and not a few of the students were from the southern colonies and also from the more distant West Indies, with occasionally a few from New York and New England.

The usual number in the whole institution was between two hundred fifty and four hundred, but more than one half of these were in the charity school and one half of the remainder students of the academy only. Only some thirty or forty were taking the college course, with perhaps as many more the medical course. The average number of graduates for the twenty years was about seven yearly. Fourteen was the largest number to receive the degree of Bachelor of Arts in any one year. Quite a number pursued their studies nearly to graduation but for one reason or another did not take their degree.

The graduate who passed the longest and probably most varied and influential life was Hugh Williamson. He was a clergyman, became professor of mathematics in college, then a physician, a businessman, and a politician. He went to England to appear before the British Privy Council concerning the tea episode in Boston Harbor. He represented North Carolina in the Continental Congress, in the Constitutional Convention, and in Congress afterwards. He wrote a number of books, essays, and papers on a variety of subjects and died finally in New York City at the ripe age of eighty-four.

Provost Smith, in the University of Pennsylvania, succeeded in demonstrating very clearly what an old-fashioned university with a curriculum founded on medieval Scholasticism could accomplish in making scholarly, conscientious citizens who were ready to risk their lives, their fortunes, and their sacred honors for what they considered their duty and the liberty of the people. Surely it may be said of him and the institution he created, "By their fruits ye shall know them."

8

THE COLLEGE OF RHODE ISLAND (BROWN)

The College of Rhode Island and Providence Plantations, subse-   *249*
quently (1804) called Brown University after a benefactor, came
into existence as the result of discussions in the Philadelphia Baptist
Association in 1762 and 1763.[1] The charter was granted March 2,
1764. Rhode Island, as the colony founded by Roger Williams,
Baptist in origin and attachment, was selected as the location of the
new college. Reverend Mr. Manning, a graduate of Princeton, was
elected the first president.

The charter arranged for the perpetuation of Baptist influence. The president of the college, eight of the twelve fellows, and
twenty-two of the thirty-six trustees had to be, by charter provision,

---

1. Nicholas Brown, after whom the college was named for his donation of
$5,000 in 1804, continued his benefactions for many years, until their total
was nearly $160,000. The Browns are represented on the campus by the John
Carter Brown Library of Americana, the premier collection of its kind. The
Annmary Brown Memorial, a library of editions of fifteenth-century printers,
established by General Rush Hawkins in memory of his wife, Annmary, is
just off the campus.

of the Baptist denomination. Four of the board were to be members of the Congregational Church, five were to be Episcopalians, and the remaining five were to be Quakers.[2]

250   Professor William MacDonald, George L. Littlefield professor of American history at Brown University, said in an address delivered on a university occasion March 24, 1905 (I owe the quotation to Professor Adams), "The founders intended to establish in Rhode Island under the fostering care of the Baptist denomination but with the aid of the Episcopalians, Congregationalists and Friends whom for this purpose they admitted to a share of control, a college in which there should forever be alike for students and officers perfect freedom in matters of faith."

In the original charter itself appear the following provisions:

> Into this Liberal and Catholic Institution shall never be admitted any Religious Tests but on the Contrary all the *251*   Members hereof shall forever enjoy full free Absolute and uninterrupted Liberty of Conscience.
>
> The Sectarian differences of opinion shall not make any part of the public and Classical instruction.

---

2. In recent years, this Baptist preponderance has been lessened to a very great extent. Professor James P. Adams, vice president of Brown, writes me, "This specification concerning the presidency written into the original charter in 1764 was removed by an amendment in 1926. As a result of this amendment it is no longer necessary for the president to be affiliated with the Baptist denomination.

"This charter amendment also modified the provisions with respect to the members of the corporation by adding six members to the Board of Trustees who may be chosen without regard to denominational affiliations. As the charter now stands the Board of Fellows consists of twelve members of whom eight shall be Baptists and 'the rest indifferently of any or all Denominations.' The Board of Trustees consists of forty-two members of whom twenty-two shall be Baptists, five shall be Quakers, four shall be Congregationalists, five shall be Episcopalians, and six shall be chosen without regard to denominational affiliation."

> The public teaching shall in general respect the sciences.

In comment on this, Dr. Faunce, late president of Brown University, in the university sermon upon the occasion of the sesquicentennial celebration in 1914 said,

> The Brown University charter therefore speaks with the accent of those who have surveyed the past and are planning for the ages to come. When "liberal" was esteemed a dangerous word—as it is still in some quarters—the charter applied that word to the college that was to be. When "Catholic" was esteemed a sectarian appellation the charter claimed the word and fearlessly described the new college as both liberal and Catholic—terms which I think no other college in America has ever used to describe itself. When science—at least in the sense of physical science—was esteemed hostile to the Bible and to morals, our charter at Brown University calmly announced "the public teaching shall in general respect the sciences."

The theses broadsides issued at commencement time at the College of Rhode Island and Providence Plantations, of which some thirty are still extant,[3] demonstrate very clearly that Baptist influence rigidly maintained during the colonial period did not cause the modification in any material way of the curriculum of the college, which continued until the nineteenth century to be strikingly similar to those of the other early colleges. At Brown as elsewhere, the series of theses selected for the public act on commencement day indicate indubitably that the seven liberal arts of the medieval universities, the *trivium* and *quadrivium* which continued throughout cultural Europe to be the main part of the studies

252

---

3. They may be seen in the John Hay Library or the John Carter Brown Library in Brown University. Five of the thesis sheets for the years just before the Revolution, 1769 to 1774, are preserved in a successive series and are particularly valuable for the purpose of our study here.

of university men in the centuries after the Middle Ages, were given the place of honor in the curriculum. The faculty devoted themselves mainly to the purpose of training the minds of men to think by means of logic, grammar, rhetoric, with mathematics and the three philosophies, natural, mental, and moral, that is, physics, metaphysics, and ethics. Astronomy and geography were studied under physics, and there were varied subdivisions of ethics and metaphysics, including politics. The method of teaching by disputation and the content of the curriculum were practically the same all over the colonies and represented the educational tradition which had been handed down in the schools for over a thousand years and was a direct derivative of Greek thought and education from Aristotle's time.

253   The theses at Brown are, if anything, more closely medieval in character than the theses of any of the other colonial colleges. They were deeply intent in that Baptist college in Providence on maintaining the thoroughly conservative character of the teaching. As the latest of the sects represented by a college, they took particular pride in demonstrating that there was no degeneration in the definitely rational character or philosophic breadth of university teaching.

At Providence the smallest of the colonial colleges was going through a very severe struggle to maintain itself, graduating at most half dozen students a year on the average, yet the faculty was manifestly intent on a determined effort to present theses at a public act on commencement day that were at least as ambitious in number and scope as any at the other colonial colleges. They were, as I have said, if anything more medievally Scholastic and conservative than those of the other colleges. It was of these theses issued by Brown particularly that the Right Reverend John A. Ryan, professor of moral philosophy at the Catholic University in Washington, wrote me when I sent him copies of the theses: "The observation that occurs to my mind most frequently on reading these is that scholastic requirements have considerably declined in the secular colleges since pre-Revolutionary days."

Indeed, these theses from the college subsequently to be called Brown represent very strikingly how broad and deep were the educational interests which the institution was trying to foster. *254* They demonstrate, too, what a very definite effort was being made in the youngest of the New England colleges to train the minds of young men in habits of thinking so as to enable them, as far as that was possible, to think straight and not merely accept formulas of various kinds with regard to the significance of the world around them and within them—the macrocosm and the microcosm of existence—without weighing duly the propositions in which the declarations were made.

The first president of the institution, Dr. Manning, was a graduate of Princeton, and it would naturally be expected that Princeton's methods and contents of education would prevail at this new institution. One need only glance at two or three of the theses sheets to be quite convinced that the one purpose of the faculty at Brown was to reproduce in this third of the New England colleges exactly the same curriculum as the older sister colleges had been following since the beginning of their careers. The theses summed up the teaching of the college except for such time as was devoted to the classics, and manifestly the one purpose was to exemplify the Scholastic philosophy in the propositions that had been in use in college since the Middle Ages.

The group of theses for the College of Rhode Island and Providence Plantations for the year 1769, the first year in which there were graduates, contains ten propositions in grammar, eight in rhetoric, eleven in logic, fourteen in mathematics, twenty-seven *255* in physics, seven in ontology, eight in pneumatology, thirteen in theology, ten in ethics, and six in *politia*, or politics—one hundred and four in all. The mathematical theses contained a good review of geometry and analytics. The physical theses discussed among other things the aurora borealis as best explained as an electrical phenomenon. These natural philosophy theses suggested further that vegetation was increased under the influence of electricity, discussed many phases of acoustics, declared there is no such thing as the force of suction in nature, and concluded with half a dozen rather searching questions in astronomy. This was evidently considered an extremely important department of college work, and there are some rather surprising anticipations of what are usually thought to be much more recent scientific conclusions.

The mental philosophy theses, however, under various heads, ontology, pneumatology, and natural theology, were evidently considered of even greater significance than those of natural philosophy. They were twenty-eight in number. The medieval character of these theses is readily perceived by anyone familiar with the curriculum of the medieval universities. Among the ontological theses are such propositions as "No being can create itself; therefore, God is not created"; "Every cause contains its effect." Then comes a thesis which would ordinarily be placed under the rubric *cosmology* and which demonstrates the acceptance of the old medieval doctrine of matter and form: "There is one underlying substratum common to all matter."

256

Under pneumatology are found such theses as this pair: "Spirits are not composed of parts; therefore, by their very nature they are immortal." Under that same rubric, however, there is the proposition "Freedom is a property of the will," but also the proposition "For spirits considered in themselves there is no location" (*nullum est ubi*). Under theology comes the rather surprising proposition, evidently advanced on what is presumed to be biblical authority, "Animals were not given as food to the people who lived before the deluge." There is also the surprisingly Scholastic proposition, in terminology at least, "Original sin cannot be imputed until the suppositum becomes a person; therefore, it is only imputed after the union of the soul with the body." This very first year at Brown, among the theology theses, is to be found Anselm's ontological argument for the existence of God, *Deus esse potest, ergo est:* "God can be, therefore He is." This argument, although it has very little appeal to the great majority of serious philosophers, surprisingly enough has caught and held the attention, and even secured the assent, of a great many profound thinkers down the centuries, though of course a much larger number of distinguished contributors to philosophy have refused to accept it. Even in the generation just past, men like the Italian philosopher Rosmini, as well as our own Orestes Brownson and Thomas Davidson, have been quite taken with it.

Among the ethical theses for this year (1769) at Brown, there *257* is the linked pair of theses "No one acts without incitement; therefore, no one ever acts against his will." This is followed by the rather consolatory proposition "No passion considered in its nature is vicious." Very often since, thoughtful men have insisted that there were good passions as well as bad passions, and resultant good habits that made activity for the best easy as well as bad habits that stimulated tendencies to evil. This proposition is followed in turn by the pair of propositions, "No one ever seeks evil as evil; therefore, that anyone should will his own damnation is in opposition to the law of nature." Practical morality is summed up in two propositions that year: "Moral obligation depends only on the will of God" and "The light of nature teaches us to distinguish between good and evil." They were confident in their assertions in moral philosophy; there was no hesitancy in their declaration of truth as they saw it. The last of the ethical propositions this year is one that might not have been expected to be formulated quite as early in the history of the country as the second quarter [*sic*; third quarter —ed.] of the eighteenth century. It was to shake New England to its center some generations later: "To reduce Africans into perpetual servitude does not agree with divine or human law." Almost needless to say, there were many Negro slaves in New England at that time.

Under *politia*, or politics, at Brown in 1769, there are some propositions that arrest attention because they show that the ideas *258*

203

which led to the Declaration of Independence were already fermenting in the minds of the college generation. After the definition that politics is concerned with the proper ruling of the commonwealth come a series of propositions that might be considered as representing rather radical political philosophy at that time. The two linked propositions immediately following the definition run, "All power of making laws and inflicting penalties is derived from the people; therefore, For a Senate to impose taxes upon people who are not represented in that Senate (legislative body) is not just." The well-known principle of the English common law which more than any other led up to the Revolution, "There shall be no taxation without representation," has been traced back to the thirteenth century, when so many of the basic principles of modern law were formulated, but here it is in Baptist Brown half a dozen years before the Revolution, presented for demonstration and argumentation at the public act held on commencement day. It must have had its effect on the minds not only of the students but especially on those in attendance who could read the Latin thesis sheets and then, doubtless because of the discussion that took place, on the rest of the audience who assembled for the commencement.

There follow some propositions that one is likely to hear expressed, though in a much more extended way, in commencement addresses—or that we heard when the custom of having such addresses still obtained. Here are some examples: "A state of civil liberty especially conduces to the study of arts and sciences." "Literature helps greatly to the stabilizing and efficient government of society."

259

The last of the propositions under the rubric *politia* was evidently meant to fit in with conditions as they were and to discourage any headstrong rationalizer toward revolutionary activity. The faculty was evidently discouraging the idea of revolution at this time, some seven years before the Declaration of Independence. Seven years later, Brown was ready to encourage revolution, and her faculty and students were willing to lay down their lives if necessary for their principles. This proposition is the last on the sheet.

It was printed in italics with an index, which meant that one of the prospective bachelors would be asked to demonstrate it and to answer the objections to it at the public act: "For Americans in the present state of affairs to undertake a revolution harmonizes badly with prudence in administering government."

In 1774 at Brown, there is no group of theses under the rubric *politia*, but there are no less than eighteen theses under *ethica*, some of which are very strikingly political in significance. For instance, ethical thesis 15 is "A defensive war is licit," followed by the proposition "Anyone who takes away liberty from another is unworthy to enjoy his own liberty." These propositions were followed by "'Unjust laws often impel men to make revolution."

It is evident that they were thinking very seriously about the question of war and were clearing up in the minds of students the moral principles involved, in order that they might have no hesitancy as to what it was right for them to do under the circumstances. The fourteenth proposition was "To overcome violence and defend ourselves and our possessions is commanded by nature and is permitted by virtue."

262

The seventeenth ethical proposition printed in italics, calling special attention to it, though without the index finger which would indicate that it would surely be part of the program, ran thus: "A glorious death for the sake of liberty is above all to be preferred to miserable slavery." The last of the ethical propositions with an index to emphasize it is "The dictates of conscience must always be obeyed."

Meantime, in the same set of ethical theses, the faculty of the College of Rhode Island, following up the traditions which had come down from the time of Roger Williams, was trying to bring the colonies more closely together and removing one of the most serious obstacles to concord among them by pointing out that religious intolerance is unworthy of educated men. The fourth and fifth propositions of this year (1774) run, "Those who adopt the opinions of others apart from evidence are often the most bitter

THESES ETHICÆ.

Ethica eft fcientia practica, quæ mores hominum dirigit ad felicitatem obtinendam.

1. OMNES virtutes fociales è mifericordia profluunt.
2. Felicitas humana ex prudenti habituum conformatione præcipuè exoritur.
3. Virtutum exercitatio, et ingenii cultus ex ftatu focietatis magnoperè pendent.
4. Reddere fenibus honorem, ad homines reddendos benè moratos maximè conducit.
5. Si non fuiffent propria hominibus, inter eos nunquam extitiffet injuftitia.
6. Generis humani propagationi, æquè ac virtutis confervationi, per-.neceffarium eft matrimonium.
7. Concubitus vagus, crimine quovis alio, plùs ad hominum mentes effeminatas, et mores reddendos depravatos, conducit.

THESES THEOLOGICÆ.

Theologia, quodcunque notum fieri poteft de Deo, atque ejus voluntate erga nos explicat.

1. HOMINES naturâ depravati omninò funt ac deperditi : Ergo,
2. Actiones eorum priùs Deo gratæ effe non poffunt quàm renafcuntur.
3. Dei comminationes ex conditione pendent, et·non femper funt perfectæ : At,
4. Prædictiones fine exceptis fiunt.
5. Si prædicta improbabilia compleantur, oportet a Deo effe edita confiteamur : Et,
6. Evangelii per gentes divulgatio, ut facris in fcripturis prænunciata, eventus fuit admodum improbabilis : Ergo,
7. Evidentiam habemus clariffimam fcripturas facras afflatu divino effe confcriptas.
8. Prædictiones, ad actiones voluntarias hominum referentes, ante expletionem earum non pernofcantur.
9. Ex plurimis Pfeudo-Chriftis qui exorti funt, planè conftat Jefum Chriftum verum fuiffe Meffiam.

BROWN, ETHICAL AND THEOLOGICAL THESES, 1789

THESES POLITICÆ.

Politia est scientia, quæ societatum civilium externas, at præcipuè internas administrationes benè dirigit.

1. QUOD ratio naturalis inter hominum societates constituit, jus gentium vocatur.
2. Homines, imperio ablato, fient licentiores quàm si nunquam fuissent subjecti : Ergo,
3. Libertas naturalis, imperio deperdito, est multò præstabilior.
4. Quisque statu naturali sese sentit esse inferiorem : Ergo,
5. Pax jus est primum naturæ.
6. Rerumpublicarum felicitas, ex consiliariorum prudentia et probitate, præcipuè emanat.
7. Gubernatores sæculis primis ex gubernandorum consensu sunt rerum potiti.
8. Quantò potentiores sunt magistratus, tantò eorum tempus administrandi debet decurtari.
9. Legum severitas extrema executioni earum obstat.
10. In ratione magnitudinis inversa, diminuitur imperii tranquillitas.
11. Quò magis gens quævis comitate exculta est, eò magis increscet dissimulatio.
12. Rebuspublicis luxuria, at Monarchiis egestas exitio est.
13. Possessori possessio, ex sua natura, est inferior : Ergo,
14. Æthiopes possessio esse non possunt.

☞ An Columbus Americam reperiendo generi humano benefecerit ?

BROWN, POLITICAL THESES, 1789

persecutors of those from whom they differ; therefore, Persecution on account of religion flourishes especially among the ignorant and those who are satisfied with implicit faith," that is, those who have not the explicit reasons for the faith that is in them.

263

The other thesis sheets that have been preserved for us from Brown for these years before the Revolution make it very clear that they were setting forth the principles of political government succinctly and thoroughly. For instance, among the ethical theses at Brown in 1773, the second thesis runs, "A militia well equipped but unsalaried is the best defense for a commonwealth." They were afraid of the danger to liberty that was involved in the support of a large regularly constituted standing army.

They were warning people, moreover, that even though a change of government should come, that would not be perfect and that no form of government under human conditions as they are could be without its faults. They drew a conclusion from that, in the form of paired propositions, that is very interesting to us a century and a half later: "No form of commonwealth can be organized by human wisdom that can be entirely without fault; therefore, A just distribution of punishment and rewards cannot be hoped for from our courts."

They were emphasizing more and more, as might have been expected in Roger Williams's colony, the necessity for religious toleration. Hence, the sixth of the ethical theses for that year ran, "Men must not be compelled by tortures and fines to renounce heresy."

264

It has been suggested in recent years that Roger Williams perhaps scarcely merited the reputation for lack of religious intolerance which has been connected with his name, but nowhere among the colleges will as strong expressions on this subject be encountered as are to be found in the theses at the College of Rhode Island more than a century after Williams's death. There was evidently a very strong feeling in this matter, and though it was to be nearly twenty years before toleration was secured by the federal Constitution,

Brown had been the leading schoolmaster toward that precious consummation so devoutly to be wished.

At Brown in 1773, certain *questiones* were discussed by the candidates for the degree of Master of Arts, the *laurea magistratus*. Instead of the disputation form used for the defense of the theses, these questions were evidently answered in somewhat oratorical or disquisitional form. There were four of them, one for each of the candidates:

1. Do theatrical exhibitions cause deterioration of men's morals and thus become a detriment to the republic? [This was answered in the affirmative by John Dennis.]

2. [Pointed out by an index and printed in somewhat larger type:] Has a republic the right of decreeing the rites of divine worship? [Answered in the negative by Theodore Foster]

3. Does a good purpose diminish the baseness of a lie? [Answered in the negative by Samuel Nash]

4. [This question was only three years before the Declaration of Independence] Have the American colonists the same rights as the inhabitants of Great Britain? [Answered in the affirmative by Seth Lee]

265

It is very interesting indeed to have these documents from Brown, or as it was then, the College of Rhode Island, because the academic training that made the men of the college what they were, in so far as education has an influence in strengthening character, is thus brought home to us. Brown has a happy patriotic distinction in that for some six years during the Revolution, the regular collegiate exercises were suspended because the members of the college, faculty and students, were all, almost to a man, as the tablet in their honor says, in the service of their country. That tablet, placed on the corner of University Hall nearly forty years ago, is one of the most striking testimonies to the leadership of college men in the Revolutionary movement that gave us our independence.

Brown very properly is proud of that bit of her history and of the record of patriotism which it chronicles:

> The Rhode Island Society of the Sons of the American Revolution commemorates by this tables the occupation of this building by the patriot forces, and their French allies, during the Revolutionary War. For six years all academic exercises in this university were suspended— faculty, students and graduates almost to a man were engaged in the service of their county. May all who read this inscription be stimulated by their example to response as loyally to their county's call. "Dulce et decorum est pro patria mori." Erected 1897.

On the occasion of his visit to New England, President Washington in August 1790 stopped off in Providence and received an address from the "Corporation of Rhode Island College" which was delivered by President Manning. The principal sentence of President Washington's brief reply ran, "While I cannot remain insensible to the indulgence with which you regard the influence of my example and the tenor of my conduct; I rejoice in having so favorable an opportunity of felicitating the State of Rhode Island on the cooperation I am sure to find in the measures adopted by the guardians of literature in this place for improving the morals of the rising generation and inculcating upon their minds principles primarily calculated for the preservation of our rights and liberties." He added, "You may rely on whatever protection I may be able to afford in so important an object as the education of our youth." The president of Rhode Island College thanked divine providence for having restored President Washington's health and protected his life and concluded by praying, "That you may afterwards [hereafter] receive the rewards of virtue by having the approbation of God is our most sincere desire and fervent supplication."

Part II

9

Scholastic Philosophy
Old and New

Our English colonial colleges were, as is clear from the commence-   *269*
ment theses, all mainly occupied, especially during the last two
years of the college course, with Scholastic philosophy. For a proper
understanding of that phase of our educational history and the
intellectual life of the collegians, it is important to have before us a
definite review of the place Scholasticism occupies in the history of
thought and development of education. The medieval *trivium* and
quadrivium, the so-called seven liberal arts, continued, with certain
modifications due to the growth of knowledge of the physical world
and the development of mathematics, to be the principal subject of
study at the universities not only during the medieval period but
for long afterwards, indeed, until well on in the nineteenth century,
not only in Europe but also in this country, though that fact has
utterly failed of recognition in English-speaking America.

While Scholasticism is usually supposed to date from the
later Middle Ages and especially the thirteenth century, as a matter of fact its history extends back much farther than that in the
history of education. Rev. Mother Mildred, in her college thesis   *270*

213

on *The Scholastic Synthesis* (presented at Fordham University for the degree of Doctor of Philosophy, Philadelphia, 1932), points out that there is already a beginning of Scholasticism to be traced under the Emperor Theodoric the Goth, who introduced the study of philosophy through his philosopher ministers, Cassiodorus and Boethius. Indeed, Boethius is often spoken of as the father of Scholastic philosophy, and his work *De consolatione philosophiae*, written probably during his imprisonment shortly before his death, has been widely read by all those interested in Scholasticism. The writings of these men proved of great service to later philosophers, but the Lombards put an end to their work in education. After them came the era of information and education as contrasted with thoughtfulness. This was outlined in the early medieval encyclopedists, Isidore of Seville, Venerable Bede, and then Rabanus Maurus, abbot of Fulda, afterwards archbishop of Mainz, whose work *De universo* was the favorite reference book of the Middle Ages until the issuance by Bartholomew, the English Franciscan, of his *De proprietatibus rerum* and by Vincent of Beauvais, the French Dominican, of his *Greater Mirror*. In the period of the earliest encyclopedists, there gradually came a reawakening of Scholastic philosophy in the environment from which it derived its name.

271   The definite formulation of Scholasticism as well as this distinctive name came in connection with the schools of Charlemagne—the Carlovingian renaissance—in the ninth century. The name *Scholastic* is derived from these schools. The head of the school was called *magister scholae* or *capiscola* or *scholasticus*. The last term outlived the others, and as the director of the school usually taught dialectics, out of which grew this system of teaching philosophy, the name Scholasticism was given to this new mode of philosophy. Alcuin was one of the earliest Scholastics in a certain sense of the word, and in his schools, the *trivium* (grammar, rhetoric, and logic) and the *quadrivium* (arithmetic, geometry, astronomy,

and music), the seven liberal arts as they came subsequently to be called, were definitely taught.[1]

Among the best known of the Carlovingian teachers was John Scotus Erigena, or Eriugena (Erin-born), probably but not necessarily an Irishman by birth. The tradition is that he could read Greek and knew much more than his contemporaries, at least with regard to Greek philosophy.[2] Erigena came to be known all over the *272* west of Europe, and his teaching was looked upon as representing what was most profound with regard to the meaning of life and the mystery of the universe—the metaphysics of the schools.

The true father of Scholasticism is often proclaimed to have been St. Anselm, that profound scholar and mystic who yet proved in his maturity the marvelously practical archbishop of Canterbury of the eleventh century, whose patriotism, exemplified in his love for his adopted country England, English historians have lauded so highly. This scholarly son of north Italy who, in the abbey of Bec in Normandy had been deeply influenced by Lanfranc, his predecessor in the archbishopric of Canterbury, secured the future of philosophy by giving it a firm foundation in basic principles and by raising it above the level of mere discussions in logic by efforts directed toward definite systematization of thought. He was personally such a taking character that it is not surprising that he

---

1. Music as they used the term represented a school discipline very different from what we mean by the word. It was really a division of mathematics which had come down from the time of Pythagoras and was supposed to include all the phases of sound and the various rhythms of the universe, so far as they knew anything about them at that time.

2. His knowledge of Greek probably indicated that he was an Irishman or at least had been educated in Ireland, for at that time, scholars who in western Europe could read Greek had, to quote the expression of Mrs. Richard Green in her volume *Irish Nationality*, usually been taught either by an Irishman or by someone who had been taught by an Irishman.

won the hearts of many disciples, and their devotion to his teaching gave it a vogue that assured its endurance for many generations. Indeed, Anselm's influence continues to be felt in the philosophy of our day. His ontological argument for the existence of God, *Deus potest esse, ergo est,* is to be found among the theses listed on the broadsides of the colonial colleges for their commencement dis-

273   putation, or public act. Many other exemplifications of Anselm's philosophic teaching may be noted here and there throughout these colonial college theses.

From all this, it is clear that by their definite adoption of Scholasticism as their fundamental philosophy, the colonial colleges were setting up for themselves, consciously or unconsciously, probably quite indeliberately, a background for their education of at least a thousand years in the intellectual life of Europe. It was the custom during most of the nineteenth century for educators outside of the Catholic Church to belittle the significance of Scholasticism, to speak contemptuously of it, and to disparage its content and method. But ideas that have lasted for a thousand years in the schools of the world are not likely to be merely trivial or insignificant. They must be founded on something very close to the heart of human nature, using *heart* in that sense, following the older usage, of the deeper thinking that man does when all his intellectual powers are enlisted.

In any case, the fact that Scholasticism represents the philosophic basis of Christianity in its effort to solve the riddle of existence and of the universe makes it particularly interesting that the colonial colleges should have occupied more than half of the time which their students gave to the pursuit of education with these old Scholastic theses and the phases of philosophy, mental, natural, and moral, which they represent. Those who feel that colonial college

274   education loses prestige because of its devotion to Scholasticism need only a better understanding of Scholasticism to contradict any such assumption and eradicate the inconsiderate conclusion

216

that there can be little or nothing worth thinking about in a form of philosophy so old and old-fashioned as this is.

Turner, in his *History of Philosophy*,[3] written while he was professor of philosophy at the Catholic University in Washington, sums up the significance of Scholasticism succinctly yet thoroughly, and I know no better way to provide a background for the understanding of the Scholastic philosophy which took up so much attention at the colonial colleges than to quote his paragraphs on the subject. He had himself received his training in philosophy through the Scholastic system of thought and knew it not merely from the historical standpoint but from personal experience as student and teacher for many years. He is able, then, to describe it in a way that brings out its inner meaning. He said,

> The philosophy of the schools resulted from the attempt to dispel the intellectual darkness of the age of barbarian rule, and throughout the course of its development it bore the mark of its origin. The schoolmen were the defenders of the rights of reason; and if mysticism retarded, and rationalism compromised, the Scholastic movement, the success of mysticism and rationalism was merely temporary. Abelard and Gilbert de la Porrée were succeeded by Alexander of Hales, Albert the Great, and St. Thomas of Aquin, who, while they avoided the errors into which their predecessors had fallen, adopted the idea of method for which their predecessors had contended, and succeeded in winning over even the most unyielding of the orthodox to a recognition of the just claims of human reason. The attitude of the great schoolmen towards the rights of reason appears most strikingly in the Scholastic use of dialectic as a means of arriving at a knowledge of natural truth and

275

---

3. William Turner, *History of Philosophy* (Boston: Ginn and Co., 1903), 417–420.

of obtaining a scientific, albeit an imperfect, grasp of the meaning of the mysteries of faith. ...

The trait which even more than the use of dialectic or the adoption of Aristotelianism characterized the philosophy of the schools, is the effort on the part of the schoolmen to unify philosophy and theology to discover and demonstrate the harmony of natural truth with truth of the supernatural order. This is the thought which inspired the first speculative attempts of the schoolmen and which after having manifested itself in so widely differing forms in the philosophy of Erigena, of St. Anselm, and of Abelard, was finally crystallized in the principles in which St. Thomas enunciated his definition of the relations between reason and faith. The day has long gone by when a historian could without fear of contradiction and protest represent Scholastic philosophy as the subjugation of reason to authority. It is now universally conceded that the phrase *ancilla theologiae* [handmaid of theology] implied no servility on the part of philosophy, but rather the honorable service of carrying the torch by which the path of theology is lighted. Hauréau [the French historian of Scholasticism: *Dict. du sciences phil.*, s.v. "Scholastique."] declares that one has but to look at the vast number of volumes [most of them many times larger than the average size of our books] which the schoolmen wrote to realize how much value they attached to philosophy and how inexorably they felt the need of exercising their reason. Indeed it is only the most superficial student of history who fails to recognize in the Middle Ages a period of immense intellectual activity, and the more the philosophy of that period is studied the deeper becomes the conviction that the schoolmen were far from failing to recognize the rights of human reason. If, then, Scholastic philosophy effected the most perfect conciliation of reason with faith, we must not take it for granted that the conciliation was brought about at the cost of the independence of philosophy. The schoolmen were as far removed from fideism

276

as they were from rationalism. They attached independent value to philosophy as well as to theology, while they contended that philosophy and theology can never contradict each other. In this way—and herein lies the philosophical significance of Scholastic philosophy—the schoolmen established between the natural and the supernatural the relation which the Greeks had established between matter and spirit, the relation of distinction without opposition.

This doctrine of the continuity and independence of the natural with respect to the supernatural order of truth is the core of Scholasticism. It is by this that Scholasticism is distinguished from Greek philosophy, of which the chief defect, as well as the paramount merit, was its complete naturalness. It is by this, too, that Scholasticism is distinguished from the philosophy of the new era. Modern philosophy—post-Reformation philosophy, as it may be called—was born of the revolt of philosophy against theology, of reason against faith. It adopted at the very outset the Averroistic principle that what is true in theology may be false in philosophy—a principle diametrically opposed to the thought which inspired Scholasticism. Indeed, in the first great system which appeared in the modern era, not only is philosophy divorced from theology, but mind is placed in complete antithesis to matter; for in Descartes' philosophy, the spirit of disintegration, which characterizes the modern era, is subversive not only of the work of the schoolmen but also of the best achievements of Greek speculation. Scholasticism distinguishes without separating; modern philosophy either fails altogether to distinguish (*fideism, monism*) or distinguishes and separates (*rationalism, Cartesian spiritualism*).

277

It used to be the custom to deprecate this medieval philosophy as occupied mainly with trifles, but the enthusiastic revival of Gothic architecture and art and literature which brought about the recognition of the magnificent achievements of the thirteenth century, and especially the universities which represented the

278   culmination of Scholastic philosophy, has changed all that. The men who know the most about it have been most enthusiastic in their appreciation of its philosophy as well as all the other phases of its accomplishments. Frederic Harrison, in his article "A Survey of the Thirteenth Century," published in the volume *The Meaning of History and Other Historical Pieces,*[4] does not hesitate to say that the age of Aquinas, Roger Bacon, St. Francis, St. Louis, Giotto, and Dante is the most "purely spiritual, the most really constructive and indeed the most truly philosophic … of all the epochs of effort after a new life."

For Harrison "the whole thirteenth century is crowded with creative forces in philosophy." Many others have come to express similar opinions. The more men know about Scholastic philosophy, the readier they are to praise it and the more highly laudatory is what they have to say about it. That renascence of interest in things medieval which has characterized the past generation has brought scholars to realize that a period which gave us the universities in the form in which they exist at the present time, developed Gothic architecture, and led up to the evolution of the arts and crafts in a way that has never been excelled could not possibly have been satisfied with an insignificant philosophy. The result of such reflections has been a definite promotion of attention to Scholasticism, and that is all that is necessary to make people realize its depth of meaning.

279   Since the latter half of the nineteenth century particularly, as a result of these studies, there has been a great reawakening of interest in Scholastic philosophy. This has occurred not only in Catholic colleges but also in non-Catholic institutions of learning. Scholars generally have wakened up to the thought that a philosophic method of thinking that satisfied men for a thousand years is not

---

4. Frederic Harrison, *The Connection of History from the Meaning of History and Other Historical Pieces* (New York: Macmillan, 1908).

likely to have been merely absurd or inane, though it was quite the custom fifty years ago for even teachers who had never opened a book of Scholastic philosophy in their lives to talk contemptuously of it. Indeed, the less they knew about it from actual contact with it, the readier they were to condemn and even bitterly to hold it up to deprecation. Firsthand knowledge of Scholasticism is the best possible corrective of a number of false notions with regard to it which are founded entirely on ignorance. Probably nothing illustrates better than the application of one of Josh Billings's expressions the attitude that used to be very commonly assumed with regard to Scholasticism, even by professors of philosophy a generation ago. Our American humorist said, "It isn't so much the ignorance of mankind that makes them ridiculous as the knowing so many things that ain't so." The generation before ours was very prone to think that it knew a great many things about Scholastic philosophy which prove, however, on closer investigation, to be just exemplifications of the tendency of mankind to accept "things that ain't so."

Father Rickaby, SJ, who was selected to present the subject of Scholasticism in the series Philosophy Ancient and Modern,[5] said in the preface, "It used to be assumed that philosophy lay in a trance for more than a thousand years from St. Augustine to Francis Bacon. Now it is coming to be admitted that the labors of the Schoolmen within that period do count for something in the history of human thought. This primer is an outline sketch of those labors by one who believes in their value." Father Rickaby was for many years professor of Scholastic philosophy at Pope's Hall, Oxford. He is an authoritative exponent of the subject and says, "All Scholastic philosophy is based upon the distinction between *matter* and *form*. Modern thought makes light of the distinction

280

---

5. Joseph Rickaby, *Scholasticism* (London: Archibald Constable, 1908).

but we must absolutely attend to it if we are to have any notion of Scholasticism at all. Likewise we must bear in mind the distinction of *substance* and *accident*. According to the Schoolmen substance alone fully is; accident has but a diminished being inhering in substance. The idealism of our day abolishes substance or permanent being altogether and recognizes accident not as anything permanently 'inhering' (for there is nothing left to inhere in) but as a fleeting 'state of consciousness.'"

Almost needless to say, these theses of the colonial colleges have very much to do with matter and form and perhaps even more with substance and accident. It seems well to emphasize that

281 the Schoolmen did not agree among themselves with regard to the many points of disputation that came up with regard to matter and form and substance and accident, and as Father Rickaby says, "Not only the Schoolmen were not all of one mind in philosophy but in fact they disputed with one another fiercely and in grim earnest." Sometimes it is rather difficult for our minds to see the points at issue. He adds, "The gauge on which the medieval mind ran was not our modern gauge. Which of the two is broad and which is narrow we need not argue; anyhow the gauge is different and the passage of the train of thought from the one to the other is a troublesome operation. Whatever difficulty we experience in making out the Schoolman's objective we shall be wise in presuming that he had some real question before him and that the disputations in medieval Paris and Oxford were not, as Moliére has represented them, mere wars of words." The same may be said as to the disputations in the colonial colleges, though a great many modern students of philosophy who read over the propositions inherited so often from the medieval universities are very much inclined to say that there is little meaning in them, but that is entirely because they have not as yet worked out the meaning as they should.

Father Rickaby discusses the very interesting question as to whether Scholasticism is exhausted as a philosophy and what was the cause of its decay. Ancient Scholasticism, he says, lies open to

the charge of having been over-much *a priori*, over neglectful of   *282*
experiment, of research, of observation, of nature at first hand, of
linguistic study, of history, of documentary evidence. He adds that
it must not be forgotten that Albertus Magnus and Roger Bacon
in their works nobly rebut this charge. The attitude of Albertus
Magnus and Friar Bacon as well as Thomas Aquinas to the physical
science of their day—"poor science it was no doubt but they took
care to have the best of it, the most recent"—shows their breadth of
intellectual interest. It was not so much the lack of science in Scholasticism as the lack of knowledge with regard to its real significance
that has brought about its condemnation in our day. As Father
Rickaby says, "How many educated men still derive their notions
of the doctrine of Scholastic philosophy from Moliére!" Modern
caricatures of Scholasticism accepted as serious criticism have led
modern educators into profound misunderstanding of a great system of philosophy which fortunately is coming into its own again.

The great Schoolmen of the thirteenth century, that supreme
period of Scholastic philosophy, were nearly all professors in the
University of Paris. The first of these was Peter Lombard, surnamed
the Master of the Sentences, who died bishop of Paris in 1160. His
Sentences became the favorite textbook in the schools and kept its
place for centuries. Its division into four books on God, on creatures, on virtues and beatitude, on the sacraments was adopted
almost completely by St. Thomas in his great work *Contra gentiles*.   *283*
Alexander of Hales, an Englishman from Gloucestershire, a Franciscan, was a master of the University of Paris and died in 1245,
leaving behind him a *Summa theologiae*, or *Summary of Theology*.
Alexander perfected the Scholastic method of teaching. Then came
John of Fidenza, known as St. Bonaventure, the Seraphic Doctor,
who studied and taught in the University of Paris for some fifteen
years (1242–1257). His election as general of his order took him
out of education. He was a close personal friend of Aquinas, though
they differed from each other in a number of rather important
points. After him came Albertus Magnus, the Universal Doctor,

of whom Father Rickaby says he was "the best travelled, the most erudite, the most vigorous and long lived of all the Schoolmen." He was first a soldier and did not become a Dominican until he was over thirty. He studied and taught at Cologne, Hildesheim, Freiburg, Ratisbon, Strasbourg, and finally at Paris.

Albert's pupil, St. Thomas Aquinas, the Angelic Doctor, is the chief of the Schoolmen. He came as a student to the University of Paris in 1245 and heard the lectures of Albertus Magnus, taking his bachelor's degree in 1248, when he was twenty-three years of age. He followed Albertus to Cologne but returned to Paris in 1253, taking his master's degree with St. Bonaventure, and then lectured there for some three years. The substance of those lectures is the *Summa contra gentiles.* The last of these thirteenth-century Schoolmen was John Duns Scotus, probably an Irishman by birth, known as the Subtle Doctor. He was to the Franciscans what Thomas Aquinas had been to the Dominicans. For centuries the Schoolmen were divided into Thomists and Scotists. Scotus was the glory of Oxford, St. Thomas of Paris. Scotus lectured for some ten years at Oxford over the turn of the thirteenth century. He went to Paris and lectured there for some four years and then died untimely. He had a genius for mathematics and delighted in distinctions and differences which sometimes opponents declared were unintelligible. After a time, the distinctions of some of his disciples became so fine that they were actually meaningless, and it is for this reason it is said that Scotus's first name, Duns, came to be modified into *dunce,* as applied to his disciples, signifying a man lacking in intelligence.

After the thirteenth century, there was some decadence of interest in Scholastic philosophy, mainly because there was a corresponding decadence of interest in the universities. Men were occupied with a number of other things, wars and rumors of wars. About the middle of the fourteenth century and for some time afterwards, the Black Death wandered through Europe, taking away nearly one half of the inhabitants of cities and disturbing academic interest

284

SCHOLASTIC PHILOSOPHY OLD AND NEW

very much. During the fifteenth century, the Renaissance, with its interest in the classics and particularly in Greek, pushed philosophic teaching and study into the background, and it was not until the Jesuits came in the second half of the sixteenth century that there was a great revival of Scholasticism. Men like Bellarmine and Suarez but also many others who might be mentioned set forth the great principles of Scholasticism under the aegis of Aquinas in a way that renewed devotion to that magnificent system of thought. With the suppression of the Jesuits in the eighteenth century, there came a very deep decadence of interest in Scholasticism, and this interest was not renewed until the restoration of the Jesuits and the gradual rebuilding of their colleges throughout the world. *285*

In this modern revolution of thought as to the value of Scholastic philosophy, the Jesuits particularly have been the moving factors. Scholasticism, in the strictest sense of the term, has been taught in their colleges for the past hundred years, though it needed the development of Neo-Scholasticism, largely through their efforts, to call attention to the fact that this medieval system of thought might very well prove better capable than any other of solving the problems of human life and of the universe as, with increase of knowledge, they come up insistently for solution. The Scholastics were noted particularly for trusting to their own reasoning power, and they dared to draw the logical conclusions from their premises as so many modern philosophers do not.

The great world awakening of interest in Scholasticism which has come in our generation is largely the result of the encyclical *286* of Pope Leo XIII known as *Aeterni Patris,* thus entitled, as is the custom with papal documents, from the first two Latin words of the instrument. Pope Leo himself had in his youth distinguished himself in his studies in Scholastic philosophy at the Jesuit college in Rome and was, thus, peculiarly qualified to appreciate Scholasticism at its true value.

His encyclical made it obligatory on all the Catholic seminaries throughout the world, that is, all the higher institutions of learning for the education of the clergy particularly, to teach philosophy and theology from a Scholastic standpoint. The papal document attracted the attention of the educational world generally. Quite needless to say, the encyclical was enthusiastically accepted by the Catholic world, and only a very few Catholic scholars saw any objection to this proclamation of the profound philosophy of the thirteenth century as the basis of philosophic study in our time.

A large number of scholarly minds outside of the Church were inclined to think that this proclamation of Aquinas as the supreme teacher of philosophy and theology, for that was what Pope Leo XIII's encyclical comprised, was reactionary and represented an unfortunate looking backward rather than forward. They prophesied that this would surely be sadly disturbing in its effect upon Church scholarship. It seemed like holding back progress in the realm of philosophic thought by annexing it to one mind and that one which had expressed itself nearly seven hundred years ago. It was not long, however, before many outside of the Church, attracted by the notoriety inevitably connected with a papal encyclical, took up seriously the study of Scholastic philosophy and applied themselves to the understanding of it as it had been taught in the latter half of the thirteenth century. They soon discovered that it represented a marvelous synthesis of human thought with regard to the significance of human life and the relations of man to himself and to his fellowmen and to his Creator.

287

The realization gained ground that the puzzling problems of human existence were undoubtedly better answered by Scholastic philosophy than in any other way. It was not long before there were a number of the most striking expressions on record with regard to the profound significance of Scholastic philosophy and its power to solve the otherwise inscrutable mysteries around us which came from non-Catholic authorities in philosophy.

The acknowledged leader in the Neo-Scholasticism of the twentieth century which came into existence as the result of the encyclical of Pope Leo XIII was Cardinal Mercier, the distinguished

Belgian prelate whose academic prestige was destined to be eclipsed by his recognition as one of the most prominent figures of the greatest war of human history. The Pope made him director of the Institute of Scholastic Philosophy at the University of Louvain, a Catholic university which has been in existence for some five hundred years and has had some outstanding scholars among its faculty *288* and its students and has proved fruitful of good work not only in philosophy but in physical science in the present generation. The most distinguished pupil of Louvain was Vesalius, who, some four hundred years ago after the publication of his great work, *De fabrica humani corporis* (1543), the studies for which, begun at Louvain, were completed in Italy, was hailed as the father of anatomy. But Louvain has had many distinguished scientists who reached distinction in our generation. Theodor Schwann, father of the cell doctrine, occupied a professor's chair there for a while after refusing the offer of a professorship at a German university. He preferred to teach among his brother Catholics in Belgium. Then there were Carnoy in biology and Van Gehuchten in neurology, whose names are among the most distinguished scientists of this generation.

Cardinal Mercier was no mere devotee of old and outworn theories but a thoroughly practical thinker and a stimulating teacher who endeavored to accumulate all knowledge that could be made available for application to philosophic problems. A striking demonstration of that state of mind is found in the fact that when hypnotism was attracting special attention in Paris under Charcot, Mercier made his way there to secure firsthand notions of hypnotism so far as it might be auxiliary to the progress of psychology. For a while, hypnotism seemed to represent the key to many mental problems. It is hard for us to understand now the vogue that it acquired. It proved to be only a misunderstood and exaggerated *289* phase of the power of suggestion. Everything else that might possibly help in the development of philosophy, particularly psychology, received a hearing from the director of the Scholastic Institute at Louvain, and so it is not surprising that he came to be looked upon as a leader in modern thought. As he said himself, "Psychology is not a finished science but a living, growing science. It should evolve with the biological and anthropological sciences which are its tributaries."

So thoroughly did he follow his own conception in this matter, that Louvain was one of the first universities outside of Germany to possess a thoroughly equipped laboratory of physiological psychology. Ribot, the well-known French writer on psychology so prominent in educational circles in France, declared after visiting the laboratory established under Mercier's auspices in Louvain that it was better than any psychological laboratory in France. This constitutes an index of the tendency of that Neo-Scholasticism of which Cardinal Mercier was so zealous an advocate. So far from being limited by the old Scholastic teaching, it imitated the old Scholastics in gathering as far as possible all knowledge and bringing it into the Scholastic fold in order that it might be coordinated with previous knowledge.

No wonder that when the Great War came, Cardinal Mercier's attitude brought him to the focus of world attention. His fearless stand gave him a place beside his monarch, the king of the Belgians, as a hero of the war. No wonder that when he visited this country, our universities proceeded to decorate him with degrees of many and various kinds, though I believe he refused to accept an honorary degree of Doctor of Divinity from a sectarian institution. He proved to have a thoroughgoing sense of humor and was highly amused when told by one of those who had the pleasure of meeting him during his sojourn with us that we were "making him an American 'by degrees.'"

To Cardinal Mercier we are indebted for a series of expressions gathered from his philosophic contemporaries in European universities which enable us to understand how full of significance is Scholastic philosophy even at the present time. He called attention particularly to the fact that the great encyclical of Leo XIII was

290

successful not only in restoring to favor the philosophy of the great master of Scholasticism, but it did ever so much more than that by giving unity to the teaching of the Catholic schools. A scarcely less important result was that "it brought to the attention of the learned world and of thinkers apart from Catholicity, sometimes indeed outside of Christianity, a world of profound thought generally unknown to them. As a result of this it is not unusual to find many men in non-Catholic circles proclaiming their homage to the supreme ability of St. Thomas Aquinas and to the great importance of the movement that has taken place in the philosophic world in the direction of a return to his teaching."[6]

291

In substantiation of his assertion, Cardinal Mercier quotes from a series of well-known writers on philosophy who were profoundly surprised at not having their attention called before this to the wonderful vein of profound thought contained in the writings of this father of Scholastic philosophy. For instance, Professor Rudolph von Ihering of the University of Gottingen, having had his attention called to Scholasticism and especially to the writings of St. Thomas Aquinas because of the papal encyclical and the notice which it attracted in the academic world, in a note to the second edition of his work, *Der Zweck im Recht*, said,

> Now that I know this vigorous thinker, I ask in wonder how it is that such truths as he taught were ever allowed to fall into such utter oblivion by learned Protestants. That mistake would have been avoided if his teaching had been faithfully preserved! As for myself, had I known earlier, I think I should not have written this book, because the fundamental ideas which I meant to put forward were already expressed by this powerful thinker perfectly clearly and with remarkable fertility of mind. . . .

---

6. Cardinal Mercier, *The Origins of Contemporary Psychology*, trans. W. H. Mitchell (New York: P. J. Kenedy, 1918).

292

Unfortunately, I am no longer in a position to take up medieval Scholasticism and contemporary Catholic ethics, and to repair my neglect of them. However, whatever success my book may meet with should help Protestant scholarship not to overlook such aid as it may secure from Catholic theological learning.

Another Protestant—a Frenchman—M. Charles Gide, wrote, "The renaissance of Catholic Scholasticism and also of Thomism makes a study of these supposedly fossilized doctrines indispensable, and in unearthing them one is astonished to find how living they are, and how they resemble those of today, and how little progress we have made, after all!" In Holland, Professor van der Vlugt, commenting on the surprise in store for those who, having known St. Thomas only through adverse criticism, read his own writings, exclaims, "Such a man is not of an age but for all time. All honour to this initiator! All honour to his work!"

These quotations are taken from distinguished non-Catholic thinkers in countries so different from one another as Germany, France, and Holland, countries which are usually considered in the modern time to have been the foster mothers of philosophic minds of distinction. It is perfectly possible, moreover, to cap these quotations with one from an English source that is very surprising. Huxley, the well-known English biologist, was stirred to give his attention to Scholastic philosophy, and above all the teaching of St. Thomas, not by any extraneous circumstance but by his own desire to get the truth at firsthand. His experience with the history of educa-

293 tion while doing research for his address as lord rector at Aberdeen caused him to turn to the *Summa* of St. Thomas, and he was deeply affected by it. He was himself a man of profoundly logical cast of mind who found a special appeal in Aquinas's extremely logical treatment of all the subjects he takes up. Huxley is not likely to be suspected of any undue partisanship for Scholasticism or medievalism, and yet his words of praise of the great medieval philosopher who put the capstone on this mode of thinking have seldom been surpassed by even the most enthusiastic Thomists. Huxley said,

> Nowhere in the world at that time [the thirteenth century] was there such an encyclopedia of knowledge in the three departments [of theology, philosophy, and nature] as was to be found in these works. The Scholastic philosophy is a prodigious monument of the patience and skill with which the mind of man undertook the enterprise of building up a logical theory of the world with the help of such material as it possessed. On the other hand, a number of men of extraordinary culture and learning devote themselves thereto as the best theory of things yet put forward. And what is still more remarkable, they are men who use the language of modern philosophy, and yet think as the schoolmen thought.

For those who may be surprised that the colonial colleges should have continued until the nineteenth century to teach Scholastic philosophy, some of these expressions of men who have found that philosophy of immense significance as an illustration of *296* the thinking powers of mankind, and of the solution of the riddle of existence that it represents, will be illuminating. The revival of interest in this mode of thought in the modern time, when there is so much confusion of thinking, has brought with it the realization that the colonial Fathers built better than they knew when they thus continued in their colleges the study of the old-fashioned philosophy and accepted the teaching that had been handed down in the European universities for some seven hundred years.

Probably the best evidence for this is to be found in that twentieth-century scholar whose contributions to present-day thought attracted so much attention and brought his generation to look back so much more sympathetically on medieval

THESES TECHNOLOGICÆ.

TECHNOLOGIA de artibus et scientiis versatur.

1. Literatura et eruditio elegans artes et scientias prægrediuntur.
2. Pictura gradum inferiorem poeticâ habet, tanquam ad illam illustrare solùm, ad hanc docere quoque, pertinet.
3. Scientiæ principium non habent, priusquam luxus irrepsit; non enim accipientur, donec utiles.
4. Chymia eundem locum in artibus, ac mathematica in iis scientiis, quæ ab ea deducunt originem, habet.
5. Artes, quæ victum hominibus afferendo maxime versantur, a scientiis minimè procedere, dignum est dictu.
6. Doctrinæ humanæ progressus et regressus, non a quibus facere mortalibus datur, sed a naturæ vicissitudinibus, nasci videntur.

JOHANNES COTTON.

THESES GRAMMATICÆ.

COGITATIONES rectè communicandi rationem edocet Grammatice.

1. Quoniam inter homines eruditos communicatio prompta ad literas colendas pernecessaria, et utilis est doctrina solùm perinde ac disseminatur, maximi momenti est linguæ principiorum cognitio.
2. Grammatice civilis est ars scriptorum eximiorum usu et auctoritate conformata; sed grammatice generalis aut philosophica est scientia ratiocinatione pendens.
3. Linguas quales nunc sunt, usu vitiatas *civilis* exhibet; *philosophica* ad fontes suas linguarum anomalia per omnes variationes investigat.
4. Quoniam usus mutabilis est linguæ arbiter, etymologia vocum significationem non semper ostendit.
5. Nulla abstrahendi facultas sine lingua homini esset.
6. Linguæ generalis et philosophicæ inventio, quamvis sæpe tentata, hactenùs fieri non potuit; et multis de causis, lingua Latina omni usui philosophico aptata esse videtur.
7. Aut substantivo aut verbo cæteræ omnes sermonis partes deducuntur.
8. Adjectivum nihil aliud est, quàm substantivum, ita variatum ut aliæ voci conveniret.
9. Participium est verbum adjectivum, id est, verbum ita variatum, ut aliæ voci conveniret.
10. Participium terminans in *ing* Anglicanum nec modi nec temporis discrimen denotat.
11. Voces particulæ denominatæ tantùm contractiones sunt aut linguæ variationes.
12. Conjunctiones multæ modi imperativi verba olim fuerunt.
13. Adverbia et præpositiones substantiva aut verba fuerunt.
14. Interjectiones linguæ principia, ut creditur, fuerunt, et substantivorum animi affectus significantium vim habuerunt.
15. Nominum et verborum inflectiones, multis in linguis inveniendæ, olim fuerunt voces disjunctæ, quas nomini aut verbo nunc coalescere usus coegit; sed reverà auxiliariæ sunt æque ac illæ, quæ separatim leguntur. Ergo,
16. Tempora Anglicana ad duo diminuere, ut propositum fuerit, absurdum esset.
17. Græcæ inflectiones omnium sunt perfectissimæ; sed etiam in iis est et redundantia et defectus.

GULIELMUS GIBBES HUNT.

THESES RHETORICÆ.

7 Quantò major est termini alicujus generalis extensio, tantò minus comprehendit: et, vice versâ.
8. Omne propositum affirmat.
9. Quæcunque tribuimus generi, specierum unicuique; et, quodcunque speciei, singulis qui in illa continentur, tribuere licet: non autem vice versâ.
10. Syllogismi, quamvis vani ad vera invenienda, in eisdem explicandis multùm proderint, utrùm accuratè disceptatur tentando, et quæ sunt falsa detegendo.
11 In syllogismum argumentum quodvis integrum redigere licet: et, demonstrationem quamvis in eorum seriem.
12. Analogicè arguere nihil quidem penitus evincit; valdè autem prodest in re explicanda, et illustranda; et, veris aliundè firmatis, inimicorum impetus avertit.
13. In disceptando Enthymemâ plerumque utimur: exemplo sit:— "Ordo, in arguendo, maximè est usui; quia, illic nititur plurima vis in comprobando." Subauditur qui dicitur terminus major.

SAMUEL FISHER.

THESES METAPHYSICÆ.

METAPHYSICA est scientia, quæ mentis leges et principia explicat.

1. Mens est una et simplex, atque omnes suæ operationes existentiæ sunt modi.
2. Animo sunt intellectus et voluntas, quorum ille judicat, hæc autem ad agendum impellit.
3. Quando res externæ sensibus nostris subjectæ sunt, res ipsas, non imagines earum nec formas, percipimus.
4. Quo modo res externæ percipiuntur ne omnino quidem intelligimus.
5 Perceptio ex voluntate non pendet.
6 Inter perceptionem et memoriam hoc maxime interest, ut, quando aliquid percipimus, id tum existere, et idem in mentem postea memoriâ revocatum quondam extitisse, dubitare non possumus.
7 Quicquid aut vidimus aut sensimus, id *conceptione* postea contemplari possumus.
8 Quando absentium formas inducit conceptio, ad tempus, quo antea perceptæ sunt, haud spectat.
9. Est homini potentia rerum quæque propria seorsum investigandi, sine qua omnes nostræ cogitationes de rebus singulis necessariè essent.
10. Multa sunt verba, quibus cum utimur ratiocinando, omnia ab iis significata in mentem non veniunt.
11. Cogitationes nostræ non casu in animis succedunt, sed, aliæ cum aliis, quodam nexu, inter se consociantur.
12. Hujus consociationis tanta est vis, ut cogitationem prorsus non ullam mens suo arbitrio excitare potest.
13 Usque ad hoc mens suis cogitationibus præest, ut, ex multis, alia in aliam instante, quamlibet seligere, detinere, et aliquod tempus in ea omni studio versari, potest.
14. Quæ consociata sæpe animis insunt, ex quo habent quoddam vinculum, et quasi cognatione quadam inter se continentur, ea, facillimè condita, etiam facillimè expromuntur.
15. Magnæ inter hominum intellectus varietates ex consuetudinibus diversis, quibus suæ inter se cogitationes consociantur, proficiscuntur.
16. Quicquid animi motus sedare et ab omni exercitatione studioque abstrahere potest, somnum inducit.

dum erit; "ut quisque maximè opis indigeat, ita ei potissimùm opitulari."
17. Leviora sunt crimina, quæ, repentinò perturbatione aliqua animi accidunt; quam ea, quæ meditata et præparata inferuntur.
18. Fiducia in promissis et pactis ad vitæ commercium et societatem est maximè necessaria.
19. Promissa et pacta, quæ legibus naturæ congruunt, semper servanda et peragenda.
20. Promissa, quæ coactus quis vi injussa, vel quæ deceptus dolo malo promiserit, non servanda.
21. Etiamsi commoda legem violando pariantur, majora incommoda eodem partu nata fuerint:
22. Quapropter, ut bona eveniant, mala facere non licet.
23. Leges naturæ negligere facinus animadvertendùm; hoc qui faciunt pœna digni sunt.

JONAS WHEELER.

THESES POLITICÆ.

SCIENTIA Politica rerum publicarum institutiones docet.

1. In hâc scientia sapientes ratiocinandi modos habent valdè diversos; alii jura hominum, alii utilitatem sibi regulam proponentes.
2. Qui de juribus ab utili disjunctis disserunt, frustrà sudant.
3. Jura sunt enim ab utilitate derivata; aut etiamsi jus per se existeret, vel nocens, vel inutile nequaquam pretium esset curæ.
4. In re privatâ non quæritur num juris sit cuivis fabro fieri? num mercatori? verùm sitne usûs?
5. Idem in re politicâ faciendum; utile tantùm quærendum est; aut si de juribus, utilitati sunt referenda.
6. Sic, in populi principatu, non quia de eâ re aliquid mysterium in juribus hominum *Natura* edoceat, sed quiá utile, pluribus pauciores concederent.
7 Sic non potest asseri universaliter populi jus esse, ad libitum gubernatores suos vi ejicere novosque eligere, vel Rempublicam ipsam funditùs novare.
8. Jus enim hoc, aut ex pacto, aut ex utili oritur.
9. Sed non secus res se habet in publicâ ac in privatâ; sine ullo nostrûm pacto in familiâ filii, in Republicâ cives facti sumus.
10. Idcirco, utrùm magistratui an parenti æquius resistere foret, in dubio est.
11. Nam alicui aut filio aut civi, omnibus denique, quicquid utile videtur, illi facere liceat: quod videtur, id est illi.
12. Tamen quòd jus sit patrem ex aquâ crinibus trahere, aut metu necis ab illo defugere, aut a scelere ejus manum avertere, minimè ad libitum in caput parentis manus sacrilegæ tollendæ.
13. Ergo, esse resistendi jus quibus videtur, illi faciant; sed periculum sit sibi: insanus enim quanquam non malus in communem salutem vinculis est tenendus.
14. Attamen, quoniam ex utili est jus derivatum, aut præ utilitate est desiderandum, cùm clamor de juribus tollitur, minùs ex justitiæ amore quàm ex potestatis invidiâ id exoriri est decernendum: et quàm conjunctissima est invidiæ cupiditas!
15. Sunt qui tempus non multùm abesse existimant, quo homines, doctrinâ vulgo diffusâ, mitiores redditi, sine severitate legis Rempublicam penè perfectam haberent.
16. Dubium est an cura laborque vitæ, quas mortalibus Natura imponit, omnium animos excoli sinerent: sed pro argumento conceditur.
17. Res tamen et scientibus speciem præ se ferunt non semper eandem; hinc altercatur perpetuò, cùm ignaris tùm sapientibus: sa-

ARS RHETORICA cui bene dicendi et scribendi scientia.

1. Sicut nihil à Deo oratione melius accepimus, quid tam dignum cultu ac labore ducamus, aut in quo malimus præstare hominibus, quàm quo ipso homines cæteris animalibus præstant.
2. Defendere amicos, regere consiliis senatum, populum, exercitum in eâ velit ducere, quam sit utile, conveniatque bono viro.
3. Multo labore, assiduo studio, variâ exercitatione, pluribus experimentis, altissimâ prudentiâ comitante ars dicendi.
4. Orator non dicendi modo cùmiam facultatem, sed omnes animi virtutes habeat.
5. Sit orator vir talis, qualis verè sapiens appellari possit ; nec moribus modo perfectus, sed etiam scientiâ.
6. Modestia plurimum oratori auctoritatis et fidei affert.
7. Memoria utilissima est oratori exemplorum, legum, benèque factorum quibus abundare, quasque in promptu semper habere debet orator.
8. Dicendi genera tria sunt, subtile, grande atque robustum, et floridum, quorum primum docendi, secundum movendi, tertium delectandi præstat officium.
9. In docendo acumen, in delectando levitas, in movendo gravitas videatur.
10. Dicendi genus subtile narrando probandoque consistit, floridum figuris erit jucundum, in grandi orator vehemens audiorem vel invitum cogere videtur.
11. Res duæ in omni sermone spectari, orator, quid deceat, quid expediat.
12. Omnis oratio tres habeat virtutes, ut emendatè, ut dilucidè, ut ornatè sit.
13. Habet bona pronunciatio quamdam in omnibus vim et potestatem.
14. Oratoris gratia cum iis, quæ dicuntur, consentiat.
15. Quandò quisque pius secundum naturam dicit, tunc magis efficit dicendo.
16. Gestus ac vultus oratori accommodati sint.
17. Oratoris ars latens ; si quicquid deprehenditur, perit.

EUSTAPHIUS FALES.

THESES LOGICÆ.

LOGICA est rectè ratiocinandi.

1. Ratiocinari est, è rebus pràs compertis, aut per se manifestis, aliquid ignotius probare.
2. Quæcunque à ratiocinamur, aliquid pro vero habemus ; et priùs oportet aliquid sumpta benè perspecta esse.
3. Quæ omnia ab illis inferuntur, uno datorum sequentium munere namque ; si utaeque datorum rerum tertiò consentit, inter se ipsa consentire ; et, duas res, quarum una tertiæ cuidam similis est, alteri non, inter se distinctè ipsas esse.
4. Ratiocinandi munera hæc ; primò, res sub quâlaum universis quarum propriis notis subjungere ; porteà, quæcunque attributa et propria illinc oriuntur, illis tribuere.
5. In ratiocinando res signis veris disponi oportet ; scilicet, ab hac arte decem ab omnia penitùs atque quintò ad exactiùs facta, tantò accuratè rationando via inseruntur.
6. Definitio perfectissima, ut genus proximum et species designamur, postulat.

(Right column, upper)

17. In somnus volumus se exercet ; non sæpe volumus e periculis effugere ; sed corpus voluntati haud paret.
18. In somnis cogitationes nostræ, aliæ ex aliis, animos subeunt eâdem lege quâ, nobis vigilantibus, consequuntur.
19. Ad cogitandum aliquid hæc memoriæ mentis intentio, dum de eodem cogitamus, plurimùm valet, vel potius necessaria prorsus videtur.
20. Eâ ratione animis affiguntur nostris, quæ semel tradita atque impressa. Sed,
21. Acerrimus ex omnibus nostris sensibus est sensus videndi.
22. Quare facillimè memoria teneri possunt ea, quæ aliis sensibus percipiuntur, si etiam oculorum commendatione animis tradantur.
23. Sine memoriâ qui motus aut quid sit tempus intelligere non potuissemus.
24. Actiones voluntariæ, crebra repetitione, videntur non voluntariæ ; quippe nos velle non animo conscii.
25. Non ipsos existere intuitu scimus, Deum demonstratio ostendit, omnibus aliis rebus testantur sensus.
26. Omnium facultatum par cultum, æquales eas inter se præstant, quales natura pinxit, animi est perfectio, et homines facit beatiores.

JOSEPHUS GOWING KENDALL.

THESES ETHICÆ.

ETHICA est scientia, quæ omnia ad mores dirigenda tractat.

1. Præcepta de moribus ex Dei voluntate deducenda.
2. Hæc præcipua, quæ legas naturæ appellantur, ratio homini explicatur.
3. In cognitione præceptorum ad mores pertinentium constat sapientia ; virtus in exercitatione assidua.
4. Boni et mali, virtutis et vitii differentia, a Deo constituta, immutabilis est ; quia in rerum naturâ posita.
5. Præmii et pœnæ expectatio, Dei mandato connexa, obligationi moralis propriè necessaria est.
6. Quæ felicitatem pariunt, actiones jubet Deus ; quæ autem miseriam, prohibet.
7. Felicitatem actionum nostrarum causam, Dei voluntatem communem esse oportet.
8. Felicitatis non nisi ab uno est ; quòd ! nec animus natura sua ad eam nascendam, investigandam est, an illâ ad felicitatem communem augendam, an ad levandam, pertinere videtur.
9. Legas divinæ cogitationes maximè spectant ; quia ex iis actiones pendent.
10. Actionem, ad laudem merendam præmiumque, non tantùm per se bonam esse oportet, sed ex consilio justo et voluntate divinâ reverentiâ.
11. Qui prætermittit, æquè ac ille, qui officium clarum violat, scelesto habeatur.
12. Magis ex usu, quàm ex cogitando homines agere solent.
13. Itaque studendum est, ut ad mores probos usu nosmetipsos formemus.
14. Virtutis et felicitatis fontes præcipue sunt Dei cultus et affectuum socialitas exercitatio.
15. Legas divinæ ad actiones ex animi affectibus nascentes magnopere respectant ; itaque curandum est ut affectus rationi obedientia præbeamus.
16. In omnibus benevolentiæ officiis tribuenda, hoc præcipuâ videtur.

(Right column, upper)

18. Sapientes graveque non alter ac alios dissentire et Bubuci insinuare magnum exemplum sit ; illud concilium Tridentinum, quod Pater Paulus tam clarè descripsit.
19. In omni, quoque, civitate, quæ in factiones disceuli, feré duobus acerrimè dimicatur, proceribus autem uniusque partis in partia. ac.
20. Porro, si homines indocti non superiorem, semel doctrinâ et ambitione imbuti, rusd vel æqualem ferrent.
21. Ergo, quamdiu humani generis permanent invidia, ambitio, et superbia, quæ in ipsâ naturâ ejus sunt innatæ ; tamdiu, non urbante artis imbecillate, opus erit, ad eas compescendas, vitium Potestatis ; tamdiu Politicorum illa aurea ætas in Republicâ non nisi in somniis invenietur.

JOSEPHUS SWASEY FARLEY.

THESES THEOLOGICÆ.

THEOLOGIA Dei cognitionem tractat, hominumque conditionem et officia docet.

1. Religionis duæ sunt partes ; altera naturalis appellatur, altera nostris literis sacris patefacta.
2. Religio naturalis mundi regimen morale nobis explicat, et homines universos, alium alio modo, afficit. Hoc Dei cujusdam metuitur.
3. Res omnes existentes, et consilii indicia passim permulta, Deum esse clarissimè demonstrant ; ita omnia creavit, et conservat, et regit ; et cui perfectiones omnes cum naturales tuum morales sunt attribuendæ.
4. Mundi regimen esse morale scimus, propterea quòd felicitatis ac miseriæ sensum, et facultatem, harum duarum utram aliquid factum esse securam, præcedendi habemus, et quòd in hâc vitâ virtutem felicitatem pariæ, ac certis legibus sequi, et vitium miseriam, videmus.
5. Mundum nobis esse non sola erit : quòd ! mo. animus natura sua perpetuò provehitur : 3ib. necesse est vitam alteram esse futuram, quæ æquum vitio suppliciam, virtuti præmium tribuae. Hunc,
6. Altera mercedem ac præmiorum vita erit.
7. In hâc vitâ vivendi conditium est, ut felicitate æterna nosmetipsos dignos præberemus. Hinc,
8. Homini liberè agendi potestas tribuenda est, quòd tali regimini divino hoc solùm sit consentaneum.
9. Hæc autem omnes rationis consequentias salis confirmant literis sacris patefactæ, quæ altiùs rerum ordinem, iesu salutis nostræ Auctore instituunt, ostendunt.
10. Hunc ordinem re vera esse hoc argumento patet, talem accessionem esse.
11. Fidei christianæ porro propagatio, excellentia sua, prophetarum prædictiones impletæ, et miranda Iesu facta, religionis christianæ originem et auctoritatem esse divinam manifestè probant.
12. Literis sacris patefacta legas naturæ explicavere, simul altem rerum ordinem ostendunt, qui rationis investiga aperui, sed rationi aperti ipsi.

Habita in Comitiis Universitatis Cantabrigiæ, Massachusettensis, Die Augusti XXIX, Anno Salutis CIƆIƆCCCX, Reipublicæ Americæ Summæ Potestatis XXXV.

HARVARD THESES, 1810

(Lacking Mathematics, Physics, Astronomy of the original.)

achievement. Henry Adams, in *Mont-Saint-Michel and Chartres*,[7] said of the greatest exponent of Scholasticism—Aquinas,

> St. Thomas is still alive and overshadows as many schools as he ever did; at all events, as many as the Church maintains. He has outlived Descartes and Leibnitz and a dozen other schools of philosophy more or less serious in their day. He has mostly outlived Hume, Voltaire, and the militant skeptics. His method is typical and classic; his sentences, when interpreted by the Church, seem, even to an untrained mind, intelligible and consistent; his Church Intellectual remains unchanged, and like the Cathedral of Beauvais, erect, although the storms of six or seven centuries have prostrated over and over again every other social or political or juristic shelter. Compared with it all modern systems are complex and chaotic, crowded with self-contradictions, anomalies, impracticable functions and outworn inheritances; but beyond all their practical shortcomings is their fragmentary character. An economic civilization troubles itself about the universe much as a hive of honey-bees troubles about the ocean, only as a region to be avoided. The hive of St. Thomas sheltered God and man, mind and matter, the universe and the atom, the one and the multiple, within the walls of an harmonious home.

It would not be difficult to multiply expressions equally laudatory with these on the part of modern students of Scholasticism, which would serve to make it very clear why this mode of thinking continued to maintain its position as a fundamental philosophy for centuries after the Renaissance and the Reformation so called. In the light of these, it becomes comparatively easy to understand why all the European universities continued to use this system of

297

---

7. Henry Adams, *Mont-Saint-Michel and Chartes* (Boston: Houghton Mifflin, 1913).

thought as an instrument of liberal education and why the seven liberal arts, modified to keep them *au courant* with growing knowledge, continued to be the basis of the college curriculum. The liberal arts and Scholasticism were very intimately associated.

To comprehend in any way adequately the curricula of the medieval universities and the modern colleges, including our own American institutions, down to well-on in the nineteenth century, the student must have a firsthand acquaintance with Scholastic *298* philosophy. The utter neglect of this knowledge has been the source of the complete misunderstanding and the resultant bitter deprecation of medieval education. I have quoted Huxley to the effect that the medieval college curriculum—the seven liberal arts—was "better calculated to develop the many-sided mind of man than the curriculum of any modern university."

The most important instruments for the medieval development of mind were the disputations as practised by the Scholastics. They constitute such an important feature of medieval philosophy that I cannot treat of them here at the end of the chapter on Scholastic philosophy but must reserve the discussion of them for a special chapter.

10

DISPUTATIONS

No feature of the teaching at the colonial colleges was so much emphasized by the statutes as the disputations. As we have seen, they were specifically mentioned even in some of the charters, and their proper conduct was recommended to the particular attention of the presidents in the statutes. It is rather surprising, then, to find that no feature of the curriculum of the colonial colleges has been so much misunderstood and the subject of so much deprecation as the disputations. Even superficial study of the early history of the colleges shows that the disputations were considered to be the most important academic exercises in college, particularly during the last two years of the course when the collegians were laying the foundation for the intellectual life that was as far as possible to make men of character and thinking power of them. These colonial college disputations, or disputes, are a direct inheritance from the medieval universities and from the disputations (syllogistic argumentation) which formed such an important element in the education afforded by the Schoolmen.

Most modem educators, and above all historians of education, have missed egregiously the significance of these disputations. The theses sheets which were distributed at the college *300*

237

commencements to such members of the audience as cared to take an active part in the terminal disputation, or public act, were unfortunately not in a form that would make it easy for them to be preserved. These large sheets of paper were particularly likely to be carelessly tossed aside or even used for note or wrapping paper, for paper was expensive in the colonies. As a result of this, a large number of the theses are missing. Two of the early colleges, William and Mary and Columbia, have none of their theses. Of those of the University of Pennsylvania, only three are extant, and those are not at the university but at the Pennsylvania Historical Society. Princeton has but four of the original theses sheets. Each of these colleges should have some fifty or more. Harvard has been carefully collecting her theses as originals or copies and now has well above a hundred for her nearly two hundred years of disputation history. Yale and Brown both have a majority of their theses, but there are a number of lacunae in the lists. It is more by good luck than by special attention that the theses have been preserved, and yet, as I have said, they constitute the most revealing index of the character of the teaching and the content of the curriculum during the last two years of college life.

Men who knew practically nothing at all about the disputations as they were held in the medieval universities, but who nonetheless for that presumed that they knew all about them, have not hesitated *301* to characterize these college exercises as if they represented a sort of childish occupation with trifles or conventional cut-and-dried disputes about questions of very little importance at best and with regard to which almost nothing positive could be known anyhow. They were quite convinced that the disputations represented an almost complete waste of time and intellectual energy. The striking example so often cited of what disputations had degenerated into is based on the famous, or rather infamous, story which represented the scholars at the medieval universities, and especially those which were supremely devoted to Scholasticism, as occupying themselves for long hours with disputes over such questions as "How many angels can rest on the point of a pin?"

No one has ever been able, so far as I know, to trace that story back to any original medieval source, but it has been quoted over and over again in the modern time, as if there could be no possible doubt that this was the sort of thing Scholastic philosophers of the olden time disputed about. There are such propositions to be found not only in the records of medieval universities but even among the theses at the colonial colleges as *Spiritibus nullum est ubi*, "For spirits there is no where [in space]," but quite needless to say, that is an entirely different proposition from the one about the angels and the point of a pin, and yet it helps us to understand where the caricature of this proposition probably came from.

For those unaccustomed to medieval metaphysics and their *302* true significance, it would be easy to think that many metaphysical problems were little better than nonsense, but then the fault under these circumstances is not with the metaphysics but with the minds occupied with them. Sometimes young writers of the modern time have ventured to suggest that they do not see in Dante all that ardent devotees of the great Italian poet proclaim that they find in his verses. But then the fault in this case is not with Dante, who is so full of Scholasticism as to represent Aquinas poetized, as has been said, but with modern youth jumping to conclusions. It is easy to understand, as the result of the failure of comprehension of the significance of the disputations, why it was that many modern educators, and only too often even historians of education, rejoiced that scholars and masters were set free from such elaborate trifling by the advance of modern knowledge after the Renaissance and the progress of more liberal education after the Reformation.

Many who consider themselves well informed have been quite ready to declare that the disputations consisted only of a series of petty responses to objections made on superficial grounds, with the spinning of cobwebby refinements of thought and wordy distinctions that clouded the whole subject instead of clarifying it. The idea of a serious argumentation such as the disputation actually represented is entirely lost on them. They felt that this college exercise was a hopelessly trifling occupation of time without any real significance worthy of consideration. The fact that these disputations in the colonial colleges were presided over as a rule by the president of the college, week in and week out during the year, who was required by the statutes to give his time and attention to them, is quite lost on these critics of the medieval system. That other fact that Scholasticism represented a powerful factor in training the minds of young men by a series of exercises, of which the disputation was looked upon as by far the most important, also failed to register.

Probably no one in the modern time has more thoroughly appreciated the value of Scholasticism and the place of the disputation than Professor Saintsbury of the University of Edinburgh, the well-known literary critic and historian of literature. In his volume on *The Flourishing of Romance and the Rise of Allegory,* which is one of the volumes that he himself wrote in the series of which he was the editor, Periods of European Literature, he said, "It used to be thought clever to moralize and felicitate mankind over the rejection of the stays, the fetters, the prison in which its thought was medievally kept. The justice or the injustice, the taste or the vulgarity of these moralizings, of these felicitations may not concern us here. But in expression as distinguished from thought the value of the discipline to which these youthful languages was subjected is not likely now to be denied by any scholar who has paid attention to this subject."

Professor Saintsbury is profoundly convinced of the benefit that was derived by scholars in method and matter from the teaching of Scholasticism, and he thoroughly appreciated the disputation and the training of mind and the discipline of language that went with it. He had no delusions with regard to lack of educational value in Scholasticism. He said, "There has always in generous souls who have some tincture of philosophy, subsisted a curious kind of sympathy and yearning over the work of these generations of mainly disinterested scholars, who whatever they were, were thorough, and whatever they could not do, could think."

Saintsbury has many quotable passages on this subject. He had made special studies in that culminating period of the Middle Ages, the thirteenth century, and knew whereof he talked. He resumes the objections to Scholasticism that are usually urged, and he caps his vindication with a defense of the disputation that is well worthy of being widely known in educational circles. This mode of philosophy and philosophic teaching occupied the serious attention of scholars for many hundreds of years and is the key to nearly one thousand years of education. Professor Saintsbury said,

> All the peculiarities which ignorance or sciolism used to ridicule or reproach in the Scholastics—their wire-drawness, their lingering over special points of verbal wrangling, their neglect of plain fact in comparison with endless and unbridled dialectic—all these things did no harm but much positive good from the point of view which we are now taking [that of exactness and accuracy in the use of words]. When a man defended theses against lynx-eyed opponents, or expounded them before perhaps more lynx-eyed pupils according to rules familiar to all, it was necessary for him if he were to avoid certain and immediate discomfiture to be precise in his terms and exact in his use of them.

305

Saintsbury would have resented bitterly and laughed at scornfully as ridiculous a great many of the expressions only too commonly seen even in textbooks that treat Scholastic philosophy and medieval education. Such expressions as "The teachers were mainly engaged in metaphysical speculation, and the students were occupied with exercises in logic and dialectics, learning in long drawn-out disputations how to use the intellectual implements they possessed but never actually applying them" would have aroused his satire.

241

Such others as "All knowledge was supposed to be amenable to increase by dialectic expression, and all truth was supposed to be obtainable as the conclusion of a regular syllogism" would not have escaped his pungent criticism. As has been called to special attention by recent investigators, the study of dialectics came to suffer from a similar abuse to that which has developed with regard to technics at the present time. Thousands of young men in laboratories are getting nowhere in genuine science but are being trained in technical observations of all kinds. The sublime ignorance of educators who talk about the centuries that saw the rise of the universities in connection with the erection of the great cathedrals and the creation of immortal literature in every country in western Europe as if these times had wasted their intellectual energies over nullities is only equaled by their assumption of knowledge.

306

Saintsbury points out that John Stuart Mill, who would surely be least of all suspected of any undue partiality toward Scholasticism, set on the title page of his *Logic* a quotation from the distinguished Scottish philosopher, Sir William Hamilton, who was, for some twenty years just before the middle of the nineteenth century, professor of logic and metaphysics at the University of Edinburgh: "It is to the Schoolmen that the vulgar languages are indebted for what precision and analytical subtlety they possess." Condorcet, the distinguished French philosopher, goes even farther than his Scottish colleague when, as Professor Saintsbury says, "Hardly exaggerating he lays down the proposition that 'logic, ethics and metaphysics itself owe to Scholasticism a precision unknown to the ancients themselves.'"

Many educated people in recent years have come to share this pithily expressed opinion of the distinguished Edinburgh professor. Indeed, it may be said that all of those who have devoted enough time to the study of Scholasticism and its ways and methods have come around to have a very tender feeling for it and a recognition of the thoroughgoing intellectual labor that went into its constructive philosophic teaching. Saintsbury appreciated above

307

242

all the value of the disputations for the cultivation of the habit of the distinctive use of words. He felt that the training in Scholasticism, especially in the disputation, had much to do with that verbal exactness and precision in the use of words which came into the modern languages when Scholastic philosophy was in its flourishing period at the end of the thirteenth century.

So far from the disputations going out of use four hundred or more years ago, we have seen in the first part of this volume that they constituted still one of the most important elements in practical education down to the beginning of the nineteenth century in what is now the United States, with all the colleges making use of them and all the presidents reminded by statutes and charters that one of their principal duties was to see that the disputations were carried on properly and regularly. What have been referred to as trifles prove to have been the most serious elements in education. It has become so much the custom to carp at that old-fashioned education and to condemn it as hopelessly backward that it is well to recall how much dissatisfaction there is with our own education and that this dissatisfaction began to make itself felt in the generation when the disputation went out of use.

There is so much misunderstanding of what these disputations, or disputes, really were that the only way to enable modern students of education to understand their true place and significance in the curriculum is to give a description of them in the words of one who knows them familiarly through his own practical experience with them for years. Reverend Father Schwickerath, SJ, in his volume *Jesuit Education*,[1] gives a definitely detailed description of the disputation as it is still carried on in Jesuit colleges. The disputation has always been a prominent feature in Jesuit education, taken over by Ignatius, their founder, and his first

308

1. Robert Schwickerath, *Jesuit Education: Its History and Principles Viewed in Light of Modern Educational Problems* (St Louis: B. Herder, 1903).

companions from the curriculum of the University of Paris, where they were all students together. Paris acquired its Scholasticism and the disputations connected with it during its nascent period in the later twelfth century. They became the most important elements in the curriculum in the thirteenth century when the great master of the disputation and of Scholasticism, Thomas Aquinas, was teaching there. Father Schwickerath's description of the disputation as it has been in use for some seven hundred years and even more will furnish a definite notion of its character and significance:

309

> One of the students has to study carefully a thesis previously treated in the lectures in order to expound and defend it against the objections which are being prepared in the meantime by two other students. On the appointed day the *defender* takes his place at a special desk in the front of the class, opposite him are the two *objectors*. The defender states his proposition, explains its meaning, and the opinions of the adversaries, ancient and modern, then gives proofs for it in syllogistic form—all this in Latin. After a quarter of an hour the first objector attacks the proposition or a part of it or an argument adduced in its proof, all this again in syllogisms. The defender repeats the objection, then answers in a few words to *major, minor* and *conclusion,* by conceding, denying or distinguishing the various parts of the objector's syllogism. The opponent urges his objection, by offering a new subsumptive syllogism to the defender's solution. After a quarter of an hour the second objector does the same for fifteen minutes. During the last quarter either the professor or any student present may offer objections against the defender's proposition.
>
> These disputations are regular intellectual tournaments, the objectors trying to show the weak points of the thesis, the defender striving to maintain his proposition.

It would be easy to think that such a detailedly regularized procedure as this, repeated before the same group of students every week for several years even though the participants changed from week to week, would mean very little for training in mental acuity and intellectual comprehension, and yet excellent teachers who have had continuous experience with the method for years, both as students and professors, are quite convinced now, as their predecessors had been for some seven hundred years or more before, that there is nothing that can take the place of the disputation and that it represents the best possible means of bringing out the thinking *310* powers of students that it also serves as the best possible method of engraving deeply on the minds of students the reasons for the truth of the propositions which they hold, as well as the answers to objections that can be made to them.

The great educators of the thirteenth century recognized the value of the disputation very cordially. Robert of Sorbonne, that famous founder of the great college named after him at the University of Paris, who more than any other contributed to the prestige of the university, was thoroughly aware of the value of disputations to clear up doubts and difficulties with regard to knowledge. His counsels to students as to habits of study are well known and are recognized as carrying the wisdom of the ages with them. Among his counsels is one to be sure to confer with one's companions frequently in disputation or in familiar conversation. Robert said, "This practice is of even greater service than reading, because it results in clearing up all doubts and the obscurities that may have remained after reading." His maxim was *nihil perfecte scitur nisi dente disputationis finiatur*, "Nothing is perfectly known until it has been finished off by the tooth of disputation."

Distinguished teachers in all centuries since have felt about this as Robert of Sorbonne. This is true not only during the Middle Ages but also in modern times and even in our own day. All that is needed is intimate familiarity with disputations to make one appre- *311* ciate their value as an instrument for thoughtful education.

Reverend Richard Clarke, SJ, a distinguished teacher of philosophy in England who was thoroughly familiar with the disputation system of teaching philosophical principles after long experience with it, said of it:[2]

> It is a splendid means of sifting truth from falsehood. Many of those who take part in it are men of ability and well versed in the objections that can be urged. ... Such men conduct their attack not as a mere matter of form but with vigor and ingenuity. ... Sometimes the objector will urge his difficulties with such a semblance of conviction as even to mislead some of those present. ... So far from any check being put on the liberty of the students they are encouraged to press home every sort of objection however searching and fundamental. ... In every class are to be found men who are not to be put off with evasion and a professor who was to attempt to substitute authority for reason would very soon find out his mistake.

It is not only the Jesuits, however, who have held the disputation in high esteem, but all the teaching orders of the Church have done the same thing, so that this method has been used for training the minds of the members of their orders for five hundred years or more. So far from these members of religious orders being the only ones to appreciate the method, it is perfectly possible to quote distinguished modern educators entirely out of sympathy with the Church who recognize the mental training it afforded. Professor Paulsen, professor of education at the University of Berlin, very well known for his studies in philosophy, in his *History of Higher Education*,[3] gives hearty recognition to the value of these exercises as they were conducted in the Middle Ages: "As regards the disputation it may be said that the Middle Ages were surely not mistaken. These exercises were undoubtedly fitted to produce

312

---

2. Richard F. Clarke, "The Training of a Jesuit," *Nineteenth Century* n. 40 (August 1896).

3. Friedrich Paulsen, *Geschichte gelehrten Unterrichts* (Leipzig, DE: Verlag Von Veit, 1885).

a great readiness of knowledge and a marvelous skill in grasping arguments."

Professor E. T. Whittaker, now of Edinburgh, sometime of Cambridge, writes me in answer to a query that "disputations were held at Cambridge from the thirteenth to the nineteenth century." Owing to the fact that John Harvard was a Cambridge man, the influence of the University of Cambridge was felt very much at Harvard, and it was here from its earliest commencement that the disputations were introduced into this country. Professor Whittaker says that in the eighteenth century at Cambridge, the disputations began "by the candidate known as the respondent [in this country *defender*] proposing three propositions on one of which he read a thesis. Against this three other students known as opponents had to argue. The discussion was presided over by a moderator who awarded praise or blame according to the merits of the participants. The discussions were always carried on in Latin and in syllogistic form." This is, of course, exactly what was happening also in the American colonial colleges during the eighteenth century. Indeed, the theses at Harvard show that this went on with very slight modifications even down to the earlier decades of the nineteenth century.

313

Professor Whittaker says further,

> The Elizabethan statutes which were in force in the English universities from 1570 to 1858 directed that logic should form the basis of university education and that it should be followed by a study of philosophy. Under the term philosophy came to be understood at Cambridge in the eighteenth century particularly natural philosophy, that is the Newtonian mathematical physics, and in the latter part of the century many of the candidates offered nothing else. About 1725 the moderator began the custom of summoning the candidates when the disputation was finished and asking them questions; gradually this questioning developed into a regular examination by a written paper—the mathematical tripos—and became

more important than the disputation; and in 1840 the disputation, which by that time had become a mere formality, was abolished.

This was very largely the course of things also in the American colleges. The theses gradually came to be discursive, as can be seen particularly in the Harvard theses of the second decade of the nineteenth century. Manifestly the disputation method was being abandoned, and the obligation of presenting a *thesis* for a degree, in the shape of an essay in Latin on some subject related to the course, took the place of the defense of *theses* until the disputation ceased to have any special significance.

314

"With regard to Edinburgh," Professor Whittaker says, "it must be remembered that in the seventeenth, eighteenth and nineteenth centuries the students were much younger than the undergraduates at Cambridge. The universities in Scotland had to do the work which in England was done by the grammar schools and it was quite common to begin a university course at the age of ten or eleven." Here in this country, as the result of the influence of Edinburgh, it was not an unusual thing for young men to graduate from the colonial colleges with the degree of AB at the age of seventeen, and not a few of the graduates were only past sixteen. Indeed, a limited number of those granted degrees who reached distinction in after life in this country received their diplomas when they were not yet fifteen years of age. Cotton Mather at Harvard and Benjamin Rush at Princeton are examples of this early graduation in men who made their mark in after life, but many others might readily be mentioned.

Professor Whittaker adds, "It was necessary for certain professions, e.g., for the Presbyterian ministry, that candidates should have a certificate of having attended classes at the University but it was not necessary to have a degree and in the eighteenth century very few students took the degrees. Nominally a student at the end of his course should have presented a thesis on some point of literature or science with propositions attached to it on which he was to

315

248

be questioned; but in practice this seldom or never happened." The disputes that are mentioned in connection with commencement represent this practice in America.

Professor Whittaker notes that "the 'arts course' of the Scottish universities when the taking of degrees was revived in the nineteenth century consisted of the seven subjects, Latin, Greek, English, mathematics, natural philosophy, logic and moral philosophy." These were the modern seven liberal arts, as it were, the *trivium*, quite different from the medieval *trivium*, for the people of the Middle Ages were not interested in languages as a subject of college education. All scholars read Latin and were satisfied with that in conjunction with their native languages. The Scottish university *quadrivium* represented a modification of the old medieval *quadrivium*, which had been combined with the classics in the Renaissance, the combined course developing especially in the Jesuit schools. Professor Whittaker adds, "This curriculum continued to be followed until about forty years ago when other subjects, for example history, were introduced."

Professor Whittaker's outline makes it clear that during the first half of the nineteenth century, there came an important modification of college education, in which the old medieval elements which had been so significant gradually lost their place or were completely replaced by other subjects. What happened in the English and Scotch universities had been anticipated in our American universities by the dropping of the theses and disputations during the first quarter of the nineteenth century.

316

11

THE CHANGE TO
MODERN EDUCATION

A definitely revolutionary change came over the content and the method of college and university education during the first half of the nineteenth century. As we have seen in the chapter "Disputations," this occurred not only in the United States but also in England and on the continent. Scholastic philosophy, which had been the basic element of education in practically all the institutions of learning in our Western civilization from the early Middle Ages down to this time, was gradually dropped from the college curriculum in all except distinctly Catholic educational institutions. The suppression of the Jesuits (1773) greatly reduced the number of Catholic colleges. Those that remained followed the trend of the times, so that Scholasticism went out of vogue to a great extent.

The modification of education thus brought about was so gradual that many educators scarcely realized what was taking place. It was a full generation before it was consummated. That is the reason why those as a rule who write about the history of education fail to recognize that Scholasticism continued entrenched until well on in the nineteenth century, for they presumed that

Scholasticism was a system of teaching and of thinking which belonged to the distant past.

318   Scholastic philosophy is commonly presumed to have disappeared more or less completely from college programs and classes at the end of the Middle Ages. As a result of the introduction of the classics into education and the effect produced on colleges and universities by the movement called the Renaissance, with its reintroduction of Greek into education, and then the religious revolution in Germany usually spoken of as the Reformation, Scholasticism, which is characteristically the philosophy of Catholicity, is presumed to have been crowded out of college curricula. The Renaissance and Reformation are usually considered to have carried men's minds, in Protestant countries at least, quite away from everything medieval. The Middle Ages, that is, the millennium from the fall of the Roman Empire (476) to the fall of Constantinople (1453), came to be called the Dark Ages. Their gloomy character so far as education is concerned was presumed to have been largely due to preoccupation with the obscure philosophy of the Scholastics. That thousand years was proclaimed a blank in human intellectual history, though it contains the origin of so many things, from Gothic architecture to the foundation of the universities, that we esteem among the highest achievements of human genius.

As a matter of fact, the theses presented at college commencements everywhere throughout Europe and also here in America continued to maintain their very definite Scholastic character, as we have said, until long after the Revolution and our independence

319   of European influence. These theses, which practically represented the subjects for examination in senior year, demonstrate beyond all doubt the intimate relationship of modern education to medieval teaching up to scarcely more than a century ago. Harvard's theses, as I have shown, are distinctly Scholastic until about 1810. The Yale theses at the end of the eighteenth century, the latest that are extant for that institution, still exhibit the same character. Brown,

that is, the College of Rhode Island, though a Baptist institution by charter, was the most conservative of all the American colleges, and the theses issued on commencement day in Providence continued to demonstrate the deep Scholastic influence under which they were issued until well on in the first quarter of the nineteenth century. Gradually a change is noticeable at Harvard, and after 1810 the theses lose their Scholastic quality, and manifestly the disputation is changing in significance, and disquisitions are taking the place of demonstrations. This same thing is true for all the colleges for which we have theses after the Revolution.

Almost needless to say, this alteration in the subjects to which the students devoted their efforts, especially during the last two years of their college course, involved a profound modification of the method and content of education. The acquisition of information now took the place, to a great extent, of training in thoughtfulness and in discrimination of truth from falsity on which so much emphasis had been laid in the older time. Professor John Dewey once said that "the best criterion of education *320* that we have is that it keeps people from being duped." He added that if this is the best criterion, education in our day is not only bad but is getting worse all the time, for "this is the age of bunk and hokum."

It is probably easier to fool people now than ever before. Many refuse to believe that and lay the flattering unction to their souls that we are an intelligent, discriminating people, but the stock market and its devotees, our wonder-working patent medicines, the ease with which our people fall for all sorts of frauds, as well as the prevalence of political chicanery and the naivete of voters demonstrate very clearly the ease with which our generation may be duped. We have been filling students' memories with large numbers of facts, but we have not trained them in that intellectual discrimination so important to the making of distinctions between what is true and what seems true and noting how close to each other truth and falsity may be under a great many circumstances. After all, half-truths are more dangerous than whole lies.

Thoughtful educators noted and lamented the change that was coming over education a century ago. Cardinal Newman, in his *Idea of a University*, written shortly after the middle of the nineteenth century, at a time when he was deeply occupied with educational questions because he had been charged with the foundation of a Catholic University in Dublin, called emphatic attention to the deterioration of education that was taking place in that generation as a result of the fad for superficial information with regard to many things replacing the more serious study and training in thoughtfulness about a few important subjects of the older time. He could already see clearly the harm that was being done to university life and scholarship. He foresaw much more serious consequences as the direct result of encouraging students to study many things superficially rather than a few things thoroughly. Looking back on twenty years of crowding the curricula of the colleges with all manner of subjects—provided only students could be got to take them—he deprecated grievously, as he could so well do, the dissipation of mind and the ruin of genuine education which would surely follow this newfangled method of education that was gradually finding its way into the institutions of higher learning. Probably no one in his day understood the significance of trends in education so well as Newman. It is not surprising, then, that we have a passage of his containing some wonderful sentences on that subject that are full of that accurate thoughtfulness and precision of expression which were characteristic of him and which make his opinion so valuable:

> I will tell you what has been the practical error of the last twenty years [these would be the twenty years after the elimination of Scholastic teaching]—not to load the memory of the student with a mass of undigested knowledge but to force upon him so much that he has rejected all. It has been the error of distracting and enfeebling the

321

mind by an unmeaning profusion of subjects, of implying
that a smattering of a dozen of branches of study is not
shallowness which it really is but enlargement which it
is not; of considering an acquaintance with the learned
names of things and persons and the possession of clever
duodecimos and attendance on eloquent lectures and
membership with scientific institutions and the sight of
the experiments of the platform, and the specimens of
a museum, that all this was not dissipation of mind but
progress. All things are now to be learned at once, not
first one thing and then another, not one well but many
badly. Learning is to be without exertion, without attention, without toil, without grounding, without advance,
without finishing. There is to be nothing individual in it,
and this forsooth is the wonder of the age.

322

Probably no one in the nineteenth century had thought more
deeply with regard to the problems of education than Newman,
and no one had a better right to an opinion as to what really constituted education. Few men in all the world's history have had his
penetrating power of thought. He knew that that had been made
largely available to him by the old-fashioned method of education,
which emphasized the maxim *non multa sed multum*. He foresaw
very clearly the evil fruits of this crowded pseudo-elective system,
long before it came to be so destructive as it is at the present time.
As a result of his recognition of the evil that would inevitably follow from it, he said, "Whether it be the school boy or the school
girl or the youth at college or the mechanic in the town or the politician in the senate, all have been the victims in one way or another
of this most preposterous and pernicious of delusions."

323

The great English educator, all of whose life had been devoted
to this one subject—education—foresaw quite literally the sad
deterioration of education as the result of the newer methods of
teaching with the unfortunate crowding of university courses. He
ventured to predict that even well-meaning educators, who actually knew better in their hearts, would be carried along almost in

spite of themselves into this modern current of education, where instruction and accumulation of information replaced training of mind, though they recognized the futility of it: "Wise men," he said, "have lifted up their voices in vain and at length lest their own institutions should be outshone and should disappear in the folly of the hour, they have been obliged as far as they could with a good conscience to humor a spirit which they could not withstand and make temporizing concessions at which they could not but inwardly smile." I am very much inclined to think that this expression of Cardinal Newman touches the conscience of a good many Catholic educators who have been caught up in the quest of the new in education and have failed to realize the value of the old, though it lacked some of the tinsel trimmings and popular appeal of the modern.

If Newman said this with regard to the unfortunate developments of education as he saw them in his time, what would he say with regard to the newfangled education of our day, in which it *324* would seem that the one supreme purpose of educational authorities is to secure as many students as possible for their institutions, where bigness is the one feature above all that presidents and trustees of a university strive to attain. One would like to know the great English educator's idea of universities whose most important drawing card is their athletic record and who, unless they give surpassing courses in rowing and tennis and baseball and football, cannot be expected to rank high in the academic world—nor above all hope to attract students. A Japanese university man who spent some time in this country recently defined an American university as "a stadium with a group of academic buildings gathered around it."

Teachers of our own day, two generations after Newman, who have given thought to education in our own time, re-echo Newman's expression very emphatically and have come particularly to realize the value of that old-fashioned expression that what we need in education and above all for education is much about a few subjects studied as profoundly as possible and not many things about a great many subjects studied superficially. In this respect, many deeply interested in education have felt what Miss Margaret Emerson Bailey, writing in *Scribner's* (May 1931), said so well with regard to present day education. She does not hesitate to ask whether the old curriculum of fewer courses would not be more profitable than such rich smatterings. She lays down the very important rule: "One subject taught richly can be made to give the key to the right way of tackling any other subject." Her comment on the hurried rush from one subject to another, which is so characteristic of present-day education and which almost inevitably dissipates that concentration of attention that is so important for the training of mind which really constitutes education, is, "To one who watches on the platform the resulting breathlessness is fair reason for alarm. Such bustling spurts produce no sustained interest, no intellectual discipline precise and patient and working to a sound conclusion. They lead at worst to a paralysis of the power of interest, at best they lead to the hodge-podge amateurishness, the cocksure knowing a little about everything, to the outline acquaintanceship with culture, the snap judgments that are becoming increasingly characteristic of American thought." *325*

Professor Grandgent of Harvard, in his volume *Old and New*,[1] suggested the alteration of the *Century Dictionary's* definition of the *Dark Ages* into something like this: "The *dark ages*, an epoch in the world's history beginning with or shortly after the French Revolution [when Scholasticism waned almost to nullity] marked by a general extension and cheapening of education resulting in a vast increase of self-confident ignorance. ... Never before were conditions so favorable to the easy diffusion of a false semblance of information. Cheap magazines, Sunday supplements, moving pictures,

---

1. C. H. Grandgent, *Old and New: Sundry Papers* (Cambridge, MA: Harvard University Press, 1920).

326 have taken the place of books. Quickly scanned and quickly forgotten, they leave in the mind nothing but an illusion of Knowledge."

He quotes the principal of "a big high school" who thinks that he has found the reason for this degeneracy of education in what is usually presumed to be the source of improvement in education, the supposed reduction of education to a science. The principal said, "Parents are discovering that their children are getting next to nothing in the public schools. Why is it? When I compare the men who taught me and taught me well with the present teachers who can hardly be said to teach anybody anything, I am puzzled to account for the difference. The older men were really no better scholars than the new ones and worked no harder." And then comes his formula to account for it: "The only explanation I can offer is that the earlier generation knew nothing of pedagogy."

Rev. Dr. Bernard Iddings Bell, sometime warden of St. Stephen's College, an integral part of Columbia University, in *The American Scholar* (January 1933), says,

> These seem to be the three great mistakes of the American people which have contributed to the debasing of our education: first, a feeling that the business of schools is to facilitate the production and ownership and use of things as the one great good in life, a good so great that other goods may safely be pushed into the background or in some cases wholly forgotten; second, an illusion of equality which ignores natural differentiations in human mentality, which denies that men differ in degree and kind
> *327* of ability; third, a conviction that teaching is a trade like brick laying or bookkeeping instead of a high art, that education is a mechanical process.

He adds that as a result of these errors and the compulsion which they engender, American education seems to a good many of us definitely defective in these respects:

> 1. That it is satisfied to train people who can do things, even if they be otherwise ignorant, crude, and vulgar;

258

2. That it encourages the incompetent and boorish to believe themselves adept and gentle;

3. That it tends to make able-minded people lazy, conceited, unhappy, and cynical;

4. That it has debased standards of scholarly achievement until the Ph.D. degree means little, the M.A. degree hardly enough to matter, the B.A. degree little more than the passing of time, and a high school diploma—the less said, the better;

5. That it has so ignored the practice and philosophy of religion as to have deprived most of our people of stability to endure the shock of circumstances, and has thus engendered in the citizenry at large a dangerous hysteria, sometimes approaching mania;

6. That it has substituted for teaching a Juggernaut apparatus, which flattens out personality, to the possible profit, but hardly the self-respect, of an hieratic caste;

7. That it has made American scholarship, despite a considerable number of brilliant scholars, to be regarded with disrespect by other nations; while at the same time it has engendered throughout the land an academic complacency both ridiculous and devastating;

328

8. That increasingly it obscures our vision of the great tradition, those ways of urbanity which might be our heritage, until we have largely lost the power to understand, control, or enjoy our civilization.

One of the prominent university educators, whom I have consulted a number of times with regard to the theses and never without good results, said, "The theses indicate a general interpretation of the great problems of philosophy and life which nine-tenths of our modern college students never acquire." It was just this interpretation that made the old-fashioned education so valuable for the colonial colleges.

It would be easy to multiply quotations of this kind from educators of long experience who have been deeply interested in the developments of education during the past two generations, in which they deprecate strongly the change that has come over instruction. That change, though the fact is not generally recognized, came with the relegation of Scholasticism into the limbo of discarded subjects and its replacement by a hodgepodge of courses that have little or nothing to do with the development of the mind, though they may load the memory with any number of more-or-less unrelated facts. Men who have known of the place and influence of Scholasticism from personal experience have not hesitated to say, like Father Clarke (see chapter "Disputations"), that "it is a *329* splendid means of sifting truth from falsehood." Above all it fitted young men to make such distinctions as enabled them to appreciate very definitely how close truth and falsehood might be and how important it was to find the distinctions between them. If there was one thing that the old Scholastic philosophers and teachers could do, as Professor Saintsbury said, "it was think." If there was another thing they could do, it was make young men think, so far, of course, as that was possible in accordance with the intelligence which they possessed.

12

LIFE AND EDUCATION

Almost needless to say, there is a very marked difference between *330* the education afforded the students at the colonial colleges and that provided for them at the present time. The supreme feature of that difference deserves special attention. It is that the students in the colonial colleges had their duties toward others emphasized for them, while the students of the modern time are taught ever so much more about their rights. They hear much now about the supreme importance of the development of individuality and the bringing out of personality. Then, they had repeated for them over and over again that education's aim was the benefit of the community and the doing of good for their fellow men.

The paramount purpose of education at the present time is to enable students to make a success of life. Success means above all the making of money. The supreme aim of education in the colonial times was to render students valuable to the community. Over and over again, college documents of various kinds—charters, statutes, announcements—dwell on the fact that education was to be cultivated mainly, indeed almost wholly, for the purpose of producing suitable candidates for the ministry and the magistracy, so as to provide a mentally well-trained pastorate for the churches and *331*

such candidates for political office as would assure honest administration as well as thoughtful consideration of the needs and rights
of the people. Colonial educators without exception were intent
on making students thoughtful for others rather than themselves,
while they provided the principles for the proper solution of political problems by men whose college training had been directed particularly toward making them honest, honorable, upright citizens
and officials of the community.

This training came between the ages of fifteen and twenty,
just when adolescents are most impressionable and when impressions produced are very likely to endure. This seems to us entirely
too early for graduation from college, and we have been prolonging
the period of tutelage during which young men are not encouraged
to assume their personal responsibilities but are left to take things
as they come and to consider that the less they have to devote
themselves to hard work, the better it is for them. Our generation is
inclined to think that college work completed at twenty or earlier is
surely too young, but our forefathers' generations would inevitably
have felt that our young men were wasting their time when they
were only graduated from preparatory school at nineteen or so, and
that they ought surely to have reached a higher mental development than this at that time of life.

Above all there is in our time very little teaching of the principles of morality and of right conduct in life and still less emphasis
332   on man's duties toward God and his neighbor as well as himself.
The lack of this teaching has been noted by many modern educators who have emphasized the fact that young men need such
training very much and yet agree that there is almost no place for it
in education as organized at the present time.

The years of life fifteen to twenty, which students spent in
college during the colonial period, particularly during the generation just before the Revolution, represent the time that is now
spent to a great extent in the preparatory or secondary schools.

Some of the most insistent complaints with regard to the defects of education at the present time have been heard exactly with regard to our secondary school education. Adolescents are not given that training for life nor have emphasized for them the principles of ethics which would make better men of them. Moral philosophy is a special subject of study that is very rarely met with in the curriculum of a preparatory school, though this is the impressionable age when it would be best learned and when the application of its principles may be so deeply engraved as to become habitual. As a result of this defect in secondary school education, there is no period in life when ethics as representing principles of personal conduct is taught.

With this in mind, it is interesting to take the opinion recently expressed by a preparatory schoolmaster of long experience as to just what is the matter with education in our time. He writes on the needs of present-day schools. It is rather startling to note how many of these needs as he outlines them were thoroughly responded to, or at least definitely recognized and their solution attempted, in the curriculum of our colonial colleges nearly two hundred years ago. The Founding Fathers engraved deeply on the minds of growing youth the ethical formulas that if followed would regulate conduct to a nicety. *333*

Writing in the *Atlantic Monthly* (April 1931), Mr. Frederick Winsor, who has been for more than a quarter of a century headmaster of the well-known Middlesex School in Massachusetts, expressed some emphatic opinions as to needed changes in the curricula of our secondary schools at the present time. He does not hesitate to say that there are serious lacunae in the teaching of boys during the adolescent period under present conditions. His remarks concern particularly education at the age at which boys were in college as a rule during the colonial period and when they were being taught ethics by the president of the college, when that was undoubtedly looked upon as the most important subject of the college curriculum.

Mr. Winsor points out that there are three fields of activity in life for which the pupils need preparation at this time. These are their civic relations, for they are just approaching citizenship; their family responsibilities, for after college graduation, most men think of settling down in life and getting married; and thirdly, the use of their leisure, or free time. After his long years of experience, the headmaster of Middlesex declares that the adolescent students

334   must be taught these three "not forgetting that the consideration underlying all is that the pupils must be mentally well trained." He does not propose to introduce new methods of teaching nor to suggest any novel materials. On the contrary, he says that

> the old established subjects of study will do the trick. Language, science, mathematics and history have stood the test and must always be the backbone of the curriculum. They provide training in the various kinds of thinking that men are called on to do and if the instruction is aimed not to prepare for examinations but to promote thinking, if the underlying philosophy [ethics] is more and more stressed as the pupils become more and more able to grasp it, they will provide a liberal foundation of intellectual experience which will prepare pupils to meet emergencies, to solve problems and later to acquire further knowledge for themselves to meet all the ordinary needs of life.

In discussing the three fields of activity for which youth must be prepared, and the training necessary to bring a man genuine success in life and with it happiness, Mr. Winsor finds very much to be desired in our modern education. Quite needless to say, he is but one of many who have reached similar conclusions as to the failure of our education to prepare students for life and not merely the making of a living. From his practical experience, he points out that to supply the first need, that of preparation for their civic relations, we have only certain barren courses in civics which furnish pupils with information about elections and politics, municipal depart-

335   ments and official positions, but nothing about the philosophy

of government. About established principles of liberty or about the age-long conflict between the interests of society and the interests of the individual, they learn nothing. To quote Mr. Winsor's own words, "These are inherently controversial subjects and so are avoided by the writers of textbooks." He goes on further to say, "We cannot expect in the future to avoid the disastrous mistakes in legislation and governmental organization which have littered the story of our nation's politics down to the present day unless we educate future generations in the principles of government." One cannot help but have the feeling that the headmaster of Middlesex would have delighted in the opportunity to have his boys demonstrate and defend the *theses politicae*, or the principles of politics, which constituted an important part of the teaching of ethics at the hands of the president of the colleges during the last years of the college course in colonial days.

This genuine political education was one of the subjects that the colonial colleges tried sincerely to impart, and there is no doubt that they recognized and endeavored to the best of their ability to fulfill their obligation, and they reaped splendid success. As an illustration of their well-meant efforts, take for instance the theses at Brown (the College of Rhode Island) for 1769, seven years before the Revolution. Under the rubric *politia*, or politics, they gathered a number of far-reaching principles of government and the exercise of authority. They were preparing the minds of young men for the war for independence by such propositions as "All power, that of framing the laws as well as of inflicting penalties, is derived from the people; therefore a Senate (governing body) has no right to impose taxes on a people who are not represented in the Senate." Here is the old medieval maxim of the English common law, formulated originally in the thirteenth century and enunciated by Bracton in his *Digest*, "There shall be no taxation without representation."

This formula was, at Rhode Island in the pre-Revolutionary days, being deeply impressed upon the minds of youth who some seven years later were to be the soldiers of the war of independence.

336

While they were engraving this important political principle on students' minds, the faculty of Brown were at the same time counselling prudence in the practical assertion of the principle, especially so far as a definite act of uprising against established government was concerned. One of the propositions that same year warned as to the danger of premature action in any military move for independence and argued that this would be an index of lack of capacity to rule people properly in a republic. Political principles of many kinds are to be found in the colonial theses, stressing first of all civic duties and at the same time emphasizing the rights of citizens and the necessity for maintaining these even at the cost of bloodshed. Emphasis was laid on the principle that there was only one ultimate criterion of political policy, and that was the benefit to the community and not merely the individual.

337   The second of the life activities, as Mr. Winsor would suggest it, that students should be prepared for between fifteen and twenty—that is, the preparatory school age in our time, the college student age of the colonial period—is that of marriage. He might well have said "student relations to the sex problem," but he preferred the more conservative wording. This called for education in morals, which is "a difficult and dangerous field." Mr. Winsor says that "it is hideous to think of the horrors that would be perpetrated by the unfit teacher of such a subject." He manifestly has had abundant experience as to how difficult it is to procure teachers of the right kind, and he hopes that the ideal school will be "staffed by teachers of tact, taste and understanding who can talk about sacred subjects such as love, service and altruism without making them common or ridiculous." This is, of course, one of the most serious problems in the education of youth that we have at the present time. It is interesting to recall in this regard that very much of the direct moral teaching of the old medieval universities was concerned with such self-repression as makes for high morality. The teachers themselves at medieval universities were all celibate by statute and gave an example of continence that was inspiring to

266

the young men around them so long as they too remained unmarried and yet was not in any way a discouragement of matrimony. In general, the morality of the universities was high, as will be best appreciated from the severe reaction which followed any violation of moral principles in university life.

Mr. Winsor insists that in the secondary school curriculum of the future, a definite and quite important place must be found for ethics. The old colonial colleges, all of them, devoted much time to it. The theses lists are very interesting in this regard. Usually there were more propositions to be defended in the public act on commencement day under the rubric *ethics* than any other. Some of these theses illustrate very well the cultivation of ethics. At Brown in 1769, ethics is defined as "the practical science of bringing happiness to man through virtue." Special emphasis was laid on such propositions as "No one ever acts against his will." At the same time, the teaching made it clear that there are good passions as well as bad passions and that good passions are as helpful in life as bad passions are harmful. The cultivation of good habits was emphasized. There was the proposition "No passion considered in its nature is vicious." *338*

But not only was there ethics for the individual but also for the citizen and the state. They were seeing clearly some of the problems that would have to be solved if our country was to be ruled successfully. They emphasized propositions of such practical political significance as "To reduce Africans to perpetual slavery agrees neither with Divine nor human law." At that time, there were still many colored slaves in New England and many more in the Middle States and of course in the South, so that this ethical principle was a distinct contradiction of what was a practical rule of life in most of the colonies at that time. But they went much deeper into politics, and in 1770 under *ethics* at Brown, there is the proposition "To all men by nature liberty belongs equally; therefore, every civil power owes its origin to the consent of the people." Here is the opening sentence of the Declaration of Independence in a specialized *339* form truer than the formula of the Declaration, but here above all is the Scholastic formula with regard to authority's being vested in the people and being transferred by them to the civil power so as to constitute righteous government.

They emphasized formulas with regard to the necessity of thoughtfulness for others, as "In order that one may perform the duties of life most faithfully he ought to attend especially to the cultivation of his intelligence." There are such other propositions as "The happiness of man flows to a great extent from society; therefore, those who segregate themselves entirely from society are to be condemned." Emphasis is placed on the idea that man does not live his life for himself alone, but for the benefit of others, and those others not merely his family but those of his neighborhood and his country.

Mr. Winsor feels that a return to the teaching of ethics in our secondary schools, in which boys of fifteen to twenty are in attendance, is extremely important. He feels that the course in ethics ought to be made the most vitally significant subject in the whole curriculum. Like all educators of the present day whose eyes are open, he realizes that the teaching of ethics is very seriously neglected. He says, "Everyone knows how extensively the old sanctions have been weakened and the old validities are being questioned by the young people of this generation. They do not accept any 'ought' whether it has behind it the authority of church, state, school or family without doubt and questioning. Among themselves they discuss all sorts of moral questions and more often than not their inexperience and narrow vision leads them to mistaken conclusions." He says in conclusion, "Our civilization depends for its successful continuance on the altruism of the men and women who compose it and the continuance of the dominant altruistic morality should not be left to chance."

340

One needs to be but very little familiar with the theses published at the various colonial colleges, and which represent so clearly the ethics which was studied during the very years from fifteen to twenty when our youth is at secondary schools as a rule, to make it very clear that the propositions announced in moral philosophy were not leaving thoughtfulness for others—the "altruistic morality" of our day and our terminology—to chance. On the contrary, they were making this thoughtfulness for others the basis of the outlook upon life of the students. The great distinction between their mode of education and ours is, as has been said, that instead of emphasizing the idea of success in life for one's self as the all-important aim of education, they dwelt very emphatically on thoughtfulness for others as the supreme trait of the educated man.

It is not only the headmasters of preparatory schools who see *341* the need for ethics for adolescents, but there are others who are brought closely in contact with these young men who feel that our education has sadly broken down in their regard. Usually we do not look to wardens of state prison for educational suggestions, but Warden Lawes of Sing Sing was asked to make an address before the convention of the National Educational Association (1932). He pointed out that during the last year for which statistics are available, arrests of juveniles under sixteen reached the high total of 6,302, while for those between sixteen and twenty, many of whom were just out of high school, the record reached the astounding figure of nearly forty thousand. He emphasized the fact that for these young fellows, the school system had done nothing to mold character, and there was a "missing link between education and character."

So far as character can be formed in the school, it surely would come from the enunciation of the principles of moral philosophy, that is, ethics, as they were set forth at the colonial colleges. Young men between fifteen and twenty, which is the dangerous period and so often represents the time of introduction of youth to crime, were in the pre-Revolutionary colleges being taught ethics by the president of the college. If they were of sufficient intellectual caliber to be influenced at all, they must have been deeply impressed by the solid doctrine of morals proffered to them by the man whom they most looked up to in their academic world.

342   It is often said that ignorance is the mother of crime, but a very large percentage of the criminals who have crowded our jails throughout the country are not, as might readily be expected, uneducated foreigners, but are drafted from those who have recently been going through our public schools, not a few of them through our high schools and some of them through our colleges. Warden Lawes reminded the assembled educators of the country that the prison school at Sing Sing was awarded a higher rating for intellectual competency by investigators from Columbia University than public schools of similar grades. He adds, "When graduates of public schools and high schools take to violent crime in a constantly rising proportion it is time to take stock and balance credits as against debits" in our educational system.

Of course, it would be utopian to think of even the best teacher of ethics under the most impressive circumstances lifting everybody up to a high plane of perfection of conduct, for while human nature is human nature, there will always be some men and a few women with such strong tendencies to evil or weakness of personality that crime will persist. But as it is, the rising generation, unless under very special circumstances, receives no instruction in ethics and as a result is very much inclined to question the whole idea of moral philosophy and to consider that whatever is legal is surely right and that "if one can get away with it," there is no reason why one should not proceed to do whatever suits him. Certainly,

343   nice distinctions of right and wrong have no interest for him. The training of character which should come as the result of impressive teaching of moral principles is lost.

Professor William Z. Ripley of the Harvard Department of Economics, in an article in *Scribner's* (October 1932), dwells upon the breakdown in business morale which has developed among the American people and which he feels has been to a great extent responsible for the unfortunate condition of affairs that we

270

have run into in the past few years. He points out some "pecu-liarly aggravating, disgraceful instances" of plain dishonesty on the part of wealthy men who, in the position of directors of large cor-porations, have been able to take advantage of their positions to make money for themselves at the expense of their concerns and the stockholders to whom they bear a fiduciary relation. Professor Ripley says that "deception, spoliation and extortion burst forth into full flower" in the period before the depression. He might have pointed out that graduates of our colleges in majorities sit on boards of directors of corporations which have furnished flagrant examples of what cannot but be called in plain terms dishonesty.

The great defect in our education and in the training of youth today is that, to a very large extent, there has been no teaching of conduct in our schools, no inculcation of definite moral principles which demand just solicitude for the interests of others as well as for self. Taking advantage of other people has come to be looked upon as smart if you can only escape detection or at least con-viction. Those who are able to accomplish the purpose of getting ahead of the other fellow no matter how it may be done, provided of course it is legal, command the admiration of a great many peo-ple rather than any condemnation. We even hear of "honest graft," and the sole duty of man is considered by the great majority of men in our generation to be the making of money—making it honestly if possible, but making it.[1]

344

---

1. A distinguished British educator who came to this country during the war, at a time when we were much readier to listen to criticism from our Allies than before or since, declared that our relationship of education to life might be expressed in three degrees of comparison: "Get on, get honor and get honest." Get on, that is, make a success of life, and that of course means make money in as large quantities as possible no matter how you do it; then get honor, as you surely will if you have money; and finally, get honest, that is, as far as pos-sible make it impossible for others to make money the way you did.

The supremely unfortunate element in the situation is that owing to the lack of teaching of anything like morality—that is, the principles of ethics in our public institutions of learning—there is no public conscience. Selfishness dominates public opinion, and there is actual sympathy with the lawbreaker, provided only he is clever enough to escape detection or at least indictment. There is only one commandment that is considered to be universally binding on man, and that is what is often called the eleventh commandment—"Don't get found out." There is no code of business honor inculcated. No one is bound to do anything but observe the law; conscience is scouted. I understand that the business schools or business departments of universities founded in recent years are unwilling to teach business ethics. The result is easy to understand. There is a chaos of thinking so far as moral principles are concerned.

345

No wonder that Professor Ripley of Harvard, who knows the economic life of the country probably better than anyone else, does not hesitate to say that the "obloquy is indisputable." In simpler terms, we are disgraced because we have no honesty. No wonder, either, that Professor Ripley insists that the basic remedy for the flagrant evils which have invaded business life is "of course a higher standard of business ethics."

To a great many in our day, it might seem that the teaching of principles of ethics would have little or almost no influence on human conduct, especially whenever they involve the question of real self-sacrifice for the sake of others. Man is considered to be only an animal and as such is essentially selfish, and therefore there can be little hope of modifying his character or changing his disposition in this regard. Professor Ripley points out, however, how much unselfishness has been fostered by the general acceptance of a definite code of altruistic conduct when danger to life at sea is involved: "What manly feats of courage and endurance," says Professor Ripley, "have not been witnessed as the result of the adoption of an opposite code of honor at sea." On a sinking vessel, "every

man for himself and the devil take the hindmost" is a principle that
if followed would brand a man as a contemptible coward for all
time, "but on land [to continue the quotation from Ripley]—bad
cess to it—something far more drastic seems requisite." The fact,
however, that the observation of the rule of the sea has been exemplified strikingly on a number of occasions in our own generation,
and at the cost of many important lives, shows what can be done by
the erection of standards of ethics and the inculcation of principles
and their adoption as rules for the road of life. On the Titanic and
on the Lusitania, many a wealthy man, for whom life seemed to
hold much future happiness in store, calmly faced inevitable death
for himself while he nobly helped the women and children, some
of whom were poor and with no prospects, especially without their
men folks, into the boats that meant life for them.

The students in the old colonial colleges were drilled in the
principles of morality, which fostered a sense of right and wrong
and thus helped to create a public conscience. They were given the
thorough training in ethics which Mr. Winsor now demands for
students during the corresponding years of life in our day. Moral
philosophy was a subject, as we cannot but repeat, usually reserved
for the teaching of the president himself and was looked upon as
the keystone of the arch of education which he was to set in place.
Many of these old college presidents came to be looked up to with
great reverence by their students after graduation, because of the
fact that they had received from them those principles of ethics
which they came to know afterwards meant so much for true happiness and satisfaction in life.

Ethics afforded the completion of mental training which prepared the young men of the graduating class for the proper fulfilment of their duties in life. The ethical theses touched on a great
many of the problems of daily life, not only for the individual but
also for the community. Principles were engraven not only on the
mind, but that deeper layer of human intelligence that is called the
heart, which were to remain as a precious possession all during life:

"Only the man that thinketh not in his heart says there is no God" is the scriptural expression which brings home to us the important place of the heart, that deeper element of human judgment, the conscience, which means so much for right conduct.

The great principles underlying the problems of life were given definite expression in these theses, which are so interesting for us now because they demonstrate exactly what the students of the colonial colleges were expected to devote themselves to for the formation of their characters. The theses broadsides proffered a selection of propositions presented at the disputations that had been held each week during the year. They were not merely rules of life learned by rote; they were definite moral principles to be syllogistically demonstrated at the beginning of the disputation and defended "manfully" against objections urged against them.

How deeply students were affected by this teaching of moral philosophy is very well illustrated by the effect produced upon Thomas Jefferson by the course in ethics which he received under President Small at William and Mary. Jefferson was only eighteen, but he was so deeply impressed that, as I have told in the chapter on "The College of William and Mary," he considered it a great good fortune to have had this teaching and that it "probably fixed the destinies of my life." Jefferson was probably the most intellectual man that we had in America in that generation before the Revolution. He had more influence than any other, and yet he was perfectly ready to confess that the teaching of ethics that came to him at William and Mary did more than anything else to shape his career for good.

The presidents of the colonial colleges seem to have been very well satisfied to give the time that was demanded for the teaching of ethics and often also of metaphysics and logic, because they realized how deep an influence these studies exerted over the impressionable minds of youth. They were very specific in their declarations with regard to what was good and what was evil, and no doubt was allowed to remain in the minds of their pupils with regard to right

348

and wrong. Above all there was no cloudiness or haziness such as characterizes so much of the thinking in our times in matters of morals. There was no "new"" morality, no "up-to-date decalogue" expurgated according to the desires of the individual, and above all no eclipse of the idea of duty by sordid selfishness.

Freedom of the will was proclaimed categorically, and men were declared to possess the power to do what they thought was right and avoid what they knew was wrong. There might be cir- *349* cumstances that would impair responsibility. There were condi- tions that made the choice of right and wrong much harder for some men than for others, but there was no compounding with evil and no justification of evildoing because "the easiest way" was so much more comfortable and required so much less effort than the straight and narrow path of duty. During the last two years of their college course, moral philosophy was drilled into students, and when they did wrong in after life, they knew it.

Finally, Headmaster Winsor lays definite emphasis on the idea that there must be discipline in the schools of adolescent youth. He definitely makes his confession, "I believe in discipline," which, almost needless to say, is a rather daring declaration to make in our time, when so many people who think they know all about human life and about the human mind are emphatic in their insis- tence on the elimination of discipline from the training of youth in order that everyone may develop his personality without any inhibitions or prohibitions. After thirty years of experience with adolescent youth, Mr. Winsor has no delusions as to the benefits to be derived from untrammeled freedom of development. He says, "Without discipline education becomes a flabby, effeminate, ane- mic caricature of itself. The notion that boys of secondary school age [fifteen to twenty] should be allowed to decide for themselves what they should study or what should constitute a day's work for them sickens me. They are without wisdom and without experi- ence and they need not only guidance but driving. Like a recruit *350* for the army the first thing that a new boy entering secondary school needs is discipline. It should be friendly and sympathetic, of course, but it should be firm."

Almost needless to say, discipline was one of the very strongly developed parts of education in the colonial colleges. Turn to the accounts that we have given of the discipline at Harvard or at William and Mary or at Yale or at Princeton in the chapters on these respective institutions, and it becomes clear that discipline was considered one of the most important features of college training. It is probable that our good colonial ancestors may have—through that unfortunate tendency which man by nature labors under of having the pendulum of *mores* swing too far in either direction—overdone the idea of discipline, but at least they had it, knew its necessity, and they cultivated it and put it into action. The pendulum has swung too far to the other extreme with us, and so our headmasters are emphasizing the necessity for its return.

This idea of discipline as all important in education may seem to some to belong to the old-fashioned classical tradition, but at least one well-known scientist of the generation just past, who has been deeply interested in education, has not hesitated to emphasize the paramount place that must be assigned to it. Huxley, in his address on "A Liberal Education and Where to Find It," places weighty emphasis on the teaching of moral principles and the training of character as of the greatest possible significance for the liberally educated man. He said, "If I am a fool or a knave teaching me to read and write will not make me less of either one or the other." Toward the end of his address, in setting forth what he meant by a liberal education, he said, "He has a liberal education who, no stunted ascetic, is full of life and fire but whose passions are trained to come to heel by a vigorous will, the servant of a tender conscience." There are people in our time who are inclined to think of *conscience* as a word that is a little ridiculous, with the feeling that it causes repressions and inhibitions that bring on curious psychoneurotic states as the result of them. As for a *tender conscience,* that is looked upon as little better than supreme foolishness. Huxley added in concluding his address, "Where is such an education to be found? Looking over the length and breadth of this island I can only say that one must return a negative answer to the question. Nowhere is a liberal education in that sense of the word to be secured." This was written fifty years ago. One is prone to wonder what Huxley would think of education as it developed in our day, not in England where there is still some conservatism left, but in the United States where *conservatism* is commonly considered another word for old-fogeyism.

Headmaster Winsor is but one of many who might be quoted in condemnation of our ethics-less education. Some years ago, Dean Jones of Yale, who had been a Yale student himself and after postgraduate work in Germany and Switzerland became dean *352* of the College of Engineering at the University of Minnesota and then dean of his alma mater, was quite outspoken in the proclamation of the moral dangers of student life in our day. He said that in "the acquiescence of parents to the loosening standards of morality we face a dangerous and terrifying progression." He does not hesitate to add that "we are approaching a moral crisis." The worst of it is that he is not sure whether we can avoid it by present-day education: "There was a time when I thought that we must teach in college first and foremost a knowledge of books. In these days I would bend every effort to the making of good citizens and by a good citizen I mean a man who is master of himself, earns his own living, and as far as possible in doing it is of benefit to his fellow man." The extramural courses that are taken by students in the movies, in dancing, and in the other occupations of youth have much more influence in relaxing morality and lowering moral standards than the university has in lifting them up.

Cardinal Mercier said that there were three of his teachers whom he remembered better than any others. Naturally the educational world is very much interested in knowing what these teachers taught him. It was not the intellectual branches that occupied so prominent a place in Mercier's memories of his school years. The first of these ever-to-be-remembered teachers taught him to obey; the second taught him to work and to will; the third taught him to dare. All of these represent culture of the will rather than the intelligence. Cardinal Mercier would doubtless agree with that definition of education which not a few people of long experience in the educational world are inclined to think of as representing the true inwardness of mental training better than any other. It runs, "Education is what is left after you have forgotten all that you were taught in school."

353

As regards the third activity with which the boys should be occupied, the training in the proper use of their free time, Mr. Winsor bewails the fact that "the secondary schools of today pay practically no attention to preparation for any kind of recreation except athletic sports." And yet man's leisure should, according to the old maxim from King Alfred's time, represent about one-third of his life. The three eights—eight hours for work, eight hours for sleep, and eight hours for the needs of the body and for play—are still the best apportionment of daily life for men. The vast majority of American businessmen have only two possible ways in which to use their spare time: either to be amused by someone else, whether it be at the theatre or over the air, or to play games. Within themselves they have no resources.

The old colonial colleges provided an education, including familiarity with the classics, that was very interesting from this standpoint of furnishing a resource within one's self for recreation purposes. Boys who came up from the preparatory school to college with a knowledge of Latin that enabled them to use it quite freely in disputations and whose textbooks even in mathematics were often in that language could read many of the classics without much difficulty. They were under the obligation of

354

constantly employing Latin except during recreation and therefore had a familiarity with the language which utterly did away with the deterrence that so often develops in the minds of modern students. How thorough it was, the passage from Benjamin Franklin's *Auto-biography*, in which he tells us that his single year of Latin followed intensively at the age of eight (!) proved a good foundation thirty years later for a working knowledge of Latin secured through his own efforts, shows very clearly.

Even when their Latin was almost forgotten, these young men had left in their minds a residue of interest in the classics that often caused them in after life to turn to the classic authors in translation for occupation for their leisure. Above all such studies made the history of mankind of deeper interest than it otherwise would have been and kept men from thinking that the ancients were far behind our generation in knowledge and wisdom because, through progress in the course of evolution, we were "the heirs of all the ages in the foremost files of time" and must, therefore, be far ahead of the past. We know from their biographies that many of the graduates of the colonial colleges actually did devote themselves after graduation to this solider reading which gave them breadth of view and depth of judgment. They were aided in the acquisition of these mental qualities by the old-fashioned philosophy they had been taught, founded as it was on the natural law and the divine law applicable to all men. *355*

Men like Jefferson and Charles Carroll of Carrollton, among the American Fathers, furnished admirable illustrations of the way students were trained to employ their leisure profitably and plea-surably through their education. They continued to read the classics during all the years of long lives, and they found real diversion of mind and very definite recreation in the practice of taking up the Latin and Greek authors and realizing how little human nature changes and what lessons for the humanity of any time were to be found in these old books. His most recent biographer[2] has told the story of the meeting between Macready, the well-known British actor, and the *Pater Patriae*, as he calls Charles Carroll. The occasion was a professional visit to Baltimore when Macready, like so many other Americans and foreigners, took the opportunity to wait on the venerable statesman in response to an invitation. The actor writes in his *Reminiscences*, "In my life's experiences I have never met with a more finished gentleman. At his advanced age he kept up his acquaintance with the classics." He had learned as a young man to devote himself to culture, in Matthew Arnold's sense of the word, as "knowledge of the best that has been said and thought in the world," and now it was the solace of his advancing years.

---

2. Joseph Gurn, *Charles Carroll of Carrollton, 1737–1832* (New York: J. P. Kenedy, 1932).

13

Modern Catholic College Theses

The easiest way to obtain a definite understanding of the historical *359* and educational significance of the lists of theses which were distributed on commencement day at the colleges in English-speaking America, before and after the revolution down to the early years of the nineteenth century, is to compare them with the lists of theses that are still selected every year for the candidates for the AB degree in present-day Catholic colleges. Their theses are not presented for defense on commencement day as was the custom in the old time, though occasionally what are called public acts, a term that comes down from the Middle Ages, are held toward the end of the year. These resemble the public disputations held at the colonial commencements. The lists of theses at the Catholic colleges are in the hands of the students for a month before commencement and are placed in the hands of the examiners for the final examination, usually some days before that event.

All the Jesuit colleges and nearly all the other Catholic colleges, not only throughout this country but also in Europe and indeed wherever there is a regular college curriculum, continue to have their examinations in philosophy by means of theses such as these for the last collegiate year at least and often for the last two years of the college course. In most of them, it is the custom to have the theses in Latin, for as a rule, their philosophy course, with logic, metaphysics, and ethics, including psychology, cosmology, and natural theology, is given in that language, and they have disputations on an average of once a week during the scholastic year, in which they defend syllogistically the theses in Latin, while the objectors do the same in presenting their objections to the theses. Lists of these theses will be found to correspond very closely, though not with absolute identity, with the colonial theses, but then neither will the theses presented at the various colonial colleges be found to be absolutely identical with one another, though as a rule, their only differences are a matter of words.[1]

360

Boston College constitutes a characteristic example of a Jesuit college thoroughly up-to-date in every way, one of the most beautifully situated and architecturally striking colleges of the Jesuits in this country. Internally it represents just as typical an example of what a Jesuit college should be. To take a recent set of Boston College theses (1930) is to pick out a very fair example of the functioning of a college during its last two years under the Jesuit *ratio studiorum*. Whatever similarities there are between the Boston College theses, then, and those of the colonial colleges is due to the fact that the colonial colleges, consciously or unconsciously, were

---

1. In recent years, there has been a tendency for some of the Catholic colleges to present their lists of philosophic propositions for examination in English rather than in Latin. This is true even in some of the Jesuit colleges and is due to the fact that not as much time is now given to the training in Latin as used to be the case, and as a result, the collegians are not as well prepared to understand Latin demonstrations and make replies in Latin as they used to be. Besides, it is felt that college students who have not taken the classical course ought to have the opportunity to study Scholastic—that is, Catholic— philosophy. As a result, the course is given in English, and the examination is in that language.

organizing their curriculum and arranging their examinations on the order laid down by the Jesuit *ratio studiorum* nearly three hundred fifty years ago.

Under the head of criteriology in the junior philosophy class at Boston College, 1930, the first five propositions were definite reminders of some of the propositions found under logic among the colonial college theses:

- Universal scepticism is theoretically absurd and practically impossible.

- All our cognitive faculties are *per se* infallible.

- In the natural order objective evidence is the ultimate and universal motive of certitude.

- The immediate judgments of consciousness are absolutely infallible.

- The world of bodies which we perceive with our senses is real and knowable.

Among the Boston College theses of the junior philosophy oral examination in 1930, a number of propositions referring to universals are strongly reminiscent of similar propositions to be found among the theses of Harvard and Brown, as well as of Yale and the University of Pennsylvania, in the colonial days. The theses express the medieval philosophic doctrine with regard to universals as it came to be taught toward the end of the Middle Ages:

361

- Universals are neither mere words nor mere fictions of the mind, nor yet do they exist outside the mind.

- That which we conceive by the direct universal concept is real though not in the manner in which we conceive it.

- The reflex universal concepts, however, are fictions of the mind though they too are based on reality.

Under cosmology at Boston in 1930 came propositions which were often anticipated in the colonial colleges as well as in the medieval universities. Those with regard to the composition of matter are particularly reminiscent of the colonial college theses: "The essence of a physical body consists of two substantial principles really distinct, namely, prime matter and substantial form."

Strikingly enough, under this same rubric of cosmology, there are some theses with regard to miracles. These are the same practically as are to be found among the colonial college theses. They emphasize the fact that miracles confirmed the credibility of Christianity and that they possess real evidential value. The reason for placing them under the rubric *cosmology* is that miracles represent a disturbance of the order of the material world, an exception to physical laws, an interruption, as it were, of that cosmic order which pervades the universe.

The last five propositions under the rubric *natural theology* at Boston College in senior philosophy in 1930 are distinctly similar to a number of propositions which had been presented on the colonial college broadsides, sometimes under theology but sometimes under metaphysics and ethics:

- Through the exercise of His efficacious will, God is truly omnipotent.
- God is the Creator of the world.
- God conserves all His creatures in existence.
- God's concurrence is necessary for all the operations of His creatures.
- All creatures are under the sway of Divine Providence.

362

Among the theses in psychology in Boston College for 1930 were a number that are similar or almost identical with those we have quoted from the lists of colonial commencement theses. The colonial theses declared that the soul was the seat of a mental faculty, the intelligence, and a determinative faculty, the will. The old-time philosophers argued very determinedly for the freedom of the will. Here are three theses on the subject of mind and will as they were outlined in Boston College in 1930:

- Man is endowed with an immaterial perceptive faculty called the intellect which in this life is only extrinsically dependent on the brain. [The colonials argued that the human mind could act independently of matter.]

- Man is endowed with a material appetitive faculty called the will.

- The human will in many of its acts enjoys a true freedom of choice. [The commonest proposition in the colonial colleges was the formula which announced the absolute freedom of the will. The Boston thesis shows a readiness to distinguish between a true and false freedom of choice.]

Such metaphysical propositions as "The human soul is a spiritual being" and "The human soul is *de jure* and *de facto* immortal" are to be found almost in similar words in the colonial theses.

The most important collection of theses as a rule in the broadside theses lists of the colonial colleges came under the rubric *ethics*. As we have said, the teacher was often the president of the college, and the subject was considered to be of great importance. When the colonial college ethics is read beside that of the modern Catholic colleges, it becomes perfectly clear that the two must have come from the same source.

Under ethics at Boston College in 1930, there was a series of propositions that had many reminders of the ethics of the colonial colleges. This can readily be seen by anyone familiar with the sets of theses, old and new, as they were set forth for defense by the students aspiring to the bachelor's degree: *363*

- An act done through fear is simply volitional; as a rule it is positively involuntary after a fashion; but fear so long as it does not destroy the right use of reason is never destructive of freedom.

- As a consequence of freedom every volitional act is imputable to the free agent whose act it is.

- Man has the duty of never taking his own life directly and on his own authority.

- Man has the duty of never lying. A broad mental reservation is not a lie but even its unconditional use is unlawful; when, however, there is a grave reason proportionate to its character, a broad mental reservation is not illicit. [The colonials were stricter than the Jesuits in this matter.]

- Man has the right to use physical force against an unjust aggressor even to the taking of his life, always with due regard for the limitations of blameless self-defense.

- The natural law forbids polyandry and polygamy as also divorce from the matrimonial bond.

- (1) Civil society is a natural society; (2) Its supreme authority arises immediately from God.

- The proximate cause of the moral union of minds and wills respecting the common end in civil society is the consent of the multitude.

- The primary and necessary subject possessing supreme authority and receiving it immediately from God is the whole community as such, which has all the right of power but only "radicitus" as regards its exercise. The community determine by their consent who shall formally exercise this supreme authority.

- War is not of itself opposed to the natural law. The conditions for lawful offensive war are (1) legitimate authority; (2) justice of cause; (3) just methods of warring.

It might readily be thought that at least in natural theology, there would be a marked difference between the theses set forth for the Boston collegians in 1930 and those of nearly two hundred years before in the Protestant colleges of the eighteenth century. The surprise, however, is to find how many resemblances there are

between the examination theses on this subject at the two long-   *364*
separated periods. For instance, at Boston under the rubric *natural
theology*, the first proposition is "The so-called ontological argument cannot be accepted as proof for the existence of God." At the
College of Rhode Island and Providence Plantations just before the
revolution, the ontological argument for the existence of God was
definitely set forth as a proposition to be defended: "God can be,
therefore He is." This absolute contradiction would seem to demonstrate how different were the two theologies, but it must not be
forgotten that there were distinguished Catholic philosophers who
maintained the ontological argument all down the ages to our own
time, when the negative decision of the Church with regard to it
was proclaimed. It originated with Anselm, the great archbishop
of Canterbury, or at least was given its most striking expression by
him, and many other churchmen since, equally as orthodox as he,
have held it.

The other theses at Boston can be paraphrased, though not
always exactly, from the various sets of theses from the colonial
colleges, for instance, "The existence of God as the Unproduced
Cause of the universe is proved with certainty by the *a posteriori*
method of demonstration." This is followed by the corollary, "God
as the Unproduced Cause must be a self-sufficient Being." Then
there are a series of other propositions, most of them quite like
certain of the theological propositions in the colonial colleges:

- The existence of God as a Supreme Being ruling
  the universe is proved by the common consent of
  mankind.

- God as a self-sufficient Being must be absolutely infinite in perfection.

- God as a self-sufficient and necessary Being must be
  absolutely simple.

- God in His own intrinsic Being is both physically and
  morally immutable.

Among the propositions which my own class at Fordham, that of 1884, had to defend in disputations during the year and in a public act toward the end of the year were theses strongly reminiscent of those of the colonial theses of a hundred years before. The propositions that we had to demonstrate the truth of and then defend against objections were those which had been used in Jesuit schools for some three hundred years, that is, from the time when the Jesuits became the most prominent factor in European education.

Like those of the colonial colleges, our theses were in Latin, and they can readily be seen in the textbooks of our teacher, Father Jouin, SJ, on mental and moral philosophy (New York, 1910). The ethical theses are strikingly like those which were defended especially in our pre-revolutionary colleges. Father Jouin's moral philosophy is divided into four principal parts. The first treats of the last end of man, the second is on the nature of human acts, the third on the rights and duties which must be maintained, and the fourth on the social obligations of men. This latter includes domestic or civil law and also international law. These divisions are found also in certain of the colonial college theses.

In the senior class at Fordham in 1930, the candidates for the degree of AB were required to defend altogether fifty-one theses. Twenty-six of these were with regard to psychology and natural theology, and twenty-five of them with regard to ethics. Practically every one of these Fordham theses of the second quarter of the twentieth century can be paralleled by theses from the colonial colleges nearly two hundred years before. Almost needless to say, these theses defended at Fordham in 1930 are practically identical in their philosophic content with those which have been selected for examination of the graduates of Jesuit colleges for some three hundred fifty years. Some of the exceptions only serve to prove the rule. The thesis on spontaneous generation is now worded differently from what it would have been two hundred years ago, because at that time, philosophers generally believed in the possibility of abiogenesis.

The thesis on evolution is a response to the scientific interest of the past generation. The arguments for the existence of God and for creation and the theses in epistemology are practically identical with those to be found in the colonial theses.

Insofar as ethics is concerned, if due consideration is given to the terminology which is tinctured very much by its direct translation into derivative Latin words as far as possible, the ideas are the same. It is perfectly easy to make some very striking parallels in the theses that are separated by one hundred fifty to two hundred years, and it is only a comparison of this kind that enables one to understand just what the meaning of the theses in the colonial colleges was. Here, then, are the Fordham theses of 1930. They represent, in concise and clearcut language, what were the great principles underlying a great many of the truths as to how knowledge is acquired and the principles by which conduct must be regulated. Some very nice distinctions have to be made in defending these propositions from objections that could be made against them, but after a young man has had to defend them once, he has a better grasp of their meaning than he could secure in any other way. At the same time, he has been acquiring the power of using his mind for discrimination between truth and falsity in a way that will sharpen his judgment and keep him from being easily led into error or from being too ready to accept the appearance of truth for the reality.

366

ETHICS (Fordham, 1930)

1. The absolutely ultimate intrinsic end of man's volitional activity is blessedness.

2. The final perfection and happiness of man consist in the perfect knowledge and love of supreme truth and supreme goodness, that is, God.

3. The proximate norm of goodness in man's volitional activity is rational nature looked at in itself and in all its essential relations; the ultimate norm is the divine nature.

4. There are actions which, independently of any will, either human or divine, are intrinsically and of their very nature morally good or bad.

5. The specific determinants of moral good and evil in man's volitional activity are the end of the action, the end of the agent, and circumstances intrinsically affecting either.

6. The right, objectively considered, is an ideal of conduct obligatory in character.

367   7. Obligation arises from moral law. Moral law is imposed on us by an act of the Divine Will, and this act, presupposing the decree of creation, is a necessary act and is rightly called the eternal law.

8. The moral law, as promulgated to us by the light of reason, is rightly called the natural law.

9. The natural law is unchangeable and so far as its primary and secondary principles are concerned cannot be invincibly unknown to men whose reason is developed.

10. Conscience or reason when it applies the principles of the moral law to individual acts is to be obeyed when it is prudentially certain, even if it be invincibly erroneous. To act with a doubtful conscience is always unlawful.

11. Right, subjectively considered, or the moral inviolable power to do or hold or exact, is derived from man's obligation to observe the moral law. True rights, therefore, exist independently of any positive law.

12. While neither coactivity nor coaction constitutes the essence of a right, still coactivity is an essential property of some rights, and the exercise of coactivity, even in rights that spring from commutative justice, ought to be entrusted normally to the civil government.

13. Man has the duty towards God of internal and external worship.

14. The natural moral law forbids the direct killing of oneself on one's own authority.

15. Man has the duty of never lying.

16. A broad mental reservation under certain conditions is not unlawful.

17. Man has the right to use physical force against an unjust aggressor even to the taking of his life, due regard being always had for the limitations of blameless self-defense.

18. External material goods capable of division are by nature negatively common. Every man has the absolute right to use these things. In virtue of this right each can licitly choose for his own use any individual thing which has not because of the same right been assumed by others.

19. Every man has the congenital right to acquire permanent individual proprietary dominion.

368

20. The Socialistic state as a practical proposition is impossible. Socialism's economic principles are unsound, and its philosophic basis is false.

21. Society is natural to man, and social authority is necessary for society.

22. Conjugal society is natural society and has for its primary intrinsic purpose the procreation and education of children and for its secondary intrinsic purpose the mutual love and aid of husband and wife.

23. Conjugal society depends for its actual existence on the mutual free consent of man and woman.

24. The natural law forbids polyandry, polygyny and perfect [complete] divorce.

25. Civil society is natural society. The supreme authority in civil society looked at in itself arises immediately from God.

If we place beside these ethical theses as they are argued or disputed about in the Jesuit colleges of our own time the *theses ethicae* from Yale about the middle of the eighteenth century, it is interesting to note how much, in spite of nearly two hundred years of interval between them, they are occupied with very similar ideas. If anything, those from Yale at the middle of the eighteenth century are more mystical, more what we are accustomed to think of as medieval, than the Jesuit theses of the modern time. When the Yale theses (1751) are compared with those distributed for the examinations in the seminaries where the Jesuit students themselves are educated, it is surprising to find how extremely similar the theses are both in the mode of expression and in the matter with which they are concerned:

Ethics is the art of living according to reason.

1. The power of moral beings in a state of innocency is proportional to their obligations.

2. No creature can suffer a punishment equal to the fault of sin.

369

3. The obedience of a creature, whether active or passive, cannot satisfy for sin.

4. More of wisdom is exhibited in the rule of the moral than the physical world.

5. The more any principle is found to promote the common good, the greater is the evidence of its moral truth.

6. The highest end to be asked of authority is the opportunity of benefiting others as widely as possible.

7. Public good is the measure of all legislation.

8. [In italic capitals with an index] Penal sanction is essential to law.

9. The highest use of friendship is the mutual incitement to virtue.

10. The happiness of human nature is proportional to its perfection.

11. [Italic capitals with index] Holiness and happiness, sin and misery, are necessarily connected.

12. Remorse of conscience is the greatest torment.

13. The glory and the happiness of the saints in heaven will be unequal.

14. Even though there were no existence after death, virtue would have to be cultivated.

Here is a set of theses in ethics (originals in Latin) defended (1930) at Woodstock College, Maryland, which is a *collegium maximum*, or college of highest rank, for the education of the candidates for the Jesuit order in this country. An excellent gloss on them is provided by certain paragraphs of President Samuel Johnson's *Elementa philosophica*. The theses follow:

1. The last end of the natural man is his own happiness to be secured without fail. The all-sufficient and necessary object of this happiness is God alone.

2. Human acts are good or evil morally in so far as they agree with rational nature looked at from all sides or disagree with it.

3. There are actions intrinsically and by their very nature and therefore independently of any precept which are good or evil.

370

4. Human acts looked at in the abstract can be morally indifferent, that is neither good nor evil; in the concrete, however, as they are done by the individual, they are always either good or evil.

5. Man can by his actions acquire merit with God.

6. There necessarily exists in God an eternal law which requires that the moral order should be observed by

the rational creature and prohibiting any violation of it.

7. The same law that is revealed to man through the natural light of reason is called the natural law.

Afterword:
The Practical Value of
Classical Education

Jason T. Eberl

There are at least three main trends within higher education today. The *training model* is arguably predominant and frames higher education in terms of the development of technical skills. The *consumer model* is more recent but growing in influence and emphasizes the individual goals and learning needs of students in order to meet those goals. The *formation model* is what is defended in this text, namely, the use of classical sources to expose students to perennial wisdom that still informs contemporary social and political debates. The training model is most clearly exemplified in technical trade schools. The consumer model largely animates most large, state-funded universities in the United States, while the formation model can be found in a decreasing number of small liberal arts schools, most of which are religious. Some colleges and universities attempt to embody two or all three models to greater or lesser degrees of success due to competing pedagogical and economic pressures.

Both the training and consumer models undoubtedly have their place. When I fly overseas on an airplane, I want the engineers who designed the plane to have had the best technical education to ensure that the aircraft will function at peak performance between my departure and arrival airports. Does it matter whether they are familiar with Immanuel Kant's categorical imperative or Aristotle's three forms of friendship? Perhaps for their full formation as persons, but not for their functional role as engineers. One might say something similar for the CEOs of *Fortune* 500 companies: it does not matter whether they understand the finer points of ethics in the eighteenth century AD or the fourth century BC; all that matters is that they maximize returns for investors in the publicly traded companies of which they are the chief executive officers. Consider, though, what can happen when engineers and CEOs lose sight of fundamental values.

On October 19, 2018, a Boeing 737 Max 8 aircraft operated by Lion Air crashed into the Java Sea. A few months later, another Boeing 737 Max 8 operated by Ethiopian Airlines crashed minutes after takeoff. Post-crash investigations revealed that both incidents resulted from a failure of a novel computer system—known as the maneuvering characteristics augmentation system (MCAS)—that is unique to this 737 model. MCAS was designed as a safety feature that pushed the plane's nose back toward level flight to prevent the aircraft from stalling if its angle of attack was too steep. MCAS became deadly because of lack of pilot training. Boeing had evidently caved to economic pressure to deliver a new aircraft that would not require airlines to pull pilots from active flight duty to undergo simulator training on malfunctions in new systems. In fact, until the Lion Air crash, Max 8 pilots were not explicitly made aware of the MCAS system or how it operated, let alone how to override it in case of malfunction. Investigations by the Federal

Aviation Administration and the National Transportation Safety Board, along with an explosive Netflix documentary, revealed how the Boeing corporation allowed the pressure to maximize profits for investors to alter their previous safety-first culture.[1]

What would have happened if, at the time the Max 8 was being developed, the engineers and CEO at Boeing had been more educated about the ethics of complicity in moral wrongdoing, if they had been more inspired by historical examples of those who suffered hardships for standing up for what is right, if they understood that short-term gains should yield long-term benefits for all, and if they had a firm grasp of the inherent dignity of every human person? Would they have stood up to the new culture of maximizing returns on short-term investments instead of ensuring that airline passengers could travel safely and securely? Would the inestimable value of the lives of passengers have been at the forefront of their minds instead of the company's quarterly financial statements? Would economic security or wealth amplification have remained their most important aim?

Ethics is ubiquitous. Every conscious, intentional decision a person makes is subject to ethical evaluation. But not just ethics is at play. Many decisions we make presume metaphysical and epistemic claims about what we understand to be real and what we think we know or can know. Take, for example, the recommendations that clinical ethicists offer to the parents of an unborn child who tests positive for a severe genetically caused disability. Does this child, as a fetus, possess a *moral status* that should be taken into account?

---

1. Rory Kennedy, dir., *Downfall: The Case against Boeing*, Netflix, 2022; and William Langewiesche, "What Really Brought Down the Boeing 737 Max?," *New York Times Magazine*, updated July 2, 2021, https://www.nytimes.com/2019/09/18/magazine/boeing-737-max-crashes.html. As Langewiesche reports in his extensive investigation, blame is also shared with Lion Air and the Federal Aviation Administration.

What is his or her anticipated *quality of life?* Can we determine quality of life *objectively* from a third-person perspective or only *subjectively* from the perspective of the person living that life? Physicians and other health care professionals are often not formed in ways that equip them to answer such questions effectively or even to understand their relevance. Indeed, professionally certified clinical ethicists typically employ a *proceduralist* approach toward helping such parents navigate these and other important, life-determining questions, but their own metaphysical and moral presumptions often are hidden yet operative in the guidance they provide.[2]

Just like engineers and CEOs, health care professionals and bioethicists need to be formed in ways that go beyond the technical knowledge required to do their jobs effectively to ensure that the choices they make are oriented toward *authentic human flourishing.* As bioethics emerged as an academic and professional field in the late-1960s and 1970s, *scholar-practitioners* were among its most influential leaders. These were philosophers, theologians, and medical practitioners who had a holistic formation in such disciplines. As the field of bioethics evolved, an increased call for *professionalization* emerged, culminating in the development of a certification process for health care ethics consultants based on a set of core texts selected by the American Society for Bioethics and Humanities.[3] Contrast this approach with that taken by Leon Kass, the first chairman of the President's Council on Bioethics, who initially required all members of the council to read *The Birthmark*, a short story by Nathaniel Hawthorne about a man who seeks the

---

2. See Abram Brummett and Jason T. Eberl, "The Many Metaphysical Commitments of Secular Clinical Ethics: Expanding the Argument for a Moral–Metaphysical Proceduralism," *Bioethics* 36.7 (September 2022): 783–793, doi: 10.1111/bioe.13046.

3. American Society for Bioethics and Humanities, "Healthcare Ethics Consultant-Certified Program," ASBH, accessed October 24, 2023, https://asbh.org/certification/hcec-certification.

298

perfection of his lover's appearance, to their mutual detriment.[4] Kass understood that *narrative*, whether a first-person account or a work of literary fiction, has the power to shape human thought and influence our feelings beyond rational argumentation.

Thankfully, Kass is not alone in this view, and the field of *medical humanities* has grown alongside that of bioethics, including more recent subfields of *narrative medicine* and *narrative bioethics*. Nevertheless, as critics of contemporary secular bioethics have pointed out, there has been an unfortunate decline in contributions like those of the scholar-practitioners of yesteryear, with a corresponding increase in a reductive form of *principlism* in ethics—relying on the application of mid-level principles (respect for autonomy, beneficence, nonmaleficence, and justice) to resolve ethical dilemmas instead of tackling the deeper questions that may be involved—which leads to a technical *proceduralism* that informs the professionalization of the bioethicist's vocation. Such proceduralism has influenced educational programs, not only in bioethics but also in medicine and allied health professions, more in the direction of the technical model than the formation model.

There are many positives from professionalizing a field such as bioethics, including greater voice and acceptance among health care professionals when providing ethics consultations. Yet the further the bioethics field moves away from the primary scholarly disciplines that continue to inform how bioethicists tend to think, make decisions, and provide guidance, the more bioethicists—as with other professionals such as engineers and CEOs—may lose sight of their fundamental orientation toward authentic, holistic human flourishing.

---

4. See Keith Dow, "'Marked' Bodies, Medical Intervention, and Courageous Humility: Spiritual Identity Formation in Nathaniel Hawthorne's *The Birthmark*," *Journal of Medicine and Philosophy* 47.5 (October 2022): 625–637, doi: 10.1093/jmp/jhac022.

To give just one example of the danger at hand, let us reflect on how quality-of-life considerations typically creep into clinical decision-making and the guidance offered to patients or their families. A prominent space in which this phenomenon can be witnessed is in the purportedly non-directive practice of genetic counseling. Consider a case in which a pregnant couple are informed that their child has been diagnosed with trisomy 18, a chromosomal abnormality that results in a range of physical impairments, including severe effects on cardiac function and respiratory difficulties. While an individual genetic counselor may indeed practice non-directiveness by not explicitly recommending that the parents either terminate or continue the pregnancy, the parents may feel implicitly pressured to terminate the pregnancy if they are presented with the available options but not provided with adequate information regarding supportive resources for children with trisomy 18, contact with parental groups that can offer first-hand information about the experience of raising a child with this condition, and forms of financial assistance to cover anticipated medical expenditures. In addition, such parents will probably require psychological and spiritual support as they discern how they are being called to respond to this situation. All of this requires genetic counselors not only to be educated in the pertinent medical facts regarding diagnosis, prognosis, and anticipated quality of life but also to understand the interconnected web of issues this family may now face, the values that will inform the decision they ultimately make, and the lived experiences of children with trisomy 18 and their families. This is one reason why *disability bioethics*—comprising philosophy, theology, literary theory, history, and activism—has become an increasingly important subfield.[5]

---

5. Jason T. Eberl, ed., "Perspectives on Disability," special issue, *National Catholic Bioethics Quarterly* 20.2 (Summer 2020): 203–423.

The formation model of education for bioethicists and other professionals, particularly those in careers that have a direct effect on the lives and flourishing of human persons, does not in itself inculcate specific values or beliefs. Rather, its purpose is to provide a set of critical thinking skills, opportunities for self-reflection—one might think here of the Ignatian spiritual exercises embedded within a *ratio studiorum*—and a rich mix of historical and contemporary exemplars, from a broad range of religious and philosophical traditions, who model the type of values-driven reasoning that should underlie technical and consumerist decision-making.

Moreover, the formation model resists the pressure to douse students with a fire hose of information and accede to consumerist demands for shorter degree tracks that enable students to enter the workforce more quickly, armed with only the technical skills needed to do their jobs effectively. Education should allow time for the imagination to develop.[6] By sitting with certain texts—say, biographies of martyrs such as St. Oscar Romero or honest spiritual autobiographies such as St. Augustine's *Confessions*—and imagining suffering, physically or spiritually, for the *truth*, one starts to imagine how he or she would act under such stressors, which over time can shape one's thought patterns. As critics of John Rawls's "original position" have noted, it is very difficult—nay, impossible—for people to adopt an unadulterated "view from nowhere."[7] Rather, as the Jewish philosopher Emmanuel Lévinas has argued, ethical justification and motivation to act stems from confronting "the face of the other."[8] There is a powerful scene in the Netflix documentary *Downfall: The Case against Boeing* in which then-CEO

6. I am grateful to my colleague Jeffrey Bishop for raising this point.

7. John Rawls, *A Theory of Justice*, rev. ed. (Cambridge, MA: Harvard University Press, 1999).

8. Emmanuel Lévinas, *Totality and Infinity: An Essay on Exteriority*, trans. Alphonso Lingis (Pittsburgh: Duquesne University Press, 1969).

Dennis Muilenberg is forced to come face-to-face at a congressional hearing with the families of victims of the 737 Max 8 crashes. If only Muilenberg and other Boeing executives and engineers had cultivated the intellectual virtues necessary to take the time to imagine themselves, with foresight, as those family members or as the victims themselves, they might have been less focused on the company's short-term financial gains when designing the aircraft and hiding the new MCAS feature.

Let us return to the parents whose unborn child has just been diagnosed with trisomy 18. A merely technically trained genetic counselor will be able to inform the parents about the nature of the diagnosis and the prognosis in terms of the symptoms their child will probably experience—based on statistical data—and the accompanying hardships their family should expect. Being both technically proficient and consumer minded, the genetic counselor will solicit the parents' wishes for how they would like to move forward: continuing the pregnancy with appropriate forms of medical support or aborting their child. A holistically formed genetic counselor would do all this as well; however, he or she would also delve more deeply into the parents' values pertinent to their decision, ensure that the parents are connected with resources they may need so that they do not perceive only the anticipated burdens of raising a child with this condition but the positive, loving aspects as well, and facilitate the parents' decision-making with not only third-person facts but first-person experiences of others who have been in their position.

It is nearly impossible to think of a profession—from a fast-food worker to a university professor (full disclosure: I've been both)—that does not have a direct effect on the lives and flourishing of human persons. Thus, formational education is essential not just for those in so-called higher professions. Rather, everyone benefits from a more informed and critically astute citizenry. Consider the current sociopolitical situation in the United States, especially with respect to how it is influenced by social media, including artificial-intelligence-driven content. Furthermore, a formational education that includes development of complex critical-thinking and moral-reasoning capacities is essential in creating a populace able to navigate complex moral situations and not simply engage in virtue signaling or knee-jerk reactions of moral outrage. Certainly, some circumstances do call for moral outrage, but as has been lamented with respect to the Israeli-Palestinian conflict and 2023 attacks by the terrorist group Hamas, contemporary liberal educational institutions have largely failed to form students intellectually in ways that allow for both nuanced assessment and the moral courage to call out evident evil.[9]

I do not believe it is an overstatement to assert that never before in human history has there been a more apparent need for a public that is not merely knowledgeable (in a technical sense) but *wise*. In light of the unprecedented access to information through Google, Wikipedia, and other platforms, Pope Francis warns about the confusion of knowledge and wisdom in his groundbreaking 2015 encyclical, *Laudato si'*, arguing against what he terms the technocratic paradigm:

> True wisdom, as the fruit of self-examination, dialogue and generous encounter between persons, is not acquired by a mere accumulation of data which eventually leads to overload and confusion, a sort of mental pollution.

> We have the freedom needed to limit and direct technology; we can put it at the service of another type of progress, one which is healthier, more human, more social, more integral.[10]

---

9. Ezekiel J. Emanuel, "The Moral Deficiencies of a Liberal Education," opinion, *New York Times*, October 17, 2023, https://www.nytimes.com/2023/10/17/opinion/israel-hamas-universities.html.

10. Francis, *Laudato si'* (May 24, 2015), nn. 47, 112.

Francis subsequently established the Vatican Dicastery for Promoting Integral Human Development, which looks beyond the formulation of merely technical solutions to global problems such as poverty, disease, and ecological degradation. Francis has called for a new moral mindset, one which is actually a recovery of a more classical mindset found in ancient and medieval epochs, as exemplified by Aristotle, Confucius, and St. Thomas Aquinas, among others. This old-is-new moral mindset begins with a fundamental consideration of the *dignity* of every human person, followed by establishing sociopolitical structures that protect and affirm such dignity at every level of humans' personal existence as living, sentient, social, rational, and spiritual animals.[11] Such is the mindset that undergirds the formational educational program argued for in the present work and that higher-education institutions, especially those that are avowedly Christian, ought to devote themselves toward enacting in their curricula in line with the Jesuit pedagogical charism of *cura personalis*—care of the *whole person*.

---

11. See Jason T. Eberl, *The Nature of Human Persons: Metaphysics and Bioethics* (Notre Dame, IN: University of Notre Dame Press, 2020).

Index

312

INDEX

315